American Red Cross personnel in Vladivostok in 1920.

The Lost Children:

A RUSSIAN ODYSSEY

by Jane Swan

South Mountain Press, Inc., Publishers
Carlisle, Pennsylvania
1989

ISBN 0-937339-03-2

Photos not otherwise credited are from the author's personal collection.

Maps: The Location of the Children's Colonies, p. 218
        The Trans-Siberian Railroad, p. 219

Published and Distributed by South Mountain Press, Inc.
Please address all inquiries to the publisher:

South Mountain Press, Inc.
P.O. Box 306
Carlisle, PA 17013
Telephone: (717) 245-9251

Maps drawn by Chris Sechrist

ACKNOWLEDGEMENTS

It seems to me an eternity since I became interested in this unknown but incredible story coming out of World War I and the Russian Civil War.

During the early years of my marriage to Alfred Swan, who, with his first wife, Katia, was responsible for the success of the first part of this odyssey, I listened with fascination to his stories of this unusual adventure. More important were the meticulous diaries and account books which the Swans had kept.

While attending the University of Pennsylvania graduate school, I wrote a paper on the subject for my Master's Degree under the watchful eyes of Dr. Walther Kirchner. He kindly arranged for its publication as a joint venture in the Delaware Notes of the University of Delaware.

In the 1960's I made several trips to Russia with my husband, meeting and becoming fast friends with a number of the colonists (children no longer). Their tales made me determined to write their story in more detail.

In 1966 I chanced to come into possession of a book by Floyd Miller called "The Wild Children of the Urals". The author was chiefly concerned with the trip in its later phase. A part of the book is fiction and part fact, especially since he had no knowledge of the role of Alfred and Katia Swan. I value his written good wishes and interest in my work.

In 1972 one of the Red Cross officials, Burle Bramhall, returned to the Soviet Union to try to meet with some of the colonists. Although the trip was taken over by Soviet officials, and his meetings with the colonists were only brief and controlled, one of the more daring of the colonists slipped a note into his pocket. Only a year later when sending his coat to the cleaners did he find an almost illegible scrawl

iii

asking him to get in touch with me and begging me to come back and write the whole story. By this time word of Alfred Swan's death had reached the colonists.

In the spring of 1975, I made a trip to Leningrad where I was able to tape the reminiscences of many of the children, at times under scary circumstances. Since I was not on official business nor with a tourist group it was difficult to get food. The hotel cafeteria was opened only for breakfast with black bread, hard boiled eggs, and vodka or tea. After that it was impossible to find a restaurant that was not closed, booked up, or being renovated. I remember one day buying raw cucumbers from an old peasant woman on the street and wolfing them down. Beside the food problem, the colonists, fearful of being discovered, always insisted on the taping sessions being held late in the evening. One night while returning from one of these midnight sessions at about three in the morning, I was caught in a violent freak snowstorm. Having given all my warm clothing to my Russian friends, I was not prepared for the freezing cold wind and heavy snow. There were no taxis so I walked the two miles unable to see the streets. Crossing The Grenadiers Bridge over the Neva River, I became so disoriented and in the end was only able to get to the other side by stepping with one foot on the curb of the sidewalk and one foot in the street. It took me two hours to reach the hotel clad only in sandals, a cotton dress, and a thin sweater. But I shall always be grateful to the colonists who so bravely talked to me in spite of their evident fears.

Over the years there have been many people, including my son, Alexis Swan, who have encouraged me whenever my spirit grew weak. Of particular help was a research support group of women scholars, all colleagues of mine at West Chester University, composed of Drs. Anne D. Sessa, Pamela Hemphill, Madelyn Gutwirth, Mary E. Crawford, and Ms. Mary McCullough. I am deeply grateful to Father Serge Schenuk of Wynnewood, Pa., who willingly struggled through old letters written in cramped handwriting on bad paper. His capable daughter, Marina Schenuk, was exceptionally helpful in translating and typing the taped interviews.

Rudolf A. Clemen, Jr., Information Research Specialist in the Library at the American Red Cross headquarters in Washington, D.C., gave me access to all A.R.C. archives, and permission to copy any material and photographs useful for this account of the odyssey.

It would be difficult to mention all of my family and friends who took the trouble to read this manuscript in its earlier stages and to provide kind but searching comments. But Irene Swann, Alfred's sister-in-law, and Donald Swann, his nephew, were particularly encouraging and interested in my completing this work.

The strangest fact of all my research was that I could find only a few Russian-Soviet sources on the odyssey. One was an ugly story printed in a children's magazine about a Russian child in New York being held with all the colonists in a New York City "concentration camp". He dropped the pencil he was using and it was picked up by someone else. Somehow, after changing hands many times, the pencil got back to Russia where it started writing by itself, telling all the happy Soviet children of the terrible conditions in America for the children. The only other Russian references to the odyssey I could find were some letters to *Izvestia* which referred to the incident in connection with the return trip to the Soviet Union of the Red Cross official, Burle Bramhall.

But I should like to reserve my deepest thanks to my husband, Robert Gruen, without whom this book would not have seen the light of day. I cannot count the number of times he edited, recopied, scolded, or encouraged, when my energy began to wane—and in general supported me both figuratively and spiritually throughout.

INTRODUCTION

In May of 1918, the parents of over 800 Russian school children, between the ages of 3 and 15, sent them on a summer vacation from Petrograd to the Ural mountains for their protection and to escape the chaos and famine of the Russian Revolution.

Who could have imagined at that time that their children would have to travel around the world for two and a half years in order to get back home? Their extraordinary adventures and hardships provide one of the strangest stories of our time.

To understand how such an odyssey could have occurred, we must go back to the beginnings of the Russia of Peter the Great who was determined to open up his mediaeval but enormous and powerful kingdom to Western influences . . .

The city of St. Petersburg, from the time of its birth in 1703, conjured up images of fairy tale palaces and magic kingdoms. Conceived by Peter the Great, it was built in the far north on the swampy shores and adjacent islands of the Gulf of Finland. The land did not even belong to Russia but was still part of Sweden. It was to be the realization of a new dream by a semi-barbarian ruler who was determined to take his country from the Middle Ages to modern times in one giant leap.

From the very beginning, St. Petersburg was the most beautiful city in Northern Europe. Divided by the midnight blue waters of the Neva River, it became known as the Venice of the North because of its numerous winding canals and many bridges. The city seemed suspended, like a mirage, between the Northern pale blue sky and the dark ominous waters of the Finnish Gulf.

Memories of so many burning wooden cities made Peter decide to pass an edict that all buildings of the new city must be of marble and stone. This, along with the absence of trees, gives the city to this day the impression of cold, overwhelming grandeur. The extreme weather, with bitter icy winds, snow, and rain contrasting with the strong sun of very short, hot summers, colored the city in soft blues, greens, and ochres.

As the Russian realm expanded into a huge empire, Peter's city took on the manners and style of other European countries, and even adopted some of their languages, so that it became part of the culture of Western Europe, almost forsaking its Russian origins. Palaces and public buildings were designed by foreign architects in the Baroque, and later Neo-Classical styles.

Parks and boulevards were laid out in the French manner. Statues glorifying Russian Czars, generals, and artists were planted everywhere, but except for their features, they could have been mistaken for rulers and famous men of any other country. Huge department stores were opened. Various sections of the city took on certain distinctly European airs, such as the German sector with St. Catherine's School, or the English sector with its Anglican church.

By the end of the 19th century the city had attracted all the famous and elegant stores, jewelers, and restaurants, and became one of the necessary stops for the International set who restlessly moved throughout Europe. Leading artists, authors, singers, and, most of all, musical performers, came to St. Petersburg during the season. Even the most unimportant performance was always sold out.

But outside the city the land was still wild and largely uninhabited. There was virtually no life beyond the city limits, and the visitor, leaving the city by train or carriage, was plunged into a vast wilderness with little warning. As late as the reign of Catherine the Great in the mid-18th century, one of her ladies-in-waiting was attacked by wolves as she left the Winter Palace and walked to her waiting coach. Even to this day people venture into the nearby woods to pick enough mushrooms for a week of meals, and return while it is still daylight for their own safety.

But by the early years of the 20th century, there was no vestige of barbarism left in St. Petersburg. The long hard winters were partially tamed by incessant sports such as ice skating and tobogganing. The streets were kept open at all times for the fast moving droshkies and trolleys. Buildings were cozily heated by the Russian stoves built into the walls which circulated warm air through ducts which had openings into all rooms. Fires burned at most street corners to warm the hands and toes of outdoor vendors and waiting drivers. Even the former strident revolutionary voices seemed muted as Russia slowly but surely began working towards parliamentary government procedures. The standard of living was also gradually increasing, and if all went well, the government hoped to have illiteracy stamped out by 1922.

The summer of 1914 was warm and serene. The long, light nights, which made it possible for people to read at 11 at night without artificial light, brought all St. Petersburg out for long evening strolls, and children released from school spent their days swimming in the quiet waters of the Neva. Vacationing clerks, businessmen, rich and poor families alike spent a day, a week, or a month at nearby dachas (summer cottages) built in the outlying forests, or along the Finnish Gulf, all within 10 or 15 miles of the capital itself.

News of the murder of the Archduke Franz Ferdinand, heir to the Austro-Hungarian throne, provoked little more than a clucking of tongues and shaking of diplomatic heads. Most people thought of it as nothing more than an insane act of a young Serb having no ties with Serbian government policy.

But to the dismay of everyone, this act precipitated war. Russia entered, honorably living up to her committed alliance with England and France, trying at the same time to protect her weaker Slav brothers, and woefully unprepared for any military confrontation. In the beginning there was an outbreak of national patriotic fervor, but that quickly subsided as repeated news of lost battles and rising casualties began to spread throughout the land. Gradually a glittering world began to die, as stunning defeats at Mausurian Lakes and Tannenberg during the first months of the war became known. Russia's hard pressed armies began digging into extended trenches like rats, to hold back the combined armies of Germany, Austria-Hungary, and later, Bulgaria, which relentlessly pounded the front lines.

Life back in the beautiful city began to change. Transportation lines bringing food and fuel supplies from the South became prey to disorganization, obsolescence, and more and more to deliberate sabotage by forces within Russia herself. Discontent was fanned by formerly dormant revolutionaries who now felt they had a new cause.

Rumors abounded of a fifth column reaching into the palace itself. For example, who was this crazy Siberian peasant advising not only the Czarina but, through her, influencing the government itself? Rasputin—the very name meant "dissolute" and was given to him by his fellow peasants as a young man. He now had uninterrupted access to the court, the Czar and Czarina, and even the nursery of the children. He outraged all St. Petersburg by his flamboyant and flagrant immorality. Denounced by many, both in and outside of the church, yet seemingly approved of by the royal family, he was, of course, used by all enemies of the monarchy and its institutional supports to damn the very basis of Russia's whole civilization.

Then beyond that, rumors spread about the Czarina's German nationality—wasn't she a cousin of Kaiser Wilhelm? Surely, wasn't the only reason that their armies were losing caused by secret government information being funneled to the enemy? Public confidence in the running of the war effort was eroded by the constant change of ministers, removal of generals, and increasing food and fuel shortages. Even Rasputin begged the emperor to stockpile flour, sugar, and butter as early as October 1915, but nothing was done.

Then in December of 1916, Rasputin was assassinated, at the instigation of a member of the Duma (Parliament), an army doctor, an officer, and two first cousins of the Czar. It was one of the most bizarre events in the 20th century. Fed poisoned cakes and two glasses of poisoned Madeira wine, shot once in the back, once in the shoulder, and once in the head, kicked with heavy boots, and pushed under the ice in the Neva River, Rasputin finally succumbed to death by drowning.

The resulting publicity, with deliberately twisted accounts and intentional distortions of his activities by both friend and foe, still fascinates historians and the public to this day. But Rasputin's exploitation of the hemophilic condition of the little Czarevitch became a contributing cause to the overthrow of the Czarist regime. He cunningly played on the fears and weaknesses of the parents and their love for their only son.

More and more acts of senseless violence occurred within the city itself, and there were tales of soldiers being sent to the front without guns or ammunition and told to take weapons from any dead soldier they might find. All this, plus continuing news of losses and suffering at the front heightened the nervousness within the country and gradually eroded what little morale remained back home.

Then in a fit of courage, but unfortunate political stupidity, the Czar himself took over the command of the army against the wishes of his own government. Rumors of impending coups began to circulate from both right and left wing sources.

The month of February 1917 was one of the worst that Russia had seen in many years. The temperature hit 35 degrees below zero, and the hard pressed railroad lines from the countryside to the cities began to collapse.

Flour, butter, and sugar were not to be had in Petrograd, as it was now called to take away the Germanic sound of its original name, St. Petersburg. Fuel ran out and there was no escape from the searing cold and driving northwest wind blowing straight from the White Sea. Within the government power struggles continued. Members of the Czar's immediate family begged for reforms. Members of the Duma, even some of the most conservative, openly denounced government policy, the direction of military activities, and the Czarina because of her supposed interference in government matters.

On Thursday, March 8th, Nicholas left for a three to four week visit to the front, after first having promised the Duma to appoint a new and responsible government and then having changed his mind once again at the eleventh hour. Why that day rather than any other was chosen remains a mystery—there was no plan, no preconceived pattern, but all at once the breadlines were too long, the cold too intense, and people too tired. Suddenly mobs broke their lines and attacked the bakeries. Workers from the factories on the other side of the river crossed over and marched down the main street, the Nevsky Prospect, shouting for bread. But the icy cold winds restrained passions for the moment.

The following day more crowds poured into the streets, and by Saturday most of Petrograd's factories were closed by striking workers. Public transportation came to a halt as the workers joined the mobs, and a new ugly note was heard as shouts and banners called "Down with the German woman!"—"Down with Protopopov!" (the Prime Minister)—"Down with the war!".

The Cabinet met all that day and well into the night, offering to resign if Nicholas wished to set up a new government. At the front, Nicholas considered it just one more disturbance in the city and, underestimating the seriousness of the temper of the crowds, simply telegraphed General Khabalov, the Military Governor of Petrograd, to end the disorders.

This was probably the worst order possible, for the caliber of the troops guarding Petrograd was very low. The best men had long since vanished at the front, and the winter garrison in the city consisted of raw recruits from the country, as well as older men drawn from factories and suburbs nearby. Untrained, lacking military discipline or pride, these were the embittered soldiers Nicholas called upon to restore order. On Sunday morning government posters forbidding public meetings were pasted up everywhere. But again huge crowds took to the streets and headed across the Neva bridges towards the government buildings. Twice, orders to fire on the crowds were refused, or the soldiers fired into the air.

Once more the helpless government wired to Nicholas, who simply decided to send reinforcements and return to Petrograd himself on March 13th. Monday morning, unbeknownst to the government, power had slipped out of its hands completely. All Sunday night troops in the barracks had been arguing about their orders, and what position they would take if ordered again to fire on their own people, their fellow citizens. Violence erupted, and the following morning, when another disorderly mob came across the Alexander Bridge, they were met and joined by a regiment of soldiers. Group after group of soldiers mutinied and joined the revolutionaries. It was only a matter of hours before the Law Courts were burning; the Arsenal, the Ministry of the Interior, the Military Government building, and the headquarters of the Secret Police, all were in flames. Even the bastion of Czarist power, the Fortress of St. Peter and Paul, had opened its gates and joined the revolution. Telephone calls to Nicholas, even by his father's brother, the Grand Duke Nicholas, produced no decision.

Finally, against the wishes of the Cabinet, the Duma declared itself in charge and set up a temporary committee to restore order and try to quell the mutinous troops. But on the same day and in the same building, a rival organization was formed. It was called the Soviet of Soldiers' and Workers' Deputies. And from that moment on there were two separate governments operating in Russia.

The following Tuesday a last outbreak of fighting occurred when a motley group of older officers, a women's brigade, and a few cadets tried to save the Winter Palace under the leadership of the still loyal General Khabalov; but, faced with the enormous force of revolutionary soldiers across the river, they quietly melted away. By Wednesday, all military organizations joined in giving their loyalty to the new government of the Duma, including the Grand Duke Cyril, the first Romanov to do so.

In the meantime, Nicholas, at Army headquarters at the front, was undergoing his own renunciation of power. A barrage of telegrams arrived, most of which he did not answer. On Sunday, March 11th, he still thought that the trouble was just street outbreaks which could easily be quelled with a show of force. That night he wrote in his diary that, while standing in church, he had such chest pains he could scarcely stand through the service and was bathed in sweat from the sharpness of the pain.

On Monday he finally realized that things were getting out of hand. He boarded the imperial train late that night, still not realizing the gravity of the situation. By Tuesday, he learned of the fall of the Imperial Palace and the formation of a new government under a committee of the Duma. At 2 A.M. on Wednesday the train was stopped and told it could not proceed—revolutionary soldiers were blocking the lines just up the track. A detour was arranged via Pskov and by eight the next morning the train arrived at Petrograd. Here he heard of the defection of all the troops, including the betrayal of the Grand Duke Cyril.

Telegram after telegram poured in begging him to abdicate to save Russia from civil war. After a day spent in anguish, Nicholas finally gave in. First he abdicated in favor of his son, but then, realizing that the frail health of Alexis could not stand up to the demands, he abdicated in favor of his brother Michael.

But the anxiety of the city was not nearly over, for a struggle began at once between the Duma government and the shadow government of the Soviet.

The Provisional Government, as it became known, was immediately recognized by both the United States and Russia's allies. Prince Lvov, who headed it for a short time only, and was later replaced by Kerensky, vowed to continue the war in spite of Russia's obviously exhausted state. This, probably more than anything else, sealed its doom. The self-constituted Soviet of Soldiers' and Workers' Deputies immediately recognized the stupidity of the decision and proceeded to make capital propaganda out of it. On March 14th, the day before the official abdication of Nicholas II, they had issued the famous Order Number One, which declared that all military units should be run by elected committees, and officers could only command during tactical operations. This increased the demoralization of the rapidly collapsing front lines.

A chilling example of the results of this order was an incident which took place when the author's brother-in-law, Edgar Swan, a very young, quickly trained officer of six months, was at the front. Sitting inside a dugout with several other officers late at night, he was surprised by a group of drunken soldiers who burst in and ordered all the officers to one side of the dugout, but motioned him to stay seated. Within seconds the soldiers gunned down all the other officers and announced to the panic-stricken second lieutenant that he had been elected General of the Western Front. For several wild drunken hours he was forced to feign celebration of the event, while surreptitiously tossing the vodka over his shoulder, until all the celebrants had passed out. As morning broke, the terrified "General" escaped from his newly proclaimed army and made his way back to Petrograd, where his mother buried his epaulets and sword under the latrine of the janitor's hut in the courtyard of their apartment house.

During the eight months' life of the Provisional Government, Kerensky faced and put down two attempted coups. In spite of the chaotic conditions much liberal legislation was passed, and even for a short time a new and successful offensive was begun in Galicia. But by the end of ten days the action ground to a halt and all fighting ceased. No amount of good will, patriotism, or liberal enthusiasm could compensate for the incredibly difficult conditions of life.

The long winter of 1916–17 brought the almost total breakdown of transportation and national discipline. This unbearable winter, both at the front and in Russia itself, without adequate food, fuel, and medicine, proved too much for everybody. A thriving black market grew, but money became worthless, and only bartering could procure the bare necessities of life. Food cards were issued, but even the small amount of black bread which they supplied was filled with straw and splinters. Petrograd was hit far worse than most cities, for she was dependent upon food shipped from southern Russia. Tragically, there was plenty of bread in the South, but the collapse of the transportation system and the absence of any government control produced extremely stark conditions in the North.

Although the Provisional Government was favorable toward the peasants' demand for land, as well as pressing demands of minorities, it was philosophically tied to a liberal position of a new and freely elected constituent assembly making major changes. The Russian jurists lost valuable time working out the perfect electoral law and, in the meantime, the gulf between the Provisional Government and the people widened. In July and September the Provisional Government escaped downfall almost by a fluke.

On October 23rd, Lenin returned from his hideout in Finland and, realizing that the calling of a constituent assembly might lose the Bolsheviks their chance to seize power, convinced the executive committee of the small, but tightly knit party, that action must be taken at once. The Military Committee of the Soviet of the Soldiers' and Workers' Deputies issued its first order to the Petrograd garrison on November 4th. By this order, the troops in the Capital were asked to transfer their allegiance to the new military government, i.e., Lenin and the Bolsheviks. On the night of November 7th, the principal buildings in Petrograd were occupied by Bolshevik troops, the centers of communications were seized and the powers of government passed from Kerensky's hands into those of Lenin.

There were a few days of bloody street fighting in the major cities, but the opposition was mostly from young cadets, or a few remaining older officers still loyal to the old regime. Word quickly spread to the front lines, and within a matter of days the entire front disintegrated, with soldiers shooting their officers, then leaving the trenches and walking in the general direction of "home." Roads were clogged, all forms of transportation confiscated, and Russia entered into a four year period of total anarchy, restlessness, and civil war, which did more to destroy her former institutions than the previous three years of war with her outside enemies.

Within Petrograd living conditions became even worse than the awful winter of 1916–17, for very soon an element of lawlessness appeared. No one knew whether the man with a gun was a soldier, responsible citizen, or violent criminal. The absence of government organization or control produced incredibly difficult conditions.

Toward the end of the winter of 1917–18 most of the schools were shut down. And it was for this reason that the parents of over eight hundred school children sent them off for a never-to-be-forgotten summer vacation with unexpectedly dramatic and drastic consequences.

The
Lost
Children:
A
Russian
Odyssey

Spring 1920. A few of the girls who made the journey from Petrograd to this location at Russian Island near Vladivostok and their subsequent sea journey around the world.

CHAPTER ONE

A middle aged couple named Schmidt were about to sit down to their meager supper in their apartment in Petrograd, when their 14 year old daughter, Vera, burst into the room breathlessly.

"Mama! Papa!" she shouted. "This afternoon my geography teacher asked our class if any of us would like to go to the Ural Mountains for the summer! I was the first to raise my hand. Can I go? Can I? Please? Please?"

Her parents were stunned—happily. They never dreamed that they would be able to send their child away to a place where there would be plenty of good food to fill out her starved body. Her mother had lain awake many a night wondering if Vera would survive another year under the dreadful conditions in the city. She stared in disgust at the table before her and saw a barely adequate meal of boiled potatoes and pickled cucumbers with tea made from reused grounds. This, because of the famine in the northern regions of Russia, was their standard fare, but hardly nourishing for a growing girl.

Vera had no trouble persuading her parents to agree. Fortunately, they couldn't know that she would have to circle the globe and be two and a half years older before they would see her again.

Similar scenes were taking place in hundreds of homes in Petrograd. It all came about because of an organization called the Union of Towns, which had been formed soon after the outbreak of the European War (known later as World War I).

The Union's main purpose was to cooperate with the Russian Duma (Parliament) to aid in the war effort and to reorganize sagging and inadequate government organizations. Bad news from the war front made the Union of Towns more and more powerful. Three and a half years of war, followed by two disruptive revolutions produced anarchy in Petrograd, the capital city of Russia. Since the Bolshevik revolution in November of 1917, people were daily assaulted by the sights of death and violence on the streets of the city. No one seemed able to do anything but helplessly stand by and watch as people were gunned down on the slightest pretext by drunken soldiers or self-styled revolutionaries.

Toward the end of the winter of 1917–18, many schools had to shut down for lack of fuel. Some parents, working under the auspices of the Union of Towns, developed a temporary plan to protect the children, keep them adequately fed, and allow them to continue their education in safety.

By the spring of 1918, the plan was set in motion and the schools began to contact all parents to find out how many would like to participate. The idea was to send the children to an area where there was still peace and abundant food. Responsible teachers would be in charge of them and their safety. They would spend a pleasant summer vacation and then return in the fall when schools would normally reopen. Everybody believed that peace and order would surely prevail by then. The Union of Towns supported the plan and promised money to procure whatever supplies could be found. The necessary charge for the expenses of each child was 75 rubles a month, or nothing if the family couldn't afford that much.

In contrast to Petrograd, which was hit hardest by the collapse of the transportation system because of a large, changing itinerant population of returning soldiers, the Volga region was almost untouched by either famine or disorder. It was determined that the small, sleepy town of Myass, in the fertile Orenburg Province west of the Ural Mountains, would be an ideal place to locate the summer camp. Children could be parceled out from there to surrounding villages, with Myass serving as headquarters.

In every school in Petrograd, a teacher was appointed to offer the plan to children and their parents. At first many parents were apprehensive about their children going off so far and for such a long time. But when the plan was explained in detail their fears were assuaged, especially since they were assured that reliable teachers and school personnel would go along as leaders and counselors. As the news spread, increasing numbers of parents met with school administrators and consented to the plans. They would then attempt to equip them with new clothes and other necessaries, but that proved utterly frustrating since stores which were still open were woefully short of goods. The result was that many children were outfitted in older brothers' and sisters' castoffs. Naturally, these things did not dampen the spirits of the eager youngsters.

By May 1918, over eight hundred children were enrolled in the

Petrograd Children's Colony, as it was now called. As the plan caught on, many parents begged to enroll even younger pre-school children, to give them a few months of good food and healthy living, and to help counteract the privations of the past few years. The result was that many boys and girls brought along younger brothers and sisters; the youngest was only three years old. With conditions getting worse by the day, no one in the administration of the colony demurred.

Vera Schmidt was in the first group of colonists to leave from the Finnish Station in Petrograd on May 18th. They were headed for the Western Siberian Plains—a five hundred mile trip which should have taken at most two days and a night. Each section consisted of about thirty cars carrying a couple of hundred children. She had brought only summer clothes and a few school books as had most of the others. The plan was to have the children catch up with their lessons, missed when the schools closed during the preceding winter.

In spite of the preparations made with great care, the enormous congestion on the railroads had not been foreseen. The Russian front, which had been collapsing gradually during 1917, was now, in the spring of 1918, deserted. On March 14, 1917, just one day before the forced abdication of Nicholas II, a self-constituted Soviet of Soldiers' and Workers' Deputies had issued the famous Order Number One. That order declared that all military units should be run by military committees, and that officers could only command during tactical operations.

The direct result was that soldiers at the front dropped their weapons and began an overwhelming flight back to their homes.

Since the colony trains were given the lowest priority, they had to give way every few miles to military trains, food trains, and even ordinary passenger trains overloaded with unending traveling humanity. One of Vera's friends, Vanya Semenov, on a military hospital train, counted six hundred abandoned engines and cars before he became bored with the game and quit. Vera's train took three weeks to get to Myass, while Vanya's was a month and a day en route.

Different delays were caused by rumors and alarms. For instance, the report that the bridge over the Myatka River had been blown up kept the train stationary for two days but turned out to be false. Trains were sometimes stalled for hours or days for just such reasons, which kept the teachers in a continuous state of nerves.

Inside the cars, however, the children, who were ignorant of all these things, passed the time pleasantly with games and singing of songs. They seemed almost oblivious of the threatening problems of the world outside of the trains.

At every station children would swarm out to look for peasants with food to sell. But except for watery milk, there was little to be had until they reached the Siberian plains. One day two of the boys, Peter Azarov and a friend, were given permission to go into the village of Kotelnich in search of food. Their train had been held up indefinitely by a blockage of the line ahead. They blithely set off, happy for the chance to vary the dull routine of life on the train. What happened next was unexpected. They were grabbed from behind by two men and held in a tight grip. In their fright, they wriggled around and saw that their assailants were two rough, un-shaven soldiers in Austrian uniforms who immediately started asking them questions.

"Who are you?" one demanded. "Where did you come from?"

Before they had a chance to answer, the other asked, "How did you get here? Do you have anything to eat?"

The men released their grip somewhat, and Peter, trembling, got up the courage to tell about their trip, where they were going, and the difficulties of traveling on clogged railroad lines and discarded trains and cars. Sullenly the soldiers let them go and walked away. They were among the numerous Austrian prisoners who, because of the Treaty of Brest-Litovsk which ended the German-Russian part of World War I, had been set free. But they were essentially still captives, because, with the chaos and lack of transportation, they had no way of getting home.

On July 7th, several days after that incident, the train finally left Kotelnich, and for four days slowly made its way along the banks of the Gusev River. When it arrived at Ekaterinburg, another unexplained delay of several days was announced. Maria Gorbachova, a young teacher, scarcely older than the children, heard of a mineral museum with a large display of stuffed animals. The children were enthusiastic to have the opportunity to leave the railroad tracks and to go sightseeing and so, without delay, she organized an expedition.

They formed two lines, one led by Maria and the other by Nicholas Borsuk, an older boy, and started to walk through the town hand in hand. They began to notice that the people here seemed somewhat different from those in other towns where they had stopped. Although curious, the townspeople only stared at the children and made no attempt to speak. In other places, local people would stop to talk and often give them little gifts of postcards or sweets, but in Ekaterinburg they only stared and turned away. Also for the first time, the children saw Red soldiers on almost every street corner lounging about, seeming to have nothing to do.

En route to the museum, Nicholas, the leader of one column, took a wrong turn, but felt too embarrassed to ask questions. To lose face in front of the smaller children was too much of a demand on his adolescent dignity. They found themselves walking through the nicest section of town, when they came upon a building closely guarded by Lett (not Russian) soldiers. It was a pretentious building, two stories high, faced with white brick and heavily decorated in a Moorish style. One child overheard a remark of a bystander, and rapidly whispers spread through the column of children: "The Czar! — The Czar!". They all stopped and stared at the silent mansion, known as the house of Ipatiev, a leading merchant of the town in Czarist times.

Inside, Czar Nicholas, Czarina Alexandra, their four daughters and their little son, the hemophiliac, Czarevitch Alexis, were living in three small rooms without enough beds for all of them. At the end of April 1918, unknown to almost everyone at the time, they had been moved from Tobolsk to Ekaterinburg, which was later renamed Sverdlov after the man responsible for their murder. Here the family was housed in the second story of the building with all the windows opaqued with whitewash. The guards were of the roughest sort, and delighted in shocking and bullying their prisoners with rude words scrawled on the walls and coarse songs sung in their presence. They were not even allowed to go to the bathroom without obscene comments and spying. Mealtimes were particularly unpleasant, for the guards insisted on eating with the family as they pushed and gobbled their food. Nobody could have known then that the lifespan of the royal family was coming to a violent close, and that just a few weeks later they would be brutally murdered.

As the children stood looking at the imposing building, a soldier came toward them waving his rifle and shouting:

"Get out! Get out, you brats!"

They turned away and continued on their way toward the museum where they became far more interested in the stuffed animals than in seeing the Czar's house. Few of them later even remembered the incident.

In the last week of June 1918, three sections of the Petrograd Colony arrived on the Western Siberian plains, and the children were settled in various villages around Myass in Orenburg Province.

When the original plans for the colony were being made during the previous winter and early spring of 1918, no one could foresee that a civil war would begin. The Bolsheviks had overthrown the provisional government of Kerensky in November of 1917 and, to all intents and purposes, were firmly in control. A duly elected Constituent Assembly, had met for only one day before being chased off by Lenin and his Bolshevik troops. The exhaustion of the Russian people from three years of war and revolution left them without any organized opposition to the Bolsheviks who seemed to be securely in power. Surely, there would be no more fighting!

Unbeknownst to anyone connected with the colony, the city of Samara on the Volga had been taken by detachments of Czech soldiers, during the time that the children were en route to Myass. The capture of Samara would deal a severe blow to the colonists because it was the rail junction through which all food and supplies were transported to various destinations, both north and west. This meant that the colonists could eventually receive no fresh supplies. However, during the short summer of 1918, local supplies were ample and the effect of Samara's fall was not immediately felt.

At Myass, the teachers and other personnel quickly organized the children into groups. They were housed mostly in large summer villas whose owners formerly had lived there during the summer.

They spent the first part of each day with a few hours of lessons, and kept busy with outdoor activities the whole afternoon. Good food, fresh air, and exercise soon filled out their thin bodies which had subsisted on war diets for three years. They took expeditions into the woods and fields of the surrounding countryside which was perfect for collecting minerals and flowers. They even started a small museum for the best specimens collected and rewarded the original finder by placing his or her name under each item. In the meantime, since they lacked any real news from Petrograd, everyone remained carefree.

Because of the large number of children coming to Myass from Petrograd, not all could be accommodated there, so one large section of the train headed for Petropavlosk further east of Myass. That train never made it. The same uprising which had resulted in the retaking of Samara by the Czech and White Russian forces was the cause. Admiral Kolchak, who eventually became head of all White efforts, had assumed the title of Supreme Ruler of Russia after the murder of the Czar. He now headed westward and was joined by Czech and Austrian war prisoners. In so doing he closed the main route to Petropavlosk and the children were suddenly stranded.

Peter Vasilivitch de George was one of the teachers with this group.

He was one of the colony's original leaders, and he remained with the children to the end. While the train was on a siding, he left and managed to get on a passing passenger train. Going back and forth, crisscrossing from one little station to another, he finally located an alternate place for this colony—the little town of Kuraii. Returning to the stranded train, de George brought the entire section straight to the village. Of course, no preparations had been made for the children.

Kuraii had been a favorite summer resort for the upper class of Ekaterinburg. It was situated on the beautiful shores of the Pueshma River in the Siberian side of the Urals, directly north of Myass. With the permission of the local Soviet committee, de George commandeered a big hotel, formerly a summer resort, in a spacious park facing the river. The small village surrounding the park owed its existence to mineral springs which were thought to be efficacious for a variety of real and imagined diseases. Until the war it had been extremely popular. The smell of sulphur still permeated the town, but the ramshackle condition of the guest house which some of the children were to occupy, belied its former prosperity.

There were about 150 houses in the village, plus the inevitable onion domed church and a large courthouse built in a Moorish style. A few small shops remained, but they were all boarded up. When the children arrived, one or two opened again hoping that the children could mean a slight return to more prosperous times, but all they had to offer were some small wooden animals carved by local peasants and a few fly-specked postcards.

Boys were settled first in the guest house with a supervisor and several teachers. Each older child was told to adopt and take care of a younger one if they had no younger brother or sister in the group. Vera Schmidt headed one of the work groups which were formed to try to bring the building back to a livable condition. The buildings had been abandoned since 1915, and were desolate and filthy. They needed a thorough scrubbing of the many rooms and porches. For several nights the children slept on the floor on straw mattresses, but they were so tired from the work that no one complained. As always in Russia when traveling, each child had brought along a mattress cover and sheets with their belongings. By the end of the week, local carpenters had completed simple wooden beds and placed the straw mattresses on them.

By the second week the teachers were able to establish a formal routine. As at Myass, classes were held every morning, while the afternoon was given over to outdoor activities and free time.

With fresh memories of home and hardships, the older children went around trying to buy flour to send to parents and relatives, but the peasants refused to barter for anything but sugar. They were too suspicious of the new government rubles. The children were quick to learn how to buy sugar from the town merchants, and then scour the countryside for peasants who could supply flour. A flourishing trade began. The Kuraii post office suddenly became a very busy place, with sacks of flour being sent to Petrograd and grateful letters of thanks arriving, containing more paper rubles to buy more sugar to trade for more flour. Vera was very proud of having been able to send over twenty pounds of the precious stuff back home, and of the letters from her family telling of the extent of their dependence on her packages.

This became a very happy time for the children. They gradually got to know each other and made many lifelong friendships. They organized or invented games and the summer days were filled with laughter and the cries of splashing children echoing over the Pueshma River. They went on picnics and outings in the surrounding woods, and would sometimes catch small animals which they tried to make into pets.

Other activities were initiated with great enthusiasm. Vera joined a girls' choir which was started by the supervisor of her group, Eugenia Mazun. They gave evening concerts occasionally. Several of the boys got together and put out a magazine called "The Colonist" which reviewed all cultural events and threw in a little personal gossip as well.

Another teacher, affectionately known as Dadya (Uncle) Brantz, developed an acting company to perform Turgenev's play "An Evening in Sorrento." Vera played the lead, Naderzda Pavlovna, and borrowed a long dress from one of the teachers for the performance. Her hair was piled high on her head. Fifty seven years later she still remembered with a giggle how beautiful she felt when she saw herself in a mirror with her fancy hair style. She was very proud of the raves she received in the Colonist's review of the performance.

But against these sunny days, dark clouds began to cast their shadows. One morning in mid-July, Vera was awakened by the sound of distant gunfire. From that time on, the quietness of summer days was interrupted by the muffled thunder of cannons from the East. Then towards the end of July, strange looking men began to straggle into the village. Soon the trickle became a torrent of irregularly clad soldiers—some wearing pieces of old Czarist uniforms, some in new Red uniforms, and many in coarse working clothes which identified their loyalty.

One day after lessons were finished, some of the children who were playing in the village saw swarms of men gathering in the town square. They hurried back to the park to tell the teachers, who quickly hustled them into the buildings. Curious children peeked out from the windows and porches, while worried teachers tried to locate any stray children who might still be out of doors. By that time, the teachers knew that fighting had broken out in the Ukraine, various places in Siberia, and even north around Archangel, but there had been no warning that Kuraii was unsafe. Slowly the firing drew closer and closer, until by mid-afternoon the hotel grounds became the front line. Bullets flew through the windows. The children were hastily put into their rooms and told to lie on the floor. The battle line was sweeping rapidly westward through the hotel grounds. Now the town was filled with different strangers wearing Czech uniforms, to the amazement of the Russians.

No one could foresee that the events of that day would presage the horrors to come. By the end of the day, Kuraii was firmly in the hands of the Czechs, and their officers and men moved freely around the hotel and park. As evening approached, a line of Red soldiers, tied together with ropes, was marched up in front of the hotel veranda. The faces of these soldiers clearly showed that they were terribly frightened young peasant boys. The curious children, hanging out of the windows, watched in fascination as a dozen Czech soldiers took up a position opposite them and began to load their rifles. By the time the teachers realized that they were about to witness an execution, they had no time to move the spellbound children in, away from the windows. Then to everyone's horror, a volley of shots rang out, producing the ugly picture of the young Red soldiers sinking to the ground, some quickly, but others not quite dead, screaming and jerking until a second volley ended their agony.

Within two days the Czech detachment left town. Normally, when they left the towns they had occupied, they would leave them in the hands of remaining White Russians. But Kuraii was too tiny a village to have any effective group willing and ready to take over, which left it unprotected. So Kuraii became prey to roving gangs of detached soldiers with no allegiance to any side. Some even openly declared themselves to be robbers living off plunder. The town had no law or order and seemed to change hands almost weekly with each new invading gang. The hotel was searched repeatedly, even straw mattresses were torn apart by the marauders. In vain, teachers tried to explain that there were only children in the hotel. But there was no authority to appeal to, and things went from bad to worse.

Local food supplies became scarce, and even their large buying power was of no help. Every plea for food by the colony supervisors was met simply with a shrug of the shoulders, and there was no higher official to petition. They learned that nearby villages had some food, so finally in desperation, they sent out small children, hoping their innocent despair might move the notoriously hard-hearted peasants. For a while, kind townspeople shared what little they had, but gradually doors were shut against the never-ending appeals of hunger. Older boys went out to help with the harvest and were paid in bread. It is interesting to note that it was white bread, since the Russian staple of life, black bread, had disappeared. By early September the only hot food served was weak soup, usually bad tasting from rotting ingredients and no salt, since, by that time, salt had also vanished. Bread would be divided each day among them all until the portions dwindled to a few crumbs. Each older girl took charge of a younger one and attempted to keep her quiet, particularly when soldiers came in to search.

Vera Schmidt and a few of her friends went foraging for food one day and were delighted to find a cow loose in a pasture. Vera climbed over the fence and started to milk her, but the peasant owner spotted the girls and chased them. Catching them he gave them all a beating with a club. They returned bruised and crying to the hotel. Vera never forgot that incident nor her attempt to hide her desperation from the younger girl in her charge.

When the Czechs took the village, all communication with Petrograd had stopped. In spite of the fact that at times some Red soldiers would control the area for a few days, communication with the outside world was cut off. No more did packages go from the local post office and no more did grateful letters arrive from home.

By now the teachers and other personnel of the colony realized that they were trapped, and fears of the vicious Siberian winter haunted everyone. Even the older boys and girls began to panic as they came to understand the situation. The new rubles possessed by the teachers were useless, for even possession of them was outlawed in White territory. As a final resort their last belongings were bartered or sold for Soviet currency, including the sheets and mattress covers on their beds. There was no way of heating the hotel which had formerly been occupied only in the summer. Since they had all expected to return to Petrograd in the early fall, they had brought no winter clothes with them, and their summer clothing was outgrown and ragged after the wear and tear of three months hard use.

The future looked grim. They had no place to turn and nobody to turn to. The only possession they had was useless money. The Siberian winter was already approaching and they had no way to keep warm. Disaster seemed imminent.

A pleasant moment when the YMCA group met before leaving Samara in flight. Alia and Katia Swan are seated and are fourth and fifth from the left. At the far left wearing tie and glasses is the Y.M.C.A. secretary Bayard Christy.

CHAPTER TWO

One evening in March of 1918, a handsome young couple, Alia and Katia Swan, were sitting in their tiny two room apartment on the Nevsky Prospect in Petrograd. They were discussing the terrible problems brought on by the Russian Revolution and were clearly worried—with good reason.

After a short silence, Katia remarked, "Alia, don't you think it's time to talk seriously about our own affairs?" This was her standard remark whenever she felt that they were faced with any difficult situation.

At that time they were both teachers of children in various schools in the city, but even these had closed down through lack of heat and safety conditions for the children. There was nothing to stop them from getting away to a part of the country not affected as yet by severe food shortages and dangerous fighting. They could have no idea that they were about to embark on a strange journey that would take them to many countries and change their lives forever.

Although Russia had supposedly pulled out of World War I, conditions from three and a half years of war followed by two revolutions, had left her flat on her back. The October Revolution of 1917, which was hailed at first as a triumph of light over darkness, proved to be an idealistic dream.

Constant street agitation by soapbox orators, loss of discipline, breakdown of city services, and the disappearance of any semblance of law and order, was caused by the gradual takeover of the city by the Bolsheviks and the impending occupation by the Germans after the signing of the infamous Brest-Litovsk Treaty. Added to this was the severe famine throughout all northern cities which were cut off by the almost total breakdown in transportation from the breadbasket of the south.

Katia was a person who preferred her life to be well organized and had already devised a plan for the coming months.

She outlined her idea to Alia: "Let's go south for the rest of the winter and summer months," she said. "I hear that conditions are much better there—plenty of food, better weather, and, even more important, less danger. We can come back to Petrograd in the Fall when I imagine law and order will surely have been restored."

Alia, being a man of few words, readily agreed.

Alfred Swan had been born in St. Petersburg into an English family who had retained residence in Russia for over four generations. His Russian nanny, defying the regal English name of Alfred, promptly rechristened him Alia, a nickname which stuck to him for the rest of his life. His father, an official in the Russo-American India Rubber Company, had sent him and his three brothers to the German school of St. Catherine where Russian was taught as a second language. Alia then went to Oxford University where he studied law.

In spite of this international education, his identification with Russia was so strong that he returned home in 1912 when his education was complete, and took up work as a teacher and translator in several schools.

His insatiable love of music and considerable talent in composing and playing the violin would seem to presage a quiet gentle life. At that time, he was also surrounded by other idealistic young people who had embraced the attractive precepts of peace and non-violence promulgated by Leo Tolstoy. The first World War proved to be a shattering blow to the young idealists of that time, and Alia was no exception. Alia threw himself into teaching, increasing his work with children of conscripted soldiers and defense workers at various clubs and centers. Volunteer work included teaching games, choral singing, and staying with the children until bedtime. In this work he was joined by Katia, a beautiful Russian woman with long blond hair whose full name was Katherine Reazvia. Katia had been brought up as a lonely child by her grandmother who was quite ill and needed a lot of attention. She was very intelligent and, having few friends, gave most of her time to her studies. One of her attractions for Alia was her practice and devotion to Tolstoyan principles.

In spite of Alia's shyness, his frequent contact with the beautiful Katherine broke his reserve and blossomed into romance. They were married in June of 1915 and continued their work together at a summer colony near St. Petersburg.

In April of 1918, the Swans left the city, now called Petrograd, with only the barest necessities plus his ubiquitous violin and the latest songs of Scriabin and Rachmaninov. Of course, both of them were convinced that they were going off on a short vacation.

But they had not realized that train travel would be almost impossible. The trains were jammed with soldiers and floating populations who were fleeing from nowhere to nowhere. Attempts to transport food and supplies to starving cities were frustrating, and all of that was complicated by masses of prisoners of war trying to find a way to get home.

When they arrived at the Volga River, they boarded a comfortable river boat. Floating down the Volga was a euphoric time. Wharf after wharf of the villages were piled high with loaves of bread in unlimited quantities. Katia and Alia eagerly bought the precious loaves and stuffed themselves till they could hardly move.

Their first stop was at Saratov. It turned out to be short lived, for it was there and then that one of the first acts of civil war suddenly broke out. A group of ex-officers and soldiers were attempting to drive the Bolsheviks out — unsuccessfully. Newspapers were carefully censored and kept everyone in ignorance about the fighting. The Swans were not the kind of people to stay calmly in the midst of such uncertain dangers, so they returned up the Volga to the large town of Samara which was untouched so far by the insurrection. Settling down in rented rooms, they began to meet a number of like-minded souls and spent their time in long walks, music making, and endless conversation.

One evening while supping at a vegetarian restaurant (all young intellectual idealists who followed Tolstoy's pacifist and dietary strictures refused to eat meat), Alia watched an American desperately trying to order food in incomprehensible Russian. He offered to help, and that meeting became the start of a life-long friendship.

Bayard Christy was one of several hundred YMCA secretaries sent to Russia during the Revolution and subsequent civil war. Their purpose was to render aid, without political bias, to the masses of displaced wanderers, and specifically to help the thousands of Czech war prisoners to get back to their homeland.

The intrusion of Czech soldiers into Russian political affairs almost defies description. The Czech army had been part of the great Triple Alliance facing Russian forces which stretched from the Baltic to the Black Sea. When the Russian monarchy was overthrown in 1917, the Czecho-Slovaks serving in the Austro-Hungarian armies, being without loyalty to the Hapsburg rule, shot their officers and surrendered by companies and regiments to the Bolsheviks whom they believed to be on the side of democracy against tyranny. For a short time they were assigned a position on the Russian front fighting against Austria and almost opposite their homeland of Bohemia. Then, to their chagrin, in March 1918, a peace was concluded between the newly formed Soviet Union and the still militant central powers of Germany and Austria-Hungary. This placed the Czechs in a desperate position both politically and geographically, and a heroic decision had to be made. Their plan was to leave their exposed position, to go around the world, if necessary, in the opposite direction, and to stand on the plains of Western Europe again where they could fight their natural enemies, the Austro-Hungarians. Subsidized by French money, (France was still battling Germany and Austria-Hungary in the West), the disciplined Czech army began moving eastward. Lenin's government was glad to get rid of an embarrassing former ally and gave them permission to cross Siberia to the Pacific Ocean. But Trotsky, Commander-in-Chief of the Red Army, ordered the Czechs to surrender their arms. The Czechs unhesitatingly refused, and, when the Soviet soldiers tried to disarm them, fighting erupted all along the Volga River. Multitudes of war prisoners flocked to join them, with the sole idea of trying to get back home. Thus an army of about forty thousand men nearly doubled as it stretched all the way across Asia from west of the Ural Mountains to Vladivostok on the Japanese Sea.

On a warm, sunny afternoon in May, Katia and Alia were reading a heavily censored Bolshevik newspaper in a small square in Samara. Suddenly they heard the distinct muffled roar of guns in the distance. The sounds of fighting approached the city with great rapidity, and within an hour the rat-tat-tat of machine guns could be clearly heard against the heavy growling of big cannons.

Without warning, the square filled with soldiers, stark naked, riding horseback and wearing absolutely nothing but caps. Others ran on foot with rifles strapped to their bare backs, while trucks full of naked men careened through the streets. This extraordinary scene never ended until nightfall, but without any explanation at all. The usual wild rumors spread. Were the Germans invading? Had the Allies come from Western Europe? Was it an uprising started by the Constituent Assembly which had been overthrown by Lenin? Was the Czar returning? But finally one rumor prevailed—the Czech soldiers must be on the move. Gradually quiet descended on the town and people went to bed, hoping that this would really be the end of the disturbance.

At three the next morning, Alia and Katia were awakened by the deafening roar of guns. The din seemed to come from every direction. They heard people screaming that cannons had been placed in the square, and more than one voice shouted, "Run! Leave everything! Hurry!".

Caught up in the hysteria, the Swans fled from the house and, with bullets kicking up dust in the street or pinging off iron railings, they fled into the side streets. As he fell down from sheer exhaustion, Alia suddenly remembered that he had left all his documents behind. At a time when the careless throwing of the word "spy" could bring immediate lynching, or instant arrest, to be without documents was suicidal. No matter what, he had to return to the house. Leaving Katia in relative safety he got to their house and saw that all windows and doors had been blown out. He climbed the bullet-riddled stairs to their room where, to his relief, he found their possessions untouched and undamaged. Quickly grabbing their documents and his violin, he fled back to the place he had left Katia.

Now in a wild panic, the Swans alternately walked, staggered, and ran down the road with hordes of other terror-stricken people. Clinging to walls and hedges, only stopping occasionally to catch their breath, they finally reached the outskirts of town where the streets were deserted.

For a while the cannonading stopped but, realizing that they could not possibly tell whether or when it would start again, they kept walking toward the countryside hoping to find a small village or peasant cottage for shelter. They walked all the next day and finally came to the village of Barbushina Polyana, about ten miles out from Samara.

Wide, shady oak-lined avenues led to the edge of the Volga, and cherry orchards were in full bloom. As dusk fell, the beauty of the scene was enhanced by the cherry blossoms glimmering in the moonlight. It all would have seemed so wonderfully peaceful, were it not for the sinister roar of distant cannons and the bright red reflection of fire in the darkening sky.

At a turn in the road they came upon the gatekeeper's house of what had evidently once been a large estate. Their knock on the door was opened by a kind-looking, large blonde peasant woman.

"Come on in," she answered their question. "You're welcome to spend the night here. I warn you, though, it's not very clean and we don't have an extra bed. But at a time like this, that really shouldn't matter. Dimitri," she called to her husband. "Come and spread some old sheepskin coats on the floor."

They lost no time in dropping into the welcome embrace of the soft sheepskins, and fell into a deep sleep, no longer hearing the muffled thunder of distant cannons. But their awakening brought a new horror. They came to, clawing and slapping at their bodies. Racing from the cottage, they found their hair, clothes, and bodies covered by flat, sickly white, insects which clung to every part of them. They discovered a well nearby and tried in vain to wash the disgusting things off, but it soon became evident that it couldn't be done. In the end, their revulsion turned into dull resignation, and, unbelievably, they were never able to get rid of the bugs until they left Russia almost two years later.

The next day the cannonading continued, and, after moving to another cottage, they learned that food had become practically nonexistent. Then they remembered the river. There, sitting calmly on the bank they found a local fisherman catching "sterlyadi", a famous fish found only in the Volga. Within an hour they were able to persuade a peasant woman to make some fish soup for them which they ate on the porch of their cottage. White cherry blossom petals from a shedding cherry tree fell softly around them as distant sounds of war roared on.

Later, while having tea, the Swans heard the tramping of feet and loud voices. A crowd of Russian officers and men came up to the porch. One officer explained that they were searching for Bolsheviks hiding in the area. They invited the officers to join them at tea, while the men were sent out to search the garden. Suddenly, amidst great commotion, several of the soldiers appeared, dragging a man by his arms. He was small, with red curling hair escaping from under his cap, obviously terror-stricken, and trembling. The soldiers claimed that he was the local commissar.

Katia, unable to stand his cries of fright, pleaded for his life as a fellow human being. But the youthful officer, ineffectively trying to conceal a pained expression, quietly turned to her with, "Don't worry," and led her back to the porch. A few seconds later two shots rang out. She wrote in her diary that night: "I suddenly realized how much easier it was for me to plead, than for this young officer to execute his prisoner."

A few days later, peace seemed to descend on the village and signs of life started again. Laundry hung out, smoke rose from chimneys, and small shops reopened. Several days passed without bombing, and the Swans decided to return to Samara.

The city looked desolate with demolished buildings, collapsed walls, and shattered windows. Miraculously, their two small rooms in the boarding house were still intact, and all their possessions were just as they left them.

Alia learned that the entire YMCA staff had been jailed as Bolshevik spies, but the matter had been straightened out. Bayard Christy explained what had happened. The Czechs were retaking towns on the Volga to cover their advance to Vladivostok. Coming from the north, they overtook the Bolsheviks on the swampy plains of the Samarka River which flows into the Volga. They occupied the bridge and forced the retreating Bolsheviks to wade through the swamps and swim for their lives across the river. The Bolshevik troops stripped naked and, with only their rifles strapped to their backs, retreated into Samara. At last the Swans understood the strange flight of naked men which they had witnessed that summer afternoon just before the bombing began.

A new government was formed in Samara of Czech officials and members of the Constituent Assembly which Lenin had chased out of Petrograd so contemptuously. Order returned to the city, and Bayard Christy invited Alia and Katia to join YMCA activities. They accepted and both of them immediately found themselves overwhelmed with translations of letters, bulletins, appeals, and documents of all sorts. They also became deeply involved in relief work ranging from collecting food from local peasants to arranging for the building of outdoor latrines to taking care of the continuous flow of refugees at the feeding stations. But everyone was very much aware of the fact that Samara lay in a tiny area about 40 miles in circumference, surrounded by hostile Bolshevik territory.

On September 12th rumors began seeping in that the Bolsheviks were on the move again. Flashes of light could be seen again on the horizon and the muffled roar of cannons soon became a constant part of the background noise. Martial law was declared.

On September 14th the main street of Samara was blocked with carts bearing small, flat, very solid, wooden boxes—the gold reserve was being evacuated.

Two weeks earlier, Bayard Christy had left Samara to go to the YMCA headquarters in Moscow. He wanted to discuss the future activities of the organization in view of the rapidly deteriorating political situation. He left the Swans in charge of the operation in Samara, with instructions to transfer money and supplies to Chelyabinsk if things got too difficult. He also had laid out a plan for future relief activities, taking into account the latest news of the arrival in Vladivostok of the American Red Cross.

Christy's return to Moscow was fraught with wild experiences. He and his entire party were arrested for some unexplained reason and thrown in jail. It was only through the strongest pressure from the American government that he was released and sent back home via Finland.

By September 15th it became imperative for the YMCA personnel to leave immediately. A compartment was obtained for the Swans, who shared it with a Dutch merchant and a fleeing Finnish clergyman with his large family. Swarms of men, women, and children were pushing on the train and tried to shove their way into the compartment, but the Finnish clergyman barred the doors. That night, while the Finn slept, Katia surreptitiously opened the door to let in a young pregnant girl and her husband. Others followed, crowding onto the shelves, lying on the floor, or wherever else a body could find a little breathing space. One young Tartar moaned all night about the slaughter of his entire family in his village of Koustanai, but didn't know what soldiers had done it. When the Finn awakened he tried to drive everyone out but was forced to back down in the face of the immovable masses.

It was in Chelyabinsk that Alia heard the first reports of wild children dressed in rags and appearing to travel in packs. Ken Miller, the local YMCA secretary, had been working with the Czech soldiers and mentioned to Alia that some Czech officers reported that their men, while out on reconnaissance, told of seeing the strange children. Whenever they tried to approach and talk to them, the children would take to their heels and disappear into the woods. They showed some kind of pack loyalty, for the bigger children would quickly grab the little ones and drag them along. The age description of the children ranged from toddlers to teenagers.

Alia was not only curious but deeply touched by Miller's story. Being totally committed to the Tolstoyan philosophy of love and service to all fellow men, he determined to learn more.

He outlined the unusual story to Katia and said, "We don't know anything about these children—who they are or why they came to be here. But there must be some tragic reason for their plight. Why don't we try to find out more? Let's go back to Myass. It's only about 25 miles."

Katia promptly agreed, "After what we've seen of conditions here, it's obvious that some chance events of war or revolution probably brought those children together. They must be in desperate need of help just to survive."

They left their few bags with Miller, and returned to the railroad station. They succeeded in forcing their way into a crowded boxcar which took them to the only station near Myass. Hiring the only horse-drawn droshkey there, they drove to Myass several miles away.

Myass was a typical Siberian village with one long street petering out into the endless steppes. Katia was knowledgable about village habits, and so headed immediately for the one little bakery which was situated at one end of the town. There were several women in the shop, one of whom, a broad shouldered German woman, turned out to be the proprietress.

"Can anyone here tell us about the stories we've been hearing of ragged groups of children running around in this area?" she asked the proprietress.

Suddenly one woman ran up to Katia. She warmly kissed her and squeezed her hand. She proved to be the mother of one of Katia's childhood friends from boarding school days.

"What a strange coincidence!" she said, after excited greetings. "I happen to be one of the teachers of the children's colony. Come with me."

She led the Swans to an old building also used to house troops. They were shocked to see a small group of children far gone in demoralization and disorder. Most of the instructors had disappeared in search of work and wages, so there was only a minimum amount of supervision for the children who were wearing ragged clothes, torn tennis shoes, and living in barracks without heat. One overworked teacher told Katia that there was not one single winter overcoat among them.

Even more alarming was the information that some of the soldiers housed in the same building had already offered gifts of food and candy to a number of older girls, hoping for future favors. She also told the Swans that there were many more groups, some in even worse condition, toward the north from Tumen and as far as Irbit. She believed that they numbered almost a thousand in all. In a sketchy fashion she told how the children had gone off from Petrograd the previous spring for a joyous vacation intended to rebuild their bodies wasted from years of war and famine. But the outbreak of civil war changed the heavenly dream into a hideous nightmare.

Moved and horrified by the story and the conditions the children were living under, the Swans rashly offered to try to help, though at that time they couldn't imagine how.

It was dark when they returned to Myass and learned that no more trains would be coming through that day. At that moment, a freight train pulled into the station and they ran over to board it, but all the doors were tightly locked. Undaunted, they climbed up on the board above the emergency brakes and rode back to Chelyabinsk with icy winds piercing their bodies all the way.

For three weeks, Alia dropped everything else to send letters, reports, and telegrams, hoping to find help. He first appealed to the YMCA, but they were unable to cope with their own present problems, much less one of that magnitude. In fact, they had already closed down many of their centers after the United States entered the war in Europe. But they did suggest that he contact the American Red Cross whose representatives were just arriving in Vladivostok, via Honolulu and Japan.

He immediately sent telegrams all along the Trans-Siberian railroad in an effort to reach the Red Cross. Just as he was despairing of ever finding help, he received the following message:

ALL CHILDREN WILL BE TAKEN CARE OF BY AMERICAN RED CROSS STOP TAKE CHARGE OF WORK STOP MEET FIRST REPRESENTATIVES AT OMSK AND GET MONEY AND CLOTHING FOR CHILDREN

Alia, who had located the seven places where the children had been sent, now dispatched telegrams to all the colonies saying that help was on the way. Having done that, he and Katia suddenly began to face the difficulties of their enormous new responsibility, and to try to sort out the many problems.

"How can we get to Omsk to meet the Red Cross train and then cover thousands of miles between the various colonies to deliver supplies?" she asked.

"Katia, you know that there are only occasional freight trains, and they're filled with typhus infected people and insects carrying other diseases. Anyway, all transportation is completely disorganized and we'll never be able to hold to any kind of schedule! It seems almost hopeless, but we got ourselves into this so we better find out how to make it work."

In visits to the few remaining YMCA officials, Alia learned that the entire eastern part of the Trans-Siberian Railroad was now in the hands of the Czech army. The only way that any officials could move around was to have their own private railroad car. However, since the Czech Commandant's headquarters was in Ekaterinburg, they would have to get there somehow to try to get permission to have a car and the right to attach it to any passing train.

The trip to Ekaterinburg was unbelievably harrowing. It made the Swans realize vividly what they were up against. For hours they waited in a dense crowd. When the train pulled in at last, the heavy doors of the freight cars opened and disgorged a pushing, shouting mob, only to be met by an even bigger mob struggling to get on. But Alia, hampered by his diffident politeness, hung back and would not take part in the melee. At the last minute an exhausted train official, noticing the frightened couple, pushed open one of the heavy doors and hurled them in, baggage and all.

Chaos reigned inside.

A mother, nursing a thin baby, tried to cover herself with some nondescript rags while softly humming a melody to lull the child.

Next to them was a middle-aged couple, not daring to speak, but obviously not used to the new Russian life of mass humanity moving about aimlessly.

From the dark shelves above, six men tumbled down—strong, bull-necked, with huge muscles—and one, staring insolently at Alia, said placidly, "D'you want me to smash your mug?"

The rest laughed, but the bully seemed intent on starting a fight and continued his insults. A seventh, short and fat to the point of having no visible neck, shouted at them, and they subsided.

Unthinkingly, Katia opened her suitcase. The bully started grabbing at the few possessions in it.

"Hey, guys!" he yelled. "Come on! The lady has a bottle of wine."

"It's only denatured alcohol for my burner."

"Never mind the burner! Give us the alcohol!"

Again he lunged at Katia. Alia started to intervene while the rest of the people cringed in frozen terror and the baby began to scream. Just then the fat man jumped up and shouted at the bully and his mates. To everyone's surprise—and relief—they meekly obeyed him, climbed back onto the shelves, and fell asleep.

With the tension relieved, Katia turned around and saw a cluster of rags on the floor stirring. A young face was peering out.

"You don't have to be afraid. They're really alright," the young man said. "They're prizefighters. The fat one's their manager."

Katia began talking to him, becoming aware of the fact that he had no legs. He was still wearing a torn uniform.

"Yes, my legs are gone. The doctors gave me up, but I guess God didn't want me. I got a St. George's cross for bravery, but I can't remember why! I took a message from one post to another, I think. I'm on my way to Harbin now, because I've heard that there's a rich old lady there who takes in people like me. Maybe she'll take care of me."

Ekaterinburg still had the look of a prosperous town with no evidence of war or revolution. But, although the trees were ablaze with autumn color, a bitter wind blew, presaging the coming of winter. After a long wait to see the Czech commandant, he turned out to be very sympathetic. Hearing the story of the forgotten children, he spoke movingly with Alia about the horrors of war and the things he was forced to see and do during these dreadful times.

He immediately assigned a fourth class car to them. They were elated at their luck and rushed out to see it. But their joy turned to dismay when they saw the condition of their car. The windows had cracks and the doors at each end were so badly fitting that the wind could whistle through the car with no obstruction. It was painted black inside, and divided into compartments, each with four hard benches, one on top of the other. One candle and a dusty lantern provided what light there was. At one end sat a cast iron stove—unusable as a stove, and, with no coal to be had, unusable anyway!

On the way back to Chelyabinsk, they became uncomfortably aware that the boxcar contained a great deal more life than they had bargained for. As darkness fell the first night, the heat of their bodies attracted innumerable bugs! Fortunately for them, the railroad authorities at Chelyabinsk mercifully agreed to send a squad of carpenters to turn the car into a half-decent dwelling place with wooden beds, chairs, and even a desk. An Austrian war prisoner named Stanislav Tvorek was engaged to look after the Swans. He acted more like a nurse—cleaning, cooking, and even mending their clothes.

Picking up Ken Miller and a guard, the car was hooked onto a passing train and the party started for Omsk. It took three weeks of unpleasant cold traveling to get there.

Omsk was a forlorn town with small square log houses, muddy streets, and the office of the International Harvester Company. But there was one difference between this small Siberian town and others, and the first sight of it stunned every newcomer. The small grubby shops with their dirty fly-specked windows blazed with diamonds, rubies, and other precious stones. Flung in an insanely opulent fashion on the dirty shelves were bracelets, rings, necklaces, and even diamond tiaras, worth a king's ransom. No attempt was made to display them attractively. The reason for all this was that Omsk was a stopping place for refugees fleeing desperately ahead of the civil war and Bolshevik troops. Running out of money, they were forced to sell their treasures for whatever they could get. As a result, the most magnificent jewels could be had for ridiculously low prices.

At Omsk, the Swans had their first taste of freight car communities: a floating population of refugees, railroad workers, YMCA secretaries, missions, commissions, foreign consuls, government officials, civil servants, living under all kinds of conditions. But human life is extremely tenacious and seems to be able to adapt to anything—smells, smoke, soot and dirt, bleating sheep, mooing cows, clucking chickens, and other assorted noises including bawling children. All types of people were thrown together, most living in box cars that were divided and subdivided. The cars were usually partitioned by thin boards—people on one side, animals on the other. Some cars were filled with the sick—typhus was the great scourge. Wash hung everywhere, as women with set faces, not daring to smile or cry, cooked, scrubbed, and carried wood and water. Cars were always having to be rearranged, or pushed and pulled along the tracks to make way for through trains. This meant that sometimes cars would come together with a bump, causing pans with the family dinner to overturn, or a child to burn himself against a hot stove or even fall into a coal bin. Yet the boxcar residents were luckier than the people herded into stations. In Omsk, as elsewhere, the sick, the living, and even some of the dead, were bundled together in the waiting rooms, without heat, water, toilets, or food, only waiting for the next train—or the next—going nowhere, just going.

Upon their arrival at Omsk, Alia found a message waiting for him. He could expect the Red Cross representative to arrive at about seven o'clock that same evening. After a seemingly endless wait, a special train pulled in at 9:30 P.M. There were two sleeping cars, a dining car, and a kitchen with an impassive Chinese cook who stood at the window, staring without expression at the people. But most important and heart-warming, the rest of the train was a mile-long row of freight cars full of warm sweaters, socks, coats, and all sorts of clothing necessary for the children.

Alia brushed his hair, shook the dust off his one decent jacket, and rushed out to greet the Red Cross official. He returned to Katia within an hour in a jubilant mood.

"Oh, darling!" he exclaimed. "The children will be saved! The Red Cross man is a Bishop from Virginia in the United States. He seems rather bewildered by Siberia and the conditions here, but he's extremely nice. We're going to start work at once and I'm to be in charge!" With that he grabbed her by the waist and they danced around the car.

Supper that night on the Red Cross train was a veritable feast, with gifts from Bishop Tucker of white bread and real butter, and an unheard of luxury—canned peaches in sweet syrup from America. Afterwards, when they returned to their own car they began to discuss the situation. In contrast to their earlier joy, doubts, fears, and unanswerable questions invaded their minds.

"But Alia, how we are going to manage all those children? And what about the teachers? So many of them have gone. How can we get the supplies to the various groups? Money won't do any good—you well know that the peasants won't take the paper money of any of the rival governments."

The gloom was pervasive. "I don't know the answers, Katia. Winter's coming on and a Siberian winter at that! God help us to survive!"

The outlook at that moment seemed grimmer than ever. Alia, who was staring despondently out of the window suddenly leaped up.

"There they are! Those are the people we need! They'll help. Look! They're reaching the end of the platform. I'll get them!"

He dashed out and down the platform, and, in a few minutes, came back with three young people. Red and white stars on the sleeves of their coats indicated that they were members of the Society of Friends. They introduced themselves as Charley Colles and Gregory Welsh, who were English, and their Russian interpreter, Xenia Jukova. They were the sole remnants of the Friends mission from the district of Bozuluk near Samara. Like the YMCA missions, their work had completely collapsed because of the civil war and the constantly changing government at Bozuluk. They were now planning to return to England.

Realizing that he was dealing with Quakers whose philosophy was very close to the teachings of Tolstoy, Alia asked them to sit down and began to describe the awful conditions of the children, made even more dangerous because of the coming Siberian winter. He briefly sketched the little he knew of the children and their background. Finally, unable to come up with more logical arguments, he simply begged them to stay and help.

There was a long silence, broken by Charley, who had fiery black eyes under bushy brows. He slapped his knees and said, "I'm staying! Which colonies do you want me to take, Mr. Swan?"

"The three northern ones—Tyumen, Irbit, and Schadrinsk," Alia quickly replied. "I'll take Petropavlosk, Kurgan, Troitsk, and Uiskaya

Stanitsa. Oh! and Charley, please call me Alia."

"All right, Alia.—Xenia? You'll help of course?—Settled! We're staying."

They all exchanged hearty handshakes. Then, by the way of celebration, the five hopeful but scared young people split two small peaches left in the bottom of the last can given them by Bishop Tucker.

The following morning, Alia introduced the three newcomers to the Bishop, and they made extensive plans. Each carved out their territories, discussed what supplies they would need, and how they would tackle the jobs. The instant rapport between Charley Colles and Alia boded well for the future. Although both of them were of very different temperaments, they had embraced the same basic philosophy, and they were totally dedicated to a quiet but firm path of helping their fellow human beings in every possible way that the Lord might direct.

Bishop Tucker delivered his supplies as quickly as possible. But he felt very uncomfortable with the kind of responsibilities that he faced, and soon made his way back to the Pacific coast and Hawaii. He was replaced by a more formidable administrator, Colonel Rudolph Bolling Teusler.

A teacher with the older girls at the Petropavlosk colony.

CHAPTER THREE

On the same day that Alia had worked out the distribution of the colonies with Gregory Welsh and Charley Colles, he and Katia started out for Petropavlosk, about 200 miles west of Omsk. Remembering the living conditions of the children at Myass, they could not help but feel uneasy about what conditions they might find there. All they knew was that the colony at Petropavlosk was larger and would require more supplies of warm clothing with winter coming on. They had also heard vague hints about corruption and outright thievery involving the manager.

As the train they were attached to started up with jerks and bumps, Katia said, "Alia. It's beginning to get colder. We're going to get there early in the morning, so we'd better go to bed now. But first you'd better light a fire."

"You know I don't know anything about stoves and how to keep a fire going. But the man who fixed the stove said it's in good working condition now. So I'll try."

Alia took some of the coal and wood he had purchased that day and set a big fire intended to last the night. With great enthusiasm, but no experience, he started it, using a tremendous amount of kindling. Then they settled down to sleep, warm at last.

Within an hour, Katia awoke shivering. She shook Alia, "What's wrong with the fire, it's freezing in here!"

He jumped up and ran to the stove. His investigation showed that the heavy weight of too much coal had smothered the kindling fire. Even the bucket of drinking water was frozen solid. Katia looked out of the window and exclaimed in dismay, "Oh! Alia! Look!"

In that one hour, winter had arrived in Siberia and the entire landscape was white with snow. There would be no more warm weather or thawing until next April!

Wind whistled through the cracks in the car. The fire was beyond repair, because Alia had used all the kindling, and there was no possible communication between cars. The Swans' car had been attached to the very end of the train, and only the impenetrable wall of a freight car was in front. Hastily, they put on every article of warm clothing they possessed, even covering their heads with knitted woollen pants, but they still shivered. Thinking quickly, Katia shouted, "Let's run!" And run they did, back and forth, bundled up to their eyebrows, until hours later they saw the glow of a red frosty sunrise through the iced coating on the window. It was only the end of October.

Petropavlosk was about seven miles from the railroad station. The chief purpose of building the Trans-Siberian Railroad had been to unite the centers of European Russia with the harbours on the Japanese Sea and the Orient. Little account, therefore, was taken of small and insignificant towns which usually were five to fifteen miles away from the tracks. Stations were then erected on the railroad line as close as possible to the nearest towns and stood out in the open in the midst of the vast Siberian plains. Each station had one waiting room and sometimes a house for the station master. When a train was expected, there might be one or two droshkies waiting there with fast little Siberian ponies. There were never facilities for food and drink, and it was the habit of peasants to meet the trains with hot food and boiling water from a samovar to make fresh tea — the liquid life force of every Russian. But in the depth of winter, these niceties were not always available — certainly not during a snow storm.

With winter cold and ice, the droshkies were replaced by sleighs. The Swans, exhausted from their long freezing night and bundled up against the cold, took one to the town.

Petropavlosk was one of those prosperous villages found in the unending Siberian plains. The houses were on one long wide street and were built of whitewashed logs, or bricks. The wooden sidewalks on both sides of the street were now covered with crisp snow. As they neared the town, the Swans heard a distant high-pitched nasal call of the muezzin, and squinting their eyes, they saw him pacing atop the minaret which towered over a big mosque. People came out and began placing rugs on the snow in the middle of the street and then knelt and prostrated themselves.

A few minutes later, a caravan of camels came along covered by snow and with icicles hanging from their heads. The animals had traveled thousands of miles to bring logs to the treeless region. The camel drivers looked like Mongolian Buddhas — their heads covered with padded conical caps with fur earflaps. Their faces were rounded, flat-featured and with slant eyes, and had permanently turned a bluish purple from the cold winds of the Siberian plains.

The first stop in Petropavlosk for Alia and Katia happened to be a house where the older girls lived. There they learned that the colony had been divided into four groups separated into different houses— older boys, older girls, younger boys, and younger girls. The older girls house was very clean, tables covered with white cloths, framed photographs and books on tables and shelves. Each big girl had adopted a child from among the little girls who were about five or six years old.

The manageress of the colony was absent, and the girls gave a few guarded but mysterious hints about her traveling to visit all the other colonies for some big project. Only a housekeeper, a young woman, was left in charge, and her stony sullen air did not shed any light on the peculiar situation. Veiled remarks of possible wrong-doing came from some of the older girls, but they were too shy, or frightened, to come right out with information. They did, however, warn the Swans not to go near the bigger boys, who were in open rebellion and terrorized the girls' houses with their mischief.

The younger girls lived a few blocks away. When the Swans arrived they found a panic-stricken woman in charge. After unsuccessfully trying to get as much information from her as possible, they ended their visit, but she put on a tall Cossack fur cap and followed them to the gate. Only then did she open up with an incessant flow of grumbling about insufficient heat, food, and clothing—complaining that everyone else had more. She also warned them about the older boys, and hinted something about their head teacher being allowed to get away with anything because he had pull.

Their third visit was to the house of the small boys. They were relieved to see that here things seemed to be under better control. A capable war prisoner, Polish-Austrian, supervised everything. The boys went to school; and he had organized them into a chorus, teaching them Russian, Polish, and Czech folk songs. But again, as in both houses of girls, the Swans were cautioned about the group of big boys who lived at the other end of town. They were reported to be totally unrestrained. The rest of the colony remained purposely out of touch and fearful of them.

The Swans now had only one more group that they had to visit. Impressed by all those warnings, and with many misgivings, they gathered up their courage and headed for the house where the older boys lived. As soon as they entered the premises, their worst fears were justified. In a big room with bare grey walls, they found filthy tables and disorderly boys lounging everywhere.

"Where's the teacher in charge?" Alia asked, but could barely be heard above the din of shouts, hoarse laughter, and the continuous tinkle of a balalaika.

Finally one of the more cocksure boys spoke up, "Oh, he's only the boss' husband. He's no teacher. So we locked him in his room. He was spoiling all the fun anyway—and besides, he said he was sick!"

Alia went and freed the prisoner immediately. He turned out to be a sick-looking, meek person. His name was Pavel Ivanovitch Vosnesensky. He was indignant but quite helpless. That evening little else could be done except to try to piece together the story of how the children had arrived in Petropavlosk, and why discipline had completely broken down.

It happened that after spending the summer in Myass, it became obvious that the children could not be returned to Petrograd because of the outbreak of civil war. The only practical solution was to divide them into groups and send them to different places where they could hope to have sufficient food and winterized quarters. They were also believed to be away from the proximity to the constantly moving front battle lines.

The Vosnesenskys were placed in charge of the group assigned to Petropavlosk, and had divided the children into the four separate houses. From the very beginning, Mrs. Vosnesensky ruled the colony with an iron fist. She completely eclipsed her husband and terrorized everyone under her.

The older boys ranged in age from 14 to 16, and were given a house formerly owned by a merchant of the town. They were supposed to continue their education in the fourth, fifth, and sixth grades, but discipline rapidly broke down.

From the beginning, the boys were up to all sorts of pranks, many of them quite dangerous. For example, they would persuade their teacher to let them climb out on the roof of the house just to observe the sights of the town and the nearby Siberian plains, on the pretext that it would help their geography lessons. Instead, they would have snowball fights and end up pushing each other off the roof in mock battles. In spite of the snow below cushioning their fall, they had been lucky so far that there were no broken limbs. Vosnesensky, the teacher, was trying to break up this game when they summarily locked him in his room.

The following morning, Alia decided to go back to the house with

Katia and talk quietly with some of the boys. He planned to select a few who could be leaders and would be willing to take on responsibilities.

He began talking with one fourteen year old, Ivan, called Vanya, Semenov, who seemed amenable to counsel and persuasion. "You fellows would be so much better off if everybody had specific duties to occupy their time," he said. "And you could get some who may have musical talents to start a small orchestra and give concerts in the town or to the other children. But that needs organization, and I'll bet that you're just the one to manage it!"

When he heard that Alia himself was interested in music, he became quite open and friendly, "Wait! Let me get my friends Kotya and Volodya. I think they'd be willing to help and maybe we can do what you're asking." Vanya went on, "You know. It's funny. When we heard you were from the American Red Cross, we thought you and your wife were Americans! — That is, until you spoke! But I'm glad you're Russian!"

With that, he went off and brought the other two to meet Alia. Then began a long series of discussions designed to bring more and more of the boys into their own self-governing unit. He suggested that they were now old enough to assume responsibility for their behavior. Alia was both gratified and surprised by the speedy positive results of his tactic. The boys went ahead and elected their council, including a manager, a housekeeper, and a treasurer. Vanya turned out to be a natural born leader, so Alia put him in charge, giving the treasurer just enough money to run the household for one month.

Alia decided next to remove Pavel Vosnesensky, the teacher, from close contact with the boys, so he rented a room away from the house for him. After hiring a war prisoner to do the cooking for the boys, he and Katia left Petropavlosk. The channeling of their youthful energies into constructive self-governing activities proved so successful that, by the end of winter, and just before the colony was moved to Turgayak, the boys took their school exams and were all promoted to the next form.

While the Swans were at Petropavlosk, a typhus epidemic broke out there and spread rapidly. The hardest hit was the railway station which was, as usual, filled with half-starved refugees. Local people were beginning to come down with it too, and they were afraid that it might spread to the children. Little was known about the disease except that it was thought to be an infection of the blood, and that it was carried by body parasites. One bite from an infectious parasite would make the temperature shoot up to incredible heights, while the victim would be covered from head to foot by red burning spots. Sometimes people became delirious and had to be tied to their beds because they would brutally attack their attendants. In fact, the pain and fever frequently drove strong people mad.

The only feeble remedy known was to wrap the sick in cold wet sheets in an attempt to lower the body temperature and lessen the strain on the heart. Oddly enough, the few lucky ones with strong hearts who survived seemed to benefit from the illness. They acquired huge appetites, gained weight, and seemed immune from most bodily ailments from that time on. It was as though the typhus had somehow mysteriously cleansed the blood. So great was the fear of the disease, that any house with a typhus victim had to burn a candle in a window to warn others. The only hotel in town had been turned over to the sick because the hospital was overflowing. Since there were too few doctors, the unfortunate people in the hotel, mostly soldiers and refugees, usually died.

One night, returning to their railroad car at the station, the Swans were traveling in a small sleigh pulled by a little Siberian horse. Hitting a bump on the icy road, the sleigh overturned tossing them into a snow bank.

Fortunately the wise horse stopped and the driver, a rather inebriated Tartar, picked himself up out of the snow. "Sorry, sir! Sorry, sir!" He kept bowing profusely to them while they were trying to brush away the white stuff which filled their eyes, ears, and mouths. "I drive the best people in town, y'know. You must know Mazaeff, the fur merchant? The big boss here? I drive him! This has never happened to me before! Sorry, sir! Sorry!"

The situation was so ridiculous that Katia, spitting snow out of her mouth, began to laugh, while Alia somewhat amused but more enraged, grabbed the sleigh, lifted it, and slammed it down right side up with a crash. The little Tartar kept on mumbling.

When they arrived at the station, somewhat the worse for wear, they found that an American Red Cross typhus train had arrived. All the cars were painted with a large red cross on the side, and the windows were frosted glass. Most of the cars were dimly lit and quiet. Silhouettes of nurses showed through the windows as they moved from bunk to bunk in the wards. At the end of the train there were several brightly lit and noisy cars. The white paint was streaked and the red crosses fading. In these cars the really heroic work was being done. The sick were washed, scrubbed, and shaven to try to rid them of the typhus spreading insects. Water was flooding the cars and even flowing through the boards. Shadows in the windows, scurrying to and fro, gave some indication of the feverish activity inside. Anyone entering would have imagined they were in purgatory.

After going through the cleansing process, the sick were taken into a quiet ward to rest. But for the Swans, the noise of water splashing and loud voices going on the whole night allowed them little sleep, even though their car was on a different track.

After settling the affairs at Petropavlosk as best they could under the circumstances, they returned to Omsk to pick up Charley Colles and Xenia Jukova who awaited them there. Charley's pervading enthusiasm and optimism cheered them immensely, and the idea of successfully returning the children to their homes filled their thoughts and conversations day and night.

The four traveled north to Tyumen, the birthplace of the notorious Rasputin. It was several hundred miles away, and the location of one of the colonies assigned to Colles. As usual, the town was miles distant from the station and spread aimlessly in a disorderly fashion on the boundless plain, and the extremely wide streets ended abruptly in muddy fields. With plenty of room available, each family took as much land as they wished. When they arrived early in the morning, a dull red sun shone through the smoky purple haze giving no warmth.

In Tyumen, the children lived in a big log house with old trees leaning on it. The house had been an outpost erected during the early colonization of this part of the country. During the reign of Ivan the Terrible in the 16th century, a family of merchant warriors there, Stroganov by name, hired Cossack troops to help them in their part-commercial, part-military enterprises. This enabled Russia to reach the Pacific Ocean by the 17th century. The buildings were similar to stockade fortresses built in America during a similar penetration of northern and western lands in the 17th and 18th centuries. The log walls were strong, with very small windows to keep out both the cold and the arrows of enemies.

The big log house was amazingly quiet when the children should have been leaving for school. They could only hear the thin sound of a balalaika coming from somewhere. Entering the courtyard beyond the outer wall, the four visitors were appalled to find that the wide stairway leading into the house had been turned into a toilet. A little boy appeared on the landing to make use of it but, seeing the newcomers, beat a hasty retreat. With an effort, they waded through the filth and entered the hall. Half-clad figures were scuttling about in the dark corridor, and whispering came from all sides. Alia, groping around, found a door and opened it. Light from one dirty window showed a group of boys gathered around one who was playing a Russian dance on the balalaika with great verve. Other boys lay on cots sleeping peacefully, or were comfortably propped up reading torn, yellowish books. In the center of the great big room, a group of dishevelled boys were so absorbed in a game of cards that they didn't even notice the presence of strangers. Suddenly the room came alive. Someone grabbed all the cards, while one little boy teased an older boy who was sleeping. The balalaika stopped abruptly as all of them watched the prankster. The sleeper awoke with a wild yell and, not noticing the newcomers, proceeded to thrash the brat who had disturbed him.

In the next room there was the same disorganization—boys lying in bed, half dressed figures reading or sitting about aimlessly. In one corner some twelve year olds were having a violent argument. Without warning two of them began a fist fight, trying to get hold of something white and fluffy.

At that moment a worried looking woman appeared in the doorway. "How do you do? Are you the representatives of the American Red Cross? Oh! I'm so glad! Could this be salvation at last?" She waved her hand around, "Look what's going on here! Some of the boys have to stay in bed because they have nothing to wear. None of them have winter clothes. Most of the teachers have left to try to make a living someplace else. Some of them are nice enough to keep on helping us—but goodness! They're so few and we have so little help."

"Oh, stop it please!" the teacher cried quite helplessly, as the crowd in the corner continued fighting. "They sold all their sheets and pillowcases when winter set in and bought rabbit skins. Now they're trying to divide them to make warm caps and mittens. The girls are keeping up a little better. They're remodeling some of their old clothes and I try to help them with that." She rambled on, "Yes, we're all frightened by winter and we're not ready for it. Nobody has any shoes, and food is our greatest problem."

Realizing that talk about morals or serious study would be totally out of place, the four representatives left. They soon returned with the Red Cross supplies of clothes, shoes, and food for both the children and teachers. They then made arrangements with a nearby factory for the children to be fitted with shoes at a reduced rate. That same evening they came back with a carload of flannel.

Word of the arrival of Red Cross people and the promise of new clothes and better conditions brought about a sudden and quick transformation in the quarters. The rooms were cleaned, and the hall and stairway were thoroughly scrubbed. The news spread rapidly, even bringing one of the teachers back to the colony.

Again Alia asked the boys and girls to elect representatives among themselves to serve on an equipment committee. This seemed to bring everyone to life, and suddenly they all became quite energetic. An almost Christmas-like happiness reigned.

Within a few days, every girl had two warm dresses, and every boy two warm shirts. They all wore brand new well fitting shoes. The teachers and girls went to work to make warm coats for everyone. In a week the fortress-like house was unrecognizable.

Charley Colles now assumed official control of the colony and made a little speech. "The American people are going to take care of you. You're going to have warm clothes, and all the food you can eat, with plenty of firewood to keep you warm. But I want you to do something in return. I want you to be good citizens. No more roaming the streets to beg and steal. When we're able to get you some books, you must resume your studies. I'll come and see you every week, because I'm the boss and you must do what I tell you. I am also your friend." Thus began his stormy career.

Charley soon acquired the nickname "Charley—the Siberian Beggar." He became absorbed by his charges, and his heart ached for them constantly. Tirelessly he chased from one Red Cross office to another, often returning to Omsk, the official headquarters. There he would nag the personnel, begging or fiercely demanding some things for his children.

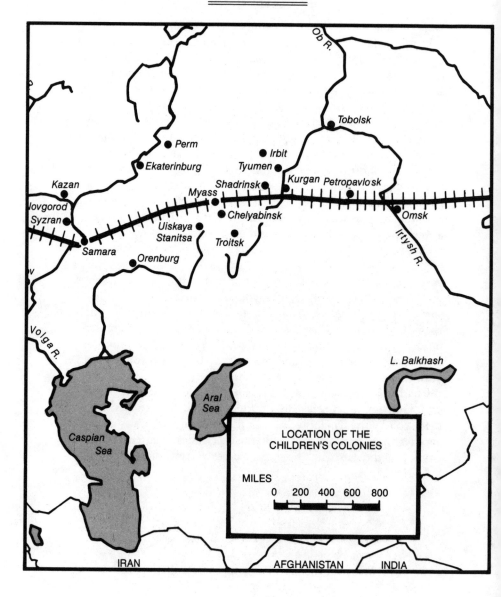

LOCATION OF THE
CHILDREN'S COLONIES

MILES

0   200   400   600   800

CHAPTER FOUR

It was now time for the four to part. Leaving Charley and the faithful Xenia behind in Tyumen with ample money and supplies, the Swans returned to their gloomy car and headed south to Troitsk where another colony was located. They had to go far past Chelyabinsk and south of the last slopes of the Ural Mountains.

They stopped en route at Ekaterinburg to see Red Cross officials and to arrange for additional supplies for the colonies. They also hoped to get up-to-date information on the present status of the civil war. If they had enough facts, they could try to plan more precisely for the children's future. Since Ekaterinburg was a fair-sized city, it should yield better factual information than the wild changing rumors which they heard daily in the smaller towns.

The civil war lines which still existed, formed an intangible and undefined front — miles long and miles wide. The Committee of the Constituent Assembly, which had moved from Samara to Omsk, seemed to be confronted by a nebulous Siberian government.

By now it was evident that the Allies were not going to send troops to help the White Russians and Czechs. In Omsk, the Swans had seen only a few forlorn, shivering British soldiers, also several French missions and commissions living on railroad tracks in luxurious cars, and a number of YMCA secretaries and Red Cross representatives. None of these were planning to go further eastward beyond Omsk. Obviously, the maintenance of the interminable front line depended on the poorly clothed and inadequately armed Russian troops as well as the better equipped Czech soldiers. But the Czechs had a strictly self-interested purpose for being there and fighting — they simply wanted to get out of Russia.

While they were in Ekaterinburg, Admiral Kolchak, the former commander of the Black Sea fleet, was proclaimed dictator of the White Russian army in order to supersede the weak Committee of the Constituent Assembly and the local Siberian government. At the same time, they heard news of the Armistice between the warring European powers which had just seeped through. But this meant nothing to Russia except bad news—the likelihood that the Allies would leave her entirely to her destiny. The sole reaction to the joyous news in Western Europe was yet another unpopular conscription of Russian soldiers in Siberia to shore up the sagging lines at the invisible front in the heart of their country.

One night while they were staying in Ekaterinburg, they visited some old friends who now lived there. This was a family which had fled in 1917 from the famine in Petrograd. One of their children had typhoid fever, but in spite of that, when they stood up to leave, Olga, their hostess, pressed them to stay overnight.

"Don't go," she said. "We can put you up for the night. We have plenty of room and we haven't seen you for so long."

Katia demurred, "You have enough of a problem with a very sick child. It's wonderful of you to ask us to stay, but really, I think we should go now. We'll keep in touch with you, though, before we leave town."

"No—no!" Olga insisted. "Look how dark it is. And you have such a long drive, and then your railroad car is so cold! Please stay!"

Alia could no longer resist. "Katia, let's do as she says. After all, it'll be wonderful to sleep in a warm room and a real bed for a change. And imagine! There will be no railway whistles and car bumps all night!"

"All right," Katia agreed. "After all, it will be unusual to get a really good night's sleep and wake up in the morning feeling healthy for a change."

But early the next morning, Katia awoke to see Alia examining his throat in a mirror. He complained to her of pain. When she examined his throat and nose, she saw that they were full of big grey spots. Furthermore, his voice had an eerie hollow sound.

Panic set in. Here they were in a strange house where one child was already very ill. What if it was infectious? The city's hospitals were already overflowing with typhus victims and the pharmacies had no supplies to sell. In desperation, Katia tried to disinfect her husband's throat with raw benzene, but he threw himself out of bed and started dashing around the room, moaning. Katia, in a fright, threw herself down on the bed, crying and hysterically clutching the pillow.

The commotion brought their hostess running into the room. She took one look at Alia and vanished, returning a moment later with some soothing drops for his nose and throat.

He quieted down after a few minutes and said meekly, "I thought my head was going to burst."

They hastily called a doctor, who examined Allia's throat as soon as he arrived and took a swab of it. Katia was elected to go to the laboratory immediately to get it analyzed. The day was sunny but bitterly cold. It took all her strength to get the specimen to the laboratory—only to be told when she arrived, out of breath, that it couldn't be done. They had no instruments in working order, and no new equipment had been acquired since the start of the war. Helpless themselves, they suggested that she try the Maternity Hospital at the Czar's Bridge. Her race to the Maternity Hospital seemed endless, as she fought time and the fearful cold. Once there, it took only half an hour for a woman doctor to hand her a certificate which confirmed her worst fears—the chemical analysis showed the presence of diphtheria bacilli. Even more distressing was the news that the hospital had had no vaccine since the beginning of the civil war. Vaccines for all of Russia came from Ufa on the western side of the Urals, which had long since been cut off from Eastern Siberia. Katia returned to her friend's house, fearful of the future. Surely they would have to leave. Diphtheria was a highly contagious disease, and one child in the house was already desperately ill with typhoid.

When she finally got back to the house, she was numb with cold and despair. She held out the torn certificate to Olga, who was just coming out of her sick child's room.

Olga wasted no time, "Oh, how dreadful!" she cried. "Let's go quickly to find a vaccine! No, I won't let you go alone. I know the town better than you do." She called to her little girl, "Tanya! Tell Nanny not to leave Kolya's bedside. I have to go out."

"But aren't you afraid of us?"

"Nonsense! You have nowhere else to go. Never mind the rest now."

For two hours they rushed around from one clinic and pharmacy to the next. Finally in a rundown hospital, cold and cheerless, on the edge of town, they found the very last vaccine available. At first the hospital insisted that Alia be brought there, but since all the beds were filled with typhus victims, and besides there was no possible means of transportation, the head doctor agreed to give the precious medicine to them. After much coaxing they were able to persuade an elderly retired doctor to go with them to administer the dose. Within a few hours, the grey spots began to disappear.

For three weeks Alia was isolated in their one room, with Katia his only companion. They cooked whatever fare their hostess sent in to them on a small sterno stove. Every day they would bundle up in all their clothes and open a window for a while, to breathe fresh air and to clean the room of sick odors. Unfortunately, one such airing brought Katia down with a sore throat and the patient suddenly became the nurse.

Near the very end of the bout, they were given another fright. Alia began to swell up in the strangest fashion — first his mouth, then, as it receded, his eyes, hands, and other parts of his body. Fearful of calling in the doctor and having their kind hostess ask them to leave, they went through this new affliction without saying anything, even though it ended with his whole body being covered with a red itching rash. Katia, surreptitiously, went back to the hospital for advice and was told that these were the direct symptoms of a stale vaccine, which could result in a temporary poisoning. Fortunately, it soon passed away.

Within three weeks Alia had recovered enough to allow them to resume their broken journey. Though they tried, they had no way to sufficiently express their grateful thanks to Olga for her Christian generosity, patience, and hospitality, which even exposed her own family to disease.

Going back to their dingy car, the Swans traveled hundreds of miles south, then west again, until they arrived at last at Troitsk in the district of Orenburg. There they found a telegram waiting for them with happy news from their former hostess. The crisis was finally over and her son, after ninety-one days of fever, was recovering nicely. Both Alia and Katia wept with happiness and thanksgiving.

The Swans were now ready to continue their visits to the colonies. Their next destination was to be the one at Troitsk. In retrospect, this would probably have turned out to be the most pleasant of all their get acquainted travels, if it were not for the unpleasant events which followed.

CHAPTER FIVE

The yellowed pages of Katherine (Katia) Kozlova's diary recounted her childhood experiences as a Troitsk colonist. Like Vera Schmidt, she also had been attending the Ivanovsky School for Girls in Petrograd and was offered the opportunity for a summer vacation in the Urals. Although her mother was worried about her going such a distance from the capital city, the situation was so grim that she agreed to the trip. The train took three weeks to arrive at Myass, but once there the summer flew by. Then, just as the children were expecting to return home, all access to Petrograd was cut off because of the fighting on various fronts. The teachers, searching for homes for the children, divided them into groups of one hundred each and Katia was one of the lucky ones.

She was sent to a convent in Troitsk and was under the direct supervision of the Mother Superior, Phenophaniya. The winter passed without incident and Katia was even promoted a grade. Even when the fighting impinged on the town itself and Ataman Dudov, a local military leader, took the city, little changed. Dudov issued his own money instead of Czarist money, but the life of the children continued to be studies, games, and a peaceful but cloistered existence.

Katia lived in a big two story house which had been used for wounded soldiers during the war. She sang in the convent choir and was paid forty rubles a month. She wrote:

"Townspeople and pilgrims came to the convent to pray and brought flour, grain, and butter. I always stood by the door and promised to pray for their departed loved ones and they would give me money. I used to go out to the town and buy horsemeat cutlets with the money. It was a Tartar town and the Tartars only ate horsemeat. Oh! They were so good! But I'm afraid I usually forgot the prayers. We all used to do this because the visitors thought that children's prayers went straight to God because we were so young and innocent. Little did they know of our mischief."

When the Swans arrived at Troitsk, they went straight to the convent and met Mother Phenophaniya. She was a tall stately old lady whose face still bore signs of her former beauty. While young whispering nuns served tea, the Mother Superior showed some of the beautiful handiwork of her nuns, all done in the minute cross stitch of Kiev.

She told them that she had been left at the nunnery at the age of six by an unknown stranger. Since that time she had never left the walled grounds of the small convent. She knew no other life than the quiet disciplined routine.

"Now times have changed so much," she said. "During the last few years we have been under shell fire so many, many times. Whenever the town changes hands we get the brunt of it, being on the outskirts and in the open. We are women here and all alone, and many of us are very old. When the shooting starts I send the sisters to their cells to pray, and give orders to ring the large bells. They shoot and we ring bells! – And we pray for those who shoot and those at whom they are shooting!"

Since the children at the convent seemed to be so well taken care of, the Swans left money with the Mother Superior to provide for their continuing needs and went on. As they departed, she presented them with a handmade bag with her own initials and a crest, a crown, indicating that she may have come from royal blood.

When they returned to their boxcar at the Troitsk station, they requested that their car be attached to the next train, only to be told that there was no next train. All trains had been shifted to another area to be used for the transfer of troops. Apparently the Bolsheviks had intercepted the railroad line.

Then, as so often happens in a situation of total chaos, the unexpected came along. A train pulled in. After much argument and the usual exchange of money, their car was hooked on. Of course, upon reaching the main junction, the whole argument had to be gone through again; but in spite of all that, at Chelyabinsk, they were unceremoniously switched to a side track and left in complete ignorance of how or when they would continue onward.

During their short stay at Troitsk while visiting the convent, they had come across a peasant woman named Fenya who was looking for work and willingly came with them to help with the chores. She took very good care of them, especially when she had her sip from the vodka bottle always kept under her pillow.

After supper that night during a tense discussion of how to get back to Kurgan, Katia inadvertantly tipped over the alcohol lamp while trying to light it with a paper taper. The spilled alcohol instantly spread and burst into flames as it ran down the floor. Black sticky smoke filled the car. Fenya rushed forward and threw a blanket into Katia's face to block the smoke, but as she leaned down her hair touched the flames. With a shriek she dashed out of the car, her head a blazing torch, and threw herself into the snow.

Alia jumped up and started searching desperately for his coat in the narrow compartment shouting. "Where's my coat? All the Red Cross money is in it!"

Groping around aimlessly, Katia found the coat on a hook right in front of her and threw it at him. Losing control, she screamed, "Let's get out! There's no water anyway! Oh! Let it burn! Let's just get out." With a frantic effort she dragged her husband out of the car and they both fell headlong into the snow.

Alia raised himself up and looked around. Taking in the horror of the situation and the possible consequences, he exclaimed, "This is madness! Where can we go?" as he dashed back into the burning car.

Fire shown behind the window panes and, through the glass Katia saw his silhouette dashing to and fro, violently battling the flames, throwing things right and left out the door at Katia and Fenya, who was still struggling with her burnt hair.

Katia, somewhat ashamed ran into the car, and, coughing from the black smoke, began to beat the flames furiously. Suddenly Alia's knickers and woolen socks caught fire. Remembering a bucket of drinking water nearby, Katia grabbed it and poured it over his legs. As soon as they stopped burning, he continued beating the flames and throwing all their movable possessions out into the snow. Even Fenya controlled her hysterics and climbed back into the car to help until the flames were subdued. The rest of the long night was spent cleaning the car with melted snow and washing themselves.

The next day their charred and battered car was hitched onto another train. But at daybreak, after three days of travel, they were again shunted to a side track by a small station. The car was cold again and Fenya was trying to light the stove, when without warning the door was thrown open and clouds of snow, freezing air, and people jammed in.

"This way folks! Come right in! There's plenty of room!" cried one of the intruders.

Bundled up women in big shawls and men in sheepskin coats with felt boots and fur caps tumbled into the car. An avalanche of wooden boxes containing all their belongings were pushed into the car. People were shoving each other, and children were pulled in crying loudly. Alia and Katia tumbled out of bed, gesticulating and trying to persuade the crowd that this was their permanent abode and not a public car. But the mob refused to budge. They were surprised and indignant and squatted down on the floor. Finally the military commander of the station learned of the invasion and forced them out. Amid the yells and curses of the mob, the car was hitched back onto a train and slowly left the station.

A few minutes later there was another noisy interruption as they heard shouts and a loud frantic knocking on the door. Since the train was already speeding up there could be no possible reason for the racket. Sliding the door open a crack, they discovered two fantastic figures clinging to the iron railings outside and shouting something inaudible over the whistling of the wind. They had no caps, but only handkerchiefs over their ears, and their faces looked frostbitten. One had a blue military coat with big shining buttons, and the other wore a flannel shirt and a short skirt. Letting them in, the Swans were almost knocked over as they brushed past them and headed for the stove.

Clapping their hands and feet, one of them said, "Don't be afraid. We mean no harm. We're Russian prisoners of war who've come all the way from Austria. We were so anxious to get home that we didn't wait to be dispatched. We just ran the minute we set foot in Russia — even without proper clothing or money. But we got lifts and were fed by generous people all the way down here. At this last station some kind people gave us a handful of change, but by the time we divided it and bought some bread and hot water, the train was pulling out and some of us were left behind. Many of our comrades have perished trying to get home."

Fenya fed them with the remains of the food in the car and at the next station, with a little extra money slipped into their pockets, they were able to join their friends in the front car.

But there never seemed to be an end to the things that could go wrong! The next day, looking out the window, they saw a bright flame leaping up from under the car. A railroad mechanic who was called, calmly announced that one of the wheels had a burning box. He patched it up, but told them to keep an eye on it as they resumed their journey. The only way they could tell was to watch the shadow of the wheel on the snow, and the whole day was spent taking turns at this tedious but frightening pursuit.

Again and again a thin line of smoke was visible against the sparkling snow followed by a small tongue of fire. As the day wore on, the smoke got denser and the flames grew higher until they started licking at the window. Fear that the wheel would fall off or the car would be set on fire again kept them all on edge. When they arrived at the tiny station of Mishkina, the train was limping badly and they were told that their car could not proceed further. Again they were sidetracked, with their destination, the town of Kurgan, still a hundred miles away. It was time for the station master to leave, and so he locked up the office, telling them that they would have to wait for mechanics to be sent from Kurgan.

Trying to make the best of their misfortune, the Swans hired a peasant with a sleigh. He wrapped them in warm Siberian homemade felt and took them for a ride. As they sped across the Siberian plain, their driver asked them if they wanted provisions and, at their nod, he took them to his home.

Inside the solidly built log house was a big square room. Along the sides were wide benches and, in the corner, one big bed. A high stove, built with white-washed bricks, stood in the center. Atop the stove was a wide platform fit to be slept on and a warm seat was scooped out of the side to serve as another bed. Hanging from the ceiling in one corner were several old icons dimly lit by lampadas (oil-burning cups with wicks).

After the driver had solemnly crossed himself three times, he offered to sell them black and white bread, jam, and eggs. He refused to accept Soviet or Siberian money, only the old Czarist rubles. And he easily made change for their 500 ruble note. Friends and relatives were called in to verify the authenticity of the bill, holding it to the window and smelling it. One helpful chap even tried to bite off a corner of it. When they were ultimately satisfied, the transaction was completed and the Swans were taken back to their car.

Once there they found that the mechanics still had not come. After three days and nights impatiently spent waiting, they finally telegraphed the British Consul at Kurgan, begging for help. The next morning they awoke to the welcome noise of hammers beating on the wheels—but their hopes were dashed when within the hour the sounds had ceased with no word of explanation. The mechanics had all vanished, the wheels were not fixed, and the station was still tightly locked.

After a few hours of helpless anxiety, not having any idea about when they could move again, they were dealt another blow. The door was flung open and seven huge men fell into the car. They were drunk to the point of stupidity.

"We'll escort you to Kurgan," one of them mumbled. "We'll get you there if you let us stay here. I already had this car switched onto the next train."

They fell down on the floor, almost where they stood, and began snoring loudly. Without warning the train gave a violent jerk and started moving. To add to their fears, the flames from the box wheel flared up within a few minutes. Fenya woke one of the men who seemed less drunk than the others. Hanging precariously out of the car, he stuffed the box with snow which he scooped up from alongside the slowly moving train. He then crawled back in again and promptly fell asleep.

A little while later, the train stopped unexpectedly in the open plain with no station or habitation in sight. Suddenly, one of the mechanics, who earlier had crawled on to an upper shelf and seemed to be in a deep sleep started up with a wild and angry look, yelling and waking his companions. One of them succeeded in quieting him down and the whole gang fell asleep once more. A few minutes later, the same man jumped up and darted at Katia and Fenya with a knife. Fenya screamed and they both ran off in different directions. The brute hit the air aimlessly and fell headlong on the floor hitting his forehead and lying motionless. Alia threw the knife out of the window and sat down to watch him in case he should come to.

A knock at the door made them open to a young man in some sort of uniform. He refused to identify himself but asked permission to stay in the car. Looking around he saw the seven mechanics.

"What are you doing here?" he said sternly, "and besides you're drunk!"

As if by magic the men came to and dragging their hurt companion, tumbled out of the door. At the next station the young man thanked them for the lift and disappeared into the night. Fenya began moaning and crying hysterically.

"My God! When that drunken bum with the knife came after me and looked so wild, I was so scared, I almost fainted. I thought he was gonna kill me." Then to Katia she moaned, "What if he had killed you, what would I have done? Thank God he fell down. O my God!"

Trying to sooth Fenya, they were again startled by a pounding at the door as the train stopped once more. This time, a little wiser, Katia peered out into the darkness and saw that they were surrounded by armed soldiers.

"Open the door! We have an order to search all cars before they are let into Kurgan!"

Alia, Katia, and Fenya began arguing, with Katia violently opposed to opening the door. Her stubbornness finally won out, and with an instinctive premonition of danger, she stamped her foot and shouted at the soldiers,

"We will not let you in! Break down the door! Shoot at us through the windows! Go ahead. But we won't open the door!"

One by one the soldiers got down, shouting a few curses, and went off. On arrival at Kurgan, they reported the incident to the military commander and station master, both of whom told them that there were no orders to search incoming trains. They thought the intruders were probably a band of lawless soldiers or Bolsheviks marauding along the railroad line and hiding in the nearby steppes and forests. But at least and at last the Swans had reached Kurgan.

The older boys at Petropavlosk 1918–19.

CHAPTER SIX

The town of Kurgan was like a magic oasis from the distant past. The cleanliness and prosperity of the place overwhelmed the Swans. What a wonderful contrast to the unpleasant and uncomfortable surroundings they had had to endure for so long! A marvelous delicatessen displayed the famous Siberian game which formerly had been shipped by the carload all over Russia. Glouhari (like wild turkey), teterki (the size of partridges), and ryabchiki (small birds with all white very tender meat), all were roasted to a golden brown and surrounded by homemade pies of meat, cabbage, and carrots. There were pickled cucumbers, pickled white mushrooms, black pressed caviar, and grayish fresh caviar. The endless varieties of freshly baked bread were surrounded by beautiful pastries. For the first time in months everyone feasted, and even the gloomy boxcar seemed brighter because of their pleasure.

The next day they met the local financier, social leader, and benefactor of the colony children. Mr. Smolin lived in a lovely home full of priceless oriental rugs and old handcarved Russian peasant furniture. He warmly greeted both Alia and Katia and, hearing of Alia's love of music, introduced them to the town doctor who had a piano. There, next to the doctor's clinic, Alia was able to satisfy his yearning for music, and perhaps even soothe some of the doctor's patients while they were being treated. For a short while the horrors of the civil war and dreadful Siberian winter were forgotten.

Mr. Smolin had loaned two of his country houses for the children to live in. Two days after their first meeting, he pulled out an old torn map from the bottom drawer of a battered desk and showed them where the houses were. He then gave the Swans elaborate directions on how to get there.

Hiring a local driver, they set out across the wide plains and came to the edge of a forest. Suddenly the driver shouted, and pulled the horse violently, as they plunged down a snowy precipice. At the bottom there was no room for the horse and sleigh, but with another shout and strong pull on the reins the horse leaped wildly up the vertical wall. The Swans hit the back of their seat with their legs straight up in the air. Then, before they realized what had happened, they were again on level ground and the horse was running swiftly while the driver acted as if nothing had happened. Before they could get over the shock the same thing happened again. Over and over again they plunged from snowdrift to precipice to gully until finally they entered the woods where the road became smooth. The trees blocked the wild winds, and they felt able to relax as they sped through the beauty of the forest with its huge white birch trees weighed down by ice-covered branches which sparkled against the blue sky.

The children lived snugly in the two houses. In front of them in a park was a lake surrounded by birches. The whole effect was like a stage setting. But this fairy tale scene turned out to be the backdrop of a nasty drama, a struggle between teachers. One of them was a business-like older woman named Mrs. Rudolph, who had been appointed head of the colony. For no apparent reason she became the scapegoat and butt of two young pretty teachers who were sisters. Evidently, the seclusion in the wilderness brought out in the sisters a vicious and petty aggressiveness, and they did everything they could think of to prevent Mrs. Rudolph from performing her duties as head of the colony. Somehow they had managed to supplant her with a mild, submissive, and inept woman doctor who forgot or lost everything. The Swans, taking stock of the situation, were appalled by the facts which were quite evident. They decided to cope with it by giving Mrs. Rudolph control of the Red Cross money and supplies.

While waiting for these things to arrive, Alia found temporary living quarters for him and Katia at the house of the British Consul, Mr. Primrose. He was a small skinny Scotsman with big teeth, dark hair, and rolls of unused skin on his body. He had been a prominent business man in Kurgan, living on the outskirts of the town where he had a large cold storage plant. Just a few days prior to the Swans' arrival, his workmen had set fire to the plant and rioted through the town. Only the black shattered walls of the plant remained, leaving no one better off, while the workmen wandered around looking for work where there now was none. Mr. Primrose's personal quarters were also in disarray, for he had sent his wife and child to England for safety several months earlier when he became aware of the first signs of trouble. The house was cold and musty and a few broken toys lay around the room given the Swans. The Consul spent most of his time in bed suffering from appendicitis. It was at this time that the first intimations of a gathering storm in the colonies occurred.

One disturbing report was given by Xenia Jukova, who had come to Kurgan from Tyumen to get supplies. Before sending her back to Tyumen, Alia asked her to go by way of Petropavlosk again to announce that he and Katia were coming soon. He was very upset by the tale of her earlier stay at Petropavlosk, when there seemed to be a number of doors closed to her with no explanation. Also any signs of interest she displayed were met with unconcealed resentment. While she was there a Swedish delegation had arrived, sent by the Red Cross to investigate the condition of the colony at the request of the children's parents. The Swedish minister, Sarve, came with a Mr. Albrecht, the father of two of the children. Somehow, Mrs. Vosnesensky, the manageress, had been able to win them over completely, with the result that they sent back a glowing report, expressing content with the well-being of the children. But Xenia, remembering her own disagreeable experiences, could not agree with their report.

A few days later, in the Kurgan colony, another more overt indication of impending trouble came. There were loud voices and noisy footsteps in the hall and the Swans heard Youla, the Consul's maid, trying to hold someone back. Katia opened her door with a sinking heart and saw a tall woman knocking violently at the Consul's bedroom door. A moment later, the appendicitis-stricken Britisher jumped out in his pajamas waving a revolver in all directions. Seeing a woman he was stunned, no doubt expecting a bunch of revolting workmen. He retreated back into his room and slammed the door. The woman turned around.

"Oh! the wrong door!" she shouted. Then, seeing Katia, "I want to see you!"

She rushed into their room without an invitation and loudly asked, "What are the intentions of the Red Cross? That's what I want to know! I'm Mrs. Siedachova, manager of the Uiskaya Stanitsa colony. We don't want any interference. We only want money to feed and clothe the children." Then suddenly, "Where am I going to sleep? We can talk tomorrow!"

Taken aback Alia said, "Please don't shout so loud, the Consul is very sick. Our railroad car's at the station, and the caretaker and Xenia Jukova, a friend of ours, are there—will you please go there?"

She exclaimed, "What an idea! In the dark?"

Taking matters into her own hands, she rushed out into the hall. "There must be some extra room in this house!"

Proceeding noisily, she went to the maid's room and flung open the door. Unexpectedly a dog jumped out of the room, barking loudly. There was a crash and a huge basket full of eggs turned over, the eggs breaking and splashing all over the floor. The disheveled Youla started crying lustily, the dog went on barking, and Alia and Katia tried to quiet everybody lest the stricken Consul should appear again brandishing his revolver. The last touch of confusion was added by the sight of an old red-faced man sleeping peacefully on Youla's bed. He did not stir but smiled broadly at some dream. It was Youla's grandfather who had come to town to sell his eggs, and was spending the night in his granddaughter's room.

The following morning, after a long sleepless night in which Alia discussed the situation with Katia from every possible angle, they realized the present helplessness of their position. Alia decided to have a talk with the Uiskaya Stanitsa manageress. He had already heard shady rumors about the woman and sensed her reluctance to have Red Cross interference in the running of the colony but, since he had not had a chance to investigate it fully, he said nothing. The conversation simply led to stony silence on most subjects or dramatic bragging about her running of the colony amidst endless difficulties. Realizing that he could get nowhere without more information he turned over a month's supply of money to her and requested an itemized list of expenses. She then departed, returning to Uiskaya Stanitsa seemingly content.

One day a telephone call came from the railroad station at Kurgan to tell them that the Red Cross supplies for the children had arrived. Would the Swans please come at once to sign for them and remove them. Alia had the flu, so Katia trotted off and, after walking a mile and a half along the tracks to the station, found a Czech soldier guarding eight huge wooden cases. She signed the receipts and listened to the station master's insistence that the cases had to be taken at once. Leaving the Czech in charge of the cases, she began to reconnoiter in town for a storeroom—but in vain.

The town was overcrowded with the usual refugees and there were no private rooms to be had. All vacant premises were registered at the office of Kolchak's Commissar, so she ended up at his office. In reply to her request there was only doubtful head shaking—not one inch of space was available anywhere.

With perfect serenity Katia looked around and said to the Commissar, "You know—you'll have to let me bring the supplies here."

"Where?" in astonishment.

"Here—to your office. Look what a nice big room you have! We won't take up much space. Please!"

"Impossible! In the morning this place is a madhouse! Jammed with people. We have too much to do here. No! No!"

"But look here! I'm responsible for all the supplies and have nowhere to take them. I can't leave them lying on the station platform. There are sweaters, socks and other things there. It's too much of a temptation for everybody!"

"But really—I can't do a thing for you," he said, looking quite shaken.

But Katia noticed that his yellow-grayish face seemed to light up as he shivered, rubbing his cold hands briskly. She was quick to catch the softened intonations of his voice at the mention of warm clothes. She continued pleading until at last he gave her permission to bring the things there.

She immediately ran into the street and hired a big sleigh to transport the boxes. Realizing that she would need at least four strong men to lift them, she looked around. Right in front of her was a big empty shop, and through the window she saw that it was filled with fantastically clad men. Blue uniform coats coupled with skirts, handkerchiefs tied around ears, or trousers in shreds, proclaimed homecoming Russian war prisoners. They had taken refuge in the empty shop until morning when they could start off again on their hazardous journey.

Asking if anyone wanted to earn a little money, she almost caused a riot and was nearly pushed off her feet. She finally selected five men. But when the sleigh started up, five more ran ahead of them all the way to the station. The boxes were loaded onto the sleigh and a hilarious procession went back up the street, with Katia balanced precariously on top of the huge load. The driver sat a few boxes lower, and some of the strangely garbed men clung to the sides of the sleigh while the rest ran behind.

In a few days, when Alia was over his flu attack, the Swans turned the Commissar's office into bedlam. Energetic hammering, squeaking boards and nails, rustling of papers, all going on in a room crowded with people. The Commissar became quite desperate, unable to hear what the people or his assistants were saying. He would send word that he could not even hear the sound of his own voice and quiet would reign for a few minutes—then the noise would start up again.

Katia later recorded in her diary that one of her deepest regrets was she never gave a Red Cross sweater to the kind, shivering Commissar. "Not from meanness," she wrote, "but from childish scrupulousness."

Leaving enough supplies at Kurgan for the children, the Swans now returned to Petropavlosk. They hoped to meet the peripatetic manageress and to put things in order. Xenia Jukova met them at the station on their arrival and again told them of her doubts. But she reiterated that she had, so far, found nothing definite to back up her misgivings. The entire mystery seemed to center about the woman in charge, who herself showed up at the station a few minutes later much to their surprise.

Mrs. Vosnesensky was tall, well built, with prematurely gray hair severely parted in the middle and pulled back into a tight knot. Above a beautifully chiseled nose and chin, rose a high forehead, – but all this was disturbed by dark glassy eyes and a vague repulsive expression around the mouth. Her speaking voice was even more repellent, and her smile had the elements of a frightening leer.

"How do you doooo? I'm glad to see you! Won't you have tea with me? Oh, not in the dismal surroundings of the colony. There's a cafe on the main street. We can have a cozy chat there – let's go right away."

She kept smiling unctuously as she put endless pastries and tea before them. Her face was the picture of affability, but a certain fear seemed to lurk in her eyes.

"You know my housekeeper, the bright-eyed woman who lives in the same house with me – she is very inaccurate in her accounts – she's not to be trusted! And the little one in charge of the second group of girls is no good at all – she's too old for the job." Pause. "I'll go and get some more pastries."

Katia said nothing, and Alia sat stiffly, his eyes fixed on the marble table top.

As she walked away, Katia said, "I simply can't stand her – I feel like throwing the whole dish of pastries into her grinning face."

Alia just said, "Please! We'll be lost if we show our feelings."

As she returned, he said, "Thank you so much, but please don't bring so many cakes."

"Oh, don't make me feel badly! Don't say you don't like them! I think that the teacher at Uiskaya Stanitsa colony has been to see you at Kurgan. She is not a nice woman."

This reminded Katia of the night at Kurgan in the house of the Consul who was suffering from appendicitis, when the "not nice" woman had suddenly appeared, and provoked the scene with the Consul in his pajamas, his maid Youla weeping, and the basket of broken eggs. She suddenly pretended to cough while stifling a giggle.

Ignoring the interruption, Mrs. Vosnesensky continued, "She has distributed all the children among the Cossacks of the village. The children have to work in the peasants' households and for this they get board and lodging. You know, she herself is having an affair with the instructor in the colony. So don't give them any money. They won't spend it on the children."

Alia stood up and broke up the party.

She smiled and said, "We will be friends, n'est-ce pas? Confidential talk like this creates ties. Don't you agree?"

Out in the street Alia and Katia paced up and down in the brilliant sunshine, tossing arguments and questions back and forth. "How to tackle this woman? She was obviously influential with the rest of the colonies, inciting them against us and the Red Cross and then exposing them to us. Why should she? You know why? She's afraid of interference and control. Now there's a thread to hang on to!"

With that kind of reasoning they decided to leave her bait in the form of enough money to run the colony for a month. This would set her mind at rest temporarily and give them time to collect facts.

After carrying out this decision they returned to the small station only to find no trace of their box car. They waded through the crowd to the station master's office and were horrified at his response.

"Sorry—very sorry," he threw his hands into the air, "Your car has been switched to a passing train by mistake. When the train was pulling out we saw the woman who takes care of your stoves shouting and gesticulating."

Meantime their cab driver had left. Petropavlosk was seven miles away and the station was packed to capacity. For a while they walked up and down the platform—but a severe frost began to chill their bones.

In desperation they decided to knock like beggars at the door of a railroad worker's hut. Russian people were hospitable by nature but in Siberia there was a special custom going back over several centuries—they would put a jug of water and a piece of black bread outside the door each night to help an escaping convict. Originally based on fear of escaping prisoners, it had long since become part of the peasant character—and, in fact, the phrase "for the unfortunate ones" was a part of every peasant's vocabulary even in the remotest areas. Knowing the tradition, they knocked at the door to beg for shelter. An extremely fat woman opened the door.

"Who are you? Oh yes! You work with the children! I know all about you. Come right in—you're very welcome and the night's so very cold."

They entered a tiny sitting room furnished with an ugly sofa upholstered in pretentious red velvet. The hostess disappeared and in a few minutes two sleepy figures wrapped in blankets moved across the sitting room carrying pillows and shivering. The hostess said cheerfully, "Please make yourselves comfortable in this room." She led them into the one bedroom. They sank with relief into the still warm beds. It was the first time they were in real beds for months.

As they relaxed blissfully, they slowly became aware that the room was getting unbearably hot. Katia jumped up and lit a candle, but it quickly went out, melted by the intense heat. In the few seconds of light they could see that the beds were squeezed in between the wall and a huge iron stove. The stove occupied the whole center of the tiny room and was red hot. Trying to open the window without getting burned was in itself a major feat. Katia climbed on Alia's back and reached the window, but lost her balance and fell down with her legs landing under the beds. They heard a clicking noise as streams of water ran from every side of the room. Not daring to move, they sat cross-legged on the bed. Striking another match and looking under the beds, they saw scores of bottles with water, many of which had been upset in domino fashion.

A head poked in the door and said, "Excuse me—have you upset the bottles? I sleep with mother in this room, and when it gets hot we drink the water."

Quite unperturbed, she mopped the floor with a rag hanging from a nail and left the room. The Swans lay down, hoping to get some rest at last, but before long they both jumped up again.

This time Alia cried out, "What's stinging? Ouch!"

Striking another match they discovered that there was a thick dark brown moving layer on themselves and on the beds—"Bed bugs!"

Flop, came another from the ceiling—flop—flop—and a whole shower of them fell.

In the morning their hostess greeted them warmly, "Good morning, have you slept well? Breakfast is ready—hot rolls with sour cream—just out of the oven. Help yourselves!" She kept pressing them to take more.

Returning to the station they were informed that their only hope of getting to Omsk would be to get permission to board an incoming train of the French Commissioner, General Janin. In a few minutes the train arrived and after some negotiation, they were invited to board. The comfort and luxury of the international sleeping cars was overwhelming. They were given a whole compartment, upholstered in green velvet. Feeling sleepy, dirty, and hungry, they could hardly bear the brightness of the electric lights and the soft seats. Timidly munching on bread, they were embarrassed by the entrance of a suave French officer inquiring in the name of General Janin if everything was all right and if they were comfortable. A little later, when they were lying down, a tall handsome officer in a spotless uniform, knocked and entered.

"Ne vous dérangez pas, je vous en prie! Je veux tellement parler avec vous. Mais si vous êtes déjà couché, alors demain matin."

This was the same General Janin who, one year later, betrayed Admiral Kolchak, titular head of the White Russian movement, by having him handed over to the local authorities who shot him within two weeks. But because they arrived at Omsk too early the next morning they did not get to see the general.

After wandering along the innumerable tracks at the Omsk station, the Swans discovered their car. Fenya began crying the moment she saw them.

"Ohhhhh, Holy Mother! I was so frightened travelling alone day and night. All sorts of people knocked at the door and there was no way of calling anybody. I thought I would be killed and never see you again! Ay! Ay!"

Amid the lamentations of Fenya, Alia hurried into the car praying that the money he had left in an unlocked barrel would still be there. He silently thanked God at finding that all the packets of Red Cross rubles were intact, just as he had left them.

Life on the rails began again—the constant scream of whistles, the bumping of freight cars as they were moved from track to track, the harsh grunts and curses of the cars' inhabitants which never ceased. The noisy passing of freight cars in the night woke everyone causing frayed nerves and short tempers.

Almost beside herself with nervous exhaustion, Katia at last fell ill and was moved to a Red Cross train on which there were a few sleeping cars. The kitchen and dining car were tended by a Czech chef and Czech waiters who cooked, scrubbed, and cleaned all the time. For several days her temperature was very high and there were no signs of improvement. One day a visitor from the Quaker mission poked his head in.

"Well, are you worse this morning? Is your temperature going up nicely? I'm sure it must be typhus!"

But fortunately he was wrong and Katia did recover. While recuperating, she plunged into temporary work as a translator for the Quaker mission still stationed in Omsk.

Meanwhile, things were not going well at the Red Cross headquarters in Omsk. As soon as Bishop Tucker had delivered the supplies, he departed. He was replaced by a Colonel, Dr. Rudolph Bolling Teusler, who had been superintendant of St. Luke's Hospital in Tokyo, and then was made commanding officer of the American Red Cross Siberian Commission. In appearance he looked like a Spanish hidalgo, behaved with enormous authority and was quick and snappy in his decisions. Alia had met Teusler, reputed to be a relative of President Wilson's wife, in Ekaterinburg when he was still convalescing from diphtheria. For the short time Teusler was there, decisions were always carried out. But then he too left to return to his old hospital in Tokyo.

His replacement in Omsk was a Colonel Thompson whose only thought was to make his escape back to civilization, away from the turmoil in Siberia. Colonel Thompson's disgust with everything Russian, including the cold, the civil war, Siberia, and all unpleasant living conditions, impinged on his work. Every morning he left his train compartment with great reluctance and went to his office in town. In the afternoon he returned to his compartment and spent the rest of the day in pajamas with no idea of what life might be like anywhere else except in his compartment and his office. He was unable to understand why the Swans did not use public transportation to visit the other colonies and why they insisted on waiting for the return of their rail car which had been loaned to some nurses who needed to go to Novonikolyevsk.

The early days of January 1919, were filled with heavy doubts—new supplies had to be taken to the colonies, the dishonest manageress had to be exposed somehow. They desperately needed their car to be able to take care of so many pressing problems, yet it still was not returned.

One day they were commissioned to take warm clothing to a colony of refugees who were encamped in cabins and underground dwellings several miles from Omsk. News of their coming preceded them and they were escorted into a large room by a big crowd. On the table in the center an ancient man with a yellow face and dark-rimmed eyes was lying. His bones seemed to stick out of his body and he was moaning feebly while two old women were praying at his feet.

"Never mind him—he's only dying—we can stay in this corner of the room," said a cheerful small boy.

But, unable to bear the sight, the Swans distributed the supplies out of doors. Returning to their truck, they found a drunken Russian soldier taunting their Czech guard, screaming at him to get out of Russia. They were able to stop his barrage of insults, but it pointed up the increasing discord between the Russians and Czechs, now that the Czechs were moving to the East in their long trek homeward.

That night there was a knock at their door in the Red Cross car, and an American doctor pushed a forlorn, wild looking little creature inside.

"Here—you like children! Do something about this girl. I picked her up on the tracks—she seems lost." The child was wearing a thin dress, a few rags and high black galoshes. Her hands were shrivelled from the cold.—Her blond hair was clipped close to her head. She seemed about five years old. She went and crouched in the corner with her chin tightly glued to her chest and would not lift her head or speak.

"Come on, let's go to the stove," Katia coaxed. "It's cold here and warm over there. We're going to eat in a minute—are you hungry?"

Temptation stronger than fright started her moving to the stove, as Katia asked, "What's your name?"

Quite unexpectedly, she said loudly, "Katia!"

After dinner they started to cut out paper dolls to amuse her, and she cut out a big-headed, thick set man without a neck and with stumpy legs. Looking at him with delight, she broke into a deep hoarse laugh.

Delicate questioning elicited the fact that both of her parents had died of typhus, so she was staying in Perm with her grandmother. When some soldiers told her that the Bolsheviks were coming and would eat her and her cat, she was so frightened that she followed them. But the soldiers left her at Omsk when they started for the front again.

Without warning she began crying bitterly and wailed, "I wish I could have my cat again!"

A few days later the Swans' car was finally returned. They felt that they had to find a home for the child. It took a while but they did at last in a local orphanage.

Now they had to go back to Petropavlosk and confront Mrs. Vosnesensky.

A few of the 800 girls and boys of the children's colonies. Note the girls with shaved heads (top photo), a precaution against the spread of typhus.

CHAPTER SEVEN

Before leaving for Petropavlosk, Alia had to complete plans and budgets for all the colonies. That done they were on their way again. New supplies were packed into freight cars, and the money hidden in a large box in the Swans' boxcar.

At that time money came in huge sheets called "kerenke," which usually contained twenty-five 40 ruble notes with one thousand rubles to each sheet. By then rubles were practically worthless and each month it took more and more for a colony to exist. There were no checks or banks; money had to be in a person's hand for any purchase. Usually five or six sheets were given to each colony for a month's expenses, but this varied depending on the then value of the ruble.

When they arrived at Petropavlosk, they were pleased to find that the American Red Cross had established a permanent typhus hospital there and had the epidemic under control.

That same day they went to visit Mrs. Vosnesensky and were again taken aback by her disagreeable and slippery personality. The girls, who lived in the building with her, and even the teachers, were obviously terrorized. The question of getting proof against her seemed almost impossible.

The first night, starting back in a sleigh on the seven mile road to the station, nature itself seemed to join all the dark forces at Petropavlosk and reinforce their depression. As they left the town and started across the plain, the cold seemed to abate a little.

Suddenly there was a muffled tremor followed by an ominous roar. The driver of the sleigh moaned, "Oh, sir! Oh, sir!" and wiggled deeper into his sheepskin coat, lifting his shoulders in an effort to cover his face.

A few seconds later the same roaring and moaning sound turned into a wild snowstorm so violent that it seemed as if the heavens had been ripped open. Even the speedy little Siberian horse slowed down, not seeing, but feeling his way. The driver shouted back to them about robberies in the area during such storms, and the horse moved even slower as the snow reached his belly. Cold crept over their finger tips as Alia and Katia clung together for warmth. The horse was finally forced to stop, and the driver, seemingly frozen or asleep, was absolutely motionless. In desperation they both began shouting, try-ing to attract attention. Their cries even brought the driver to life and he joined in.

"Aooooo-oooo-ooo" suddenly came from somewhere near.

Through the swirling snow they could make out the dim silhou-ettes of men approaching on horseback.

Fear of robbers struck them both until one rider shouted, "Hal-looo! You're stuck pretty bad! Try to move on—we'll break the snow for you! Follow us—the station's only a few hundred yards away."

It proved to be the station master coming back from town with several of his employees. In a few minutes they saw the dim glittering lights of the station and were able to make their way back to the safety of their car. They entered with a prayer of thanksgiving, but it was hours before they were really warm again.

For two nights and a day the storm continued to rage and they were forced to stay in their car. Food began to run out and their coal supply was almost at an end. But on the morning of the third day the sun appeared and the storm stopped as quickly as it had begun. Suddenly life returned to the railroad and there was feverish activity everywhere as people began digging out of the storm and cleaning the cars and tracks.

Now there was no longer any excuse not to tackle the Petropavlosk manageress. They returned to the colony and Alia closeted himself all day with Mrs. Vosnesensky, meticulously going over her accounts in the hope of finding some evidence of her misdeeds.

Katia, more or less free, decided to take a walk. As she went down the street, she saw two girls across the road whispering together and glancing at her apprehensively.

She crossed the street and said to them, "What is it? Do you want to talk to me?"

Plucking up courage, one answered, "We've got to talk with you. Could you come for a walk with us?" No sooner had they gone beyond the colony when both girls began talking fast and furiously.

"You must save us from that awful woman. She's crazy! Please do something. She's a maniac! She takes everything she can get her hands on. She took our money. We had a small amount of pocket money we brought from home. She collected it all and we've never seen it again. None of the boys got the Red Cross sweaters and socks that you brought last time you were here. She told us that the Red Cross is holding us as hostages for Americans who are being held by the Bolsheviks, and that as long as the Red Cross is in charge we will never see our parents. She told all the other colonists the same thing."

Returning from the walk, Katia went straight to the housekeeper and asked her to tell what she knew. At first the poor woman was too frightened to say anything, but finally, seeing that Katia had both authority and determination, burst out with damning evidence.

"I've been worrying for a long time about the monthly statements of food and fuel spent by the colony which Mrs. Vosnesensky made me write for her. She buys everything herself. What does she want these statements for? The girls are right about the sweaters and socks, and also about her stories concerning the Red Cross holding the children as hostages."

At that moment, Alia came out of the manageress' office and seeing Katia, exploded with, "I know she's a swindler. But how can I confront her with it unless I have some real proof?"

Katia shushed him, whispering that they would be overheard. So they left the building and began walking up and down the same lonely street where they had walked several months before, again discussing the situation. They decided at last to call a meeting the following day in their car and summon Mrs. Vosnesensky with her accounts. All the other teachers and the housekeeper would be present. And, in order to give the meeting a more authoritative appearance, Alia asked the head health officer of the American Red Cross typhus hospital, Dr. Newman, if he would attend.

Dr. Newman was an unforgettable type of Red Cross relief worker. He was a firm and courageous doctor who himself later fell victim to typhus and lingered for weeks on the brink of death before finally recovering. His successful and extraordinary work in conquering typhus in Petropavlosk was counterbalanced by an insatiable and immoral private life to which he gave free rein. He seemed to look upon the Russian expedition as an open playground for amorous escapades free of all consequences. But his presence at the meeting did help turn the scales against Mrs. Vosnesensky.

The following morning to everyone's surprise a shy trembling woman came to the meeting and tearfully acknowledged her disloyalty to the Red Cross, and her use of the housekeeper's statements as substitutes for the original bills. When the meeting was over, Alia questioned her for several hours again about the accounts. He then went through the ledger books alone, locating, kopec by kopec, proof of eleven thousand rubles which had been misappropriated. A formal list was drawn up, citing the charges against her with all the proof. When she and her husband were faced with it, she managed to produce eleven thousand rubles from her trunk. Both she and her husband were discharged but not prosecuted since all the money was returned. Now, of course, the entire colony had to be reorganized.

Mrs. Vosnesensky had divided her colony into four groups. A war prisoner was in charge of the small boys, a governess took care of the older girls, and she herself handled the little girls as well as coordinating all the groups. Her husband, whom the Swans had originally found locked in his room, was supposedly in charge of the older boys. Although he had been removed from the building and given a private room in town, he was technically still attempting to run the older boys' establishment.

Alia now changed the entire system. Each group was made independent of the others and new people found to run each section, except for the older boys. He decided that no older person should be put in charge of them, but that they should be given the responsibility of running their own group. Since these were the same boys whom he had worked with and organized on his earlier trip, Alia felt that they could be relied on to manage their own house. Six of the twenty-two boys were put in charge of various duties, such as housekeeping, cooking, cleaning, discipline, and accounts.

The two leaders were Semenov and Smolieninov. Semenov later became the lead cellist in the Maly Theatre and collected such rare musical memorabilia that his collection will be housed in a special museum after his death. Smolieninov was mature and thoughtful, but was bitterly persecuted later, being unable to knuckle down to the gray rigidity of Bolshevism.

Others who assumed definite responsibilities were Barinov, handsome but badly spoiled, Yegorov, the athletic one, and the older Schutt boy, well-meaning but stupid. Their group worked out extremely well and soon all lost books were located, instruments found, singing taken up, and organized study instituted. Alia got to know many of the boys as individuals—and fifty years later, in a different world, he was still in contact with several of them.

So well did the boys live up to the confidence placed in them that just before the Swans left, they decided to have a celebration. For a week they worked hard preparing a play, *The Bear*, a broad comedy by Chekhov.

The big night arrived and all the colonists were invited. The energy of the boys, misused for so long, showed in the constructive way they organized and presented their show. The actors of course outdid themselves trying to show off before the girls, and the whole evening was a complete success.

Katia recorded in her diary that for a few short hours they all felt that they were back in times of peace, forgetting that Russia was crumbling, that the civil war was all around them, and that typhus was heralding the coming of the new order.

But reality quickly reasserted itself. On the way back to the girls' quarters the precariousness of life was sharply brought to their attention.

The street was dark and deserted, when the quiet was broken by a volley of shots, and a loud answering volley was heard nearby. The panic-stricken girls began to run and it was quite some time before they could all be collected in a place of safety between two buildings. Eventually, by making a long detour, the girls' dormitories were reached with no harm to anyone.

The Swans had been able to hire a man named Pavel to tend the stove and see to the water supply, when Fenya, exhausted by all her upsetting experiences, quit. On their return to the boxcar that night, they found Pavel delirious and tossing in his bunk. He was one of the bits and pieces that the revolution was constantly flinging about, — a typical victim, not because of his beliefs, but simply because he had the audacity to want to eat. Originally he had come from the northern district of Novgorod in European Russia. During the famine of 1918, the aldermen of his village decided to send a group of young peasants to Perm to buy wheat and bring it back to help the villagers survive the coming winter. Pavel was one of those chosen.

The necessary funds were collected by every family in the village contributing a certain amount. The young men reached Perm safely. Here they bought the wheat, hired a boxcar from the railroad officials, and began their long journey home. At the very first stop, the government, supposedly created just for working men and peasants, decided to interfere since there was too much of individual initiative in this venture. A detachment of Bolshevik troops started firing at the boxcar loaded with wheat, and the only thing left for them to do was to run or be slain. The official answer to the peasants inquiries was that the wheat had been confiscated. They did not dare to return to their homes, for they had spent the common money and lost the wheat. The civil war soon began, and Pavel joined innumerable refugees, finally getting to Omsk and the situation he was in now.

They knew during the past week that Pavel had not been well, but in the rush of things had not paid much attention to what seemed like just one more problem.

As soon as he saw them he mumbled pathetically, "Don't worry, this isn't typhus. I've had typhus already."

They believed him. During that night he even got up to do some chores, and in the morning mended the stove. This reassured them.

Again the whirlwind of activities claimed the Swans, but gradually Alia realized that Pavel was getting worse and sent for Dr. Newman. The doctor took one look at him and diagnosed typhus. He took him off immediately to the American Hospital. Katia was told to burn all of his things outside in the snow and to have the car scrubbed and totally disinfected.

In desperation, she tossed everything belonging to him out into the snow and was preparing to scrub the place herself, when an old woman appeared at the door and offered to do the job herself for a large sum of money. At this point Katia was not in a mood to quibble, so she accepted the offer and went outside to burn Pavel's possessions. As she stepped out, she was horrified to see a crowd gathered around, gleefully grabbing his infected things.

Shouting at them to stop because they were typhus infected, one old woman retorted, "Never mind the typhus, typhus bugs are everywhere, so are all bugs, but clothing, a mattress, blankets, they can't be bought for solid gold, even if you had it."

One old man, arriving late at the scene, found only a piece of stale bread which Pavel had not finished lying in the snow. He picked it up, crossed himself, and started gnawing on it with his toothless gums.

After the removal of Pavel, the Swans were amazed to be informed that the railroad officials were preparing to rebuild and fix their car. Like magic it was cleaned, painted a soft gray, partitioned into two rooms, an office and a bedroom, furnished with a high bench for sleeping, and even a few chairs. A table was built for working and eating, and the floors and windows mended. A new war prisoner, a sulky Pole, was assigned to take care of the stove and water.

During their stay at Petropavlosk, a teacher from Uiskaya Stanitsa named Streschkovsky, and one of his colleagues showed up for another month's funds. Streschkovsky was the shady character, supposedly the lover of the manageress, Mrs. Siedachova, whose violent entrance into the British Consul's house in Kurgan had created such a stir. Alia had already heard many unfavorable reports about him, and indeed his appearance seemed to bear them out. His whole body seemed to exude a nauseating odor and his face was covered with a black beard partially concealing unpleasantly blackened teeth. Although only 27 years old, he stooped and had the air of a complete degenerate. Alia felt that he had no choice but to give him the money for the next month, March, and send him back to Uiskaya Stanitsa because he was too involved at the time in getting affairs at Petropavlosk straightened out.

Having put everything to rights by March 10th, the Swans felt free to leave Petropavlosk. They proceeded to Kurgan with their Polish war prisoner, as well as a young, 7-year-old colonist, named Vladimir Schutt who came along supposedly to run errands, but really to be babied, for he was frightfully homesick and lonely.

There they found that things had not been going well since they had reinstated the incompetent Mrs. Rudolph. Although she was a thoroughly honest woman and possessed many sterling qualities, she had an unfortunate manner in dealing with others. All her subordinates were alienated by her peevish attitude and misanthropic ways. The organization of the colony was rapidly melting away and the teachers were constantly quarreling with one another. On arriving at Kurgan, Alia saw that he had made a mistake and had to depose her at once.

In her place he appointed Dr. Yeropkina who had been a neutral outsider, taking no part in the petty feuds. She was an excellent woman for the job, old enough to command respect from the other teachers and kind enough to gain the love of all the children. Overnight the entire atmosphere changed and the whole colony began to run efficiently.

The second day of their stay the children got up a party on the spur of the moment. Everyone felt an unaccustomed sense of relief from pressures. They induced Alia to play his violin so that they could dance. Someone started a game of Cossacks and Bandits and they all took part in the general hilarity. Only Mrs. Rudolph absented herself.

Meanwhile to their surprise, their sulky war prisoner changed completely and proved to be one of the most capable men with whom they had ever dealt. It began with a whole new regime in the boxcar. He kept it clean and warm at all times. He put up shelves, and when coal ran low, the scrounging talent of Stanislav Francawich, his Russian name, assumed genius proportions. He also proved able to cook hot meals on the coal heating stove. There seemed to be no

71

end to his talents. He even produced a new pair of much-needed shoes for Alia after several days labor over a piece of leather.

Gradually he told them his life story. Coming from the Carpathian Mountains, he had become a prisoner of war on the plains of Western Siberia for four years. He showed pictures of his wife and three children, but mourned them as dead. During the fighting his village had been evacuated and the houses razed to the ground.

"I don't know where to look for my family. They're probably all killed."

After a two-day stay in Kurgan, the Swans continued on to Myass to begin the job of extricating the children at Uiskaya Stanitsa from the homes of the Cossacks and the clutches of Mrs. Siedachova and Streschkovsky.

Flight from Turgayak.

CHAPTER EIGHT

On arriving at Myass, they found difficulties there even greater than had been painted. In the first place, the colony at Uiskaya Stanitsa was almost inaccessible. Miles and miles separated it from the nearest town, and the only means of transportation was by horse and sleigh. Word had been sent ahead that the Swans were coming, but it was evidently deliberately ignored.

They decided first to collect all the information they could about the history of the colony and its present condition. To this end they introduced themselves to the Czech Commandant at Myass. He in turn introduced them to the local baker's wife, fondly called Mamasha by the entire village. She was a plump jolly woman who controlled the whole place.

Indeed, when ever the slightest crisis arose, it was the Commandant's habit to go to her and, with a joking, "Mamasha, save the revolution," ask her advice.

A YMCA car was also at Myass. It was run by a Mr. Wheeler, who by this time was reduced to the sole relief practice of selling American cigarettes to the Czech soldiers. For several evenings they met with the Czech Commandant, Mr. Wheeler, and Mamasha to discuss various plans. The original message, announcing the Swan's coming visit, had been finally answered with a warning of contagious illnesses of the children. A stronger message was sent, but the same answer came back. After that they all agreed that the only way to handle the problem would be to bring the colony to Myass because of the inaccessibility of Uiskaya Stanitsa.

Learning that there were a number of Cossack villages in the area, the Swans decided to investigate some of them to see if suitable premises could be found. Not quite realizing the distance or the dangerous conditions of the times, they rather lightheartedly hired a sleigh to start a fifty mile cross-country journey to a large Cossack settlement called Chebarkul on the shore of a lake several miles long.

The trip began pleasantly enough, riding along through the open countryside, but soon they plunged into the dense dark forests of the Ural slopes where the sky was totally obscured.

The driver gruffly replied to their questions, or just grunted—until he suddenly turned and, looking at them glumly, said, "Here at this left turn, one often sees wolves."

Along the trail were wooden crosses with small icons imbedded in the markers. With sudden eagerness in his voice, the driver began pointing them out.

"These mark the spots where people have been killed. Here's one— a man killed his mother-in-law right there. And there, by that dead tree, a small boy was murdered—he had the tough luck to ask the way to Myass of some highway thugs. They asked him if he had any money and he innocently showed them fifty kopeks. They told him the wrong way and when he was lost they grabbed him, took his money, killed him, and hung his corpse on that pine tree there. But they got caught themselves because they bragged about their cleverness and told the whole story."

Mile after mile they rode, and the driver finally lapsed into silence. Nothing was said by anyone for some time, when suddenly a shrill whistle broke the stillness. The driver stopped and whistled back. In a few seconds, two big men appeared rolling a barrel, and without a word deposited it under the driver's feet, then quickly disappeared into the woods. No one said a word. The Swans dared not ask, and they proceeded on with the trip.

Passing cross after cross, they at last emerged from the woods opposite a small frozen lake. Little black figures on the lake scurried away in all directions and hid behind blocks of ice. The driver explained that they were timid Mongolian tribesmen fishing through the ice. Reassured that they were not the only ones who were timid, the Swans signaled the fishermen to come over and show their catch. With supper in mind, they purchased several shimmering green perch from the tribesmen who were now very friendly and gathered around begging them to look at their fish.

Soon after they reached Chebarkul, a very wealthy village, the Cossacks eagerly welcomed them as soon as they spotted the barrel, which proved to contain illegal moonshine. The village turned out to be typical, with one long street, tightly clustered houses, carved windows and gate posts, opening into big yards. Tall white birches lined the street. The big, fat, red-faced Cossack alderman soon dashed their hopes—there was nothing suitable in the village and no large outlying estates where the children could be housed.

Many more journeys like that had to be taken before the Swans one day discovered the ideal spot on Lake Turgayak. After all these fruitless trips, one night Mamasha remembered hearing that some children had stayed at Lake Turgayak the summer before. She thought that there might be suitable accommodations there. Lake Turgayak was only ten miles from Myass. The lake was a lovely bowl-shaped body of water with an island at one end and, on the other, a high bank which dropped abruptly to a sandy beach below. A typical Russian village was on one side of the lake. But adjoining the village was a colony of private summer houses, all of which were now empty and had not been occupied since before the war. The place seemed ideal and, with the permission of the commandant of the district, the Swans took possession of the summer homes.

With tremendous energy they started to fit out several of the houses for the children and Stanislav Francawitch proved invaluable. He built bunks, adjusted iron stoves, fixed broken window panes, and made all other necessary repairs. They made occasional trips to Myass with a much more cheerful driver who took them in his troika. But he too pointed out all the signs of wolves found on the trail—badly mutilated carcasses of cows, horses, sheep, some with fresh blood still visible.

One night, returning to Myass in the midst of their preparations, they found that a Red Cross car had arrived bearing the new head who had come to replace the incompetent Colonel Thompson. The Reverend Doremus Scudder was a cozy little person who invariably wore steel rimmed glasses and carried a volume of Shakespeare with him. In appearance he reminded them of Goldsmith's "Vicar of Wakefield." He had previously been a minister in Honolulu and carried with him the gentle quiet ways of his former profession—even to writing poetry in his spare time.

He sent three typewritten reports of the three colonies to Red Cross headquarters for April, May, and June, 1919, and they read in part more like poems than business reports. Katia was delighted to find that he had brought some of Racine's works with him, and that he was very anxious to learn to speak Russian of which he could already read a little. Every time a Russian letter puzzled him, he would laugh cheerfully and say, "What is this little villain doing here?" Horrified at the way the Swans were living, he sent them a large supply of California canned peaches, pineapples, and a bag of granulated sugar—unheard of luxuries at that time.

During his meetings with Alia, the idea of concentrating all the colonies in one spot took shape. Dr. Scudder promptly contacted Admiral Kolchak for advice as to where the safest place might be. At that time Kolchak was winning on all sides, and so great was his optimism that he assured Scudder that Turgayak would be perfectly safe, and that by fall he would be in Moscow. Then the children could be sent home.

Inspired by such assurances, the Swans accepted the plan. The removal of the Uiskaya Stanitsa colony to Turgayak would be the first step toward bringing all the children there. Again they sent word to Uiskaya Stanitsa and again they received another stalling message. Finally, Alia was forced to ask for aid from the Czech soldiers who expressed delight at the idea of going on such an adventure. Written orders were given to them with a list of every child's name. The next day a group of well-armed soldiers set out for Uiskaya Stanitsa. A few days later, one of the soldiers returned to tell them when the children would arrive. He also told them of the trouble they were having locating each child. The rumours had been true—the children were scattered all over the village, earning their board and kept as servants in the local Cossacks' homes. The manageress refused to make any preparations to leave, so the soldiers had to take matters into their own hands.

Katia realized that the children would have to spend the night in Myass before going on to Turgayak. She went to the Russian General Stepnoy to ask for a building to house them in for one or two nights. To her astonishment, he refused aid of any sort, so she simply went right out and took over the schoolhouse. She then returned and gave the surprised General such a tongue lashing that he was speechless.

The appointed day arrived and the children came in huge wagons filled with straw and completely surrounded by Czech soldiers with their rifles. Bringing up the rear were the two trouble makers. The whole town turned out to celebrate the occasion, led by Mamasha who met the cavalcade with homemade buns and pretzels for all.

The following morning the manageress, Mrs. Siedachova, and the nauseating Streschkovsky were fired. The same day, forty sleighs left Myass and arrived at Turgayak at dusk carrying the bundled-up children and remaining teachers. The children tumbled out stretching their numbed limbs and chattering. Katia had hired some villagers to prepare a hot meal and they had set up a long table in the largest house.

In the middle of the meal one of the older boys stood up and said,

"We demand to be sent to Petrograd. We shall *not* be hostages of the Red Cross any more!"

Everyone became silent and there was an air of embarrassment over the whole room. Alia quietly rose and began to speak to the children about the situation. He explained that it was the plan of the American Red Cross to return them as quickly as possible to their parents in Petrograd, and everyone was praying and hoping that it could be accomplished by fall if the fighting would stop. He told them about Admiral Kolchak's optimistic predictions. He said that the coming summer would be just a continuation of their last summer vacation, and surely by September they could expect to be back home. He then quietly spoke of the work of the American Red Cross in taking care of the children over the preceding winter and through next summer. Soon everybody seemed to be convinced of the falsehood of Mrs. Siedachova—although later events proved that she had sown her seeds deeply in their young minds. As soon as dinner was over the tired but peaceful children were distributed into houses and went fast asleep.

The only place left for the Swans to sleep was on the big table where they had all eaten. It was bathed in moonlight streaming through the window. They were so tired that they dozed off quickly, only to be awakened by a howling wind blowing from the lake. The moon and stars had been covered by dark heavy clouds. Snow began falling and getting heavier by the minute. A terrible crash and the sound of broken glass sent them running to another house. There they were met by a small crying figure who told them that two boys had upset a table which broke a window, and the icy wind and snow were blowing into the main room. Grabbing a big piece of home-made Siberian felt from the hall floor, they were able to stuff it into the broken window. They got through the rest of the night lighting fires in the iron stoves and covering the children with torn blankets or any rags they could find.

The next few days were spent reorganizing life for the children and the teachers. Once these problems were more or less in order, the Swans began the complex task of developing a schedule to bring all the other colonies to Turgayak.

CHAPTER NINE

The Swans decided that their next move would be to pick up the children at Petropavlosk and bring them back to the newly organized Turgayak center. On the day of departure they went to the office of the Czech Commandant of the Myass station to get permission to have their car switched on to the next passing train.

The room was packed with people, and when the Commandant looked at their papers he shouted, "Hurry up! Run to the Russian military commander. He has to give the order. A train is just coming in. You might have time to switch your car, otherwise you'll have to wait for several days!"

Alia grabbed his papers and rushed out of the office. When he reached the office of the Russian commander, he discovered to his horror that his papers were gone. He frantically searched all his pockets and realized that he must have left them behind. With nervous trepidation he raced back to the Czech Commandant's rooms.

The big square room was still packed with people and confusion reigned. Suddenly out of the dense crowd an old peasant stepped forward. He was clad in a sheepskin coat, felt boots, and a fur cap. His beard and bushy hair matched his quiet gray eyes. In fact, he seemed the very image of St. Nicholas as pictured on so many Russian icons.

A slight smile was hovering around his lips as he said, "I think, Sir, that you have forgotten this booklet here—I picked it up on the counter over there."

Alia, barely taking the time to thank him, took it and rushed back to the Russian commander's office. He was vastly relieved to find the wallet intact with all his papers and the Red Cross money. To his dying day, Alia believed that St. Nicholas had somehow intervened.

The journey to Petropavlosk was uneventful and the weather grew warmer each day. With amazing speed the big snow-drifts melted away to nothing, and within a few days the steppes were green again.

On April 10th, Easter day, they arrived, still accompanied by little Vladimir Schutt. Vladimir was promptly surrounded by the other boys who tried to get him to tell about his experiences, but though he tried, he seemed unable to explain the simplest story. The others soon left him in disgust.

The return to the colony was one of the high points of the whole Siberian odyssey. Everything was working perfectly. The older boys were completely living up to the responsibilities that had been entrusted to them. Nothing had to be changed or corrected in their operation. The girls were in the care of their teachers, and the little boys were under the supervision of the war prisoner who was like a father to them. All the teachers spoke of the change in the older boys and told how much they helped in taking care of the rest of the colony. Everyone looked to them for help, and now in any decisions they were always consulted.

The entire colony joined in the Easter celebrations with the people of the village. Even the American, Dr. Newman, provided eggs and candy for the children, and they all exchanged the traditional three Easter kisses. Then they tried to crack each other's egg in the Russian game — the one child with an uncracked egg at the end would have his wish fulfilled and have good luck for the next year. Alia inwardly prayed that it might be so for all the colonists.

After Easter the long involved preparations to move the colony to Turgayak began. No one thought to doubt Kolchak's optimism. All the girls were put to sewing, and the boys repaired whatever they could and helped to pack. Several teachers went out to buy all available provisions around the countryside, and were lucky to find, at the last minute, a cheese processor and a sausage factory right in the town itself. Here, in this remote village, they were able to order barrels of Gruyere, Dutch, and other cheeses, which, with freshly baked bread and other provisions, equally fresh, were delivered to the station the morning they left. Alia had chartered a long string of boxcars, and, on April 25th, the trip began.

The weather was wonderfully warm and, since everyone expected the children to be home by fall, all the old torn winter clothing was left behind. They took nothing warmer than sweaters. As the train neared Kurgan it began to get colder and colder. Then without warning, they ran into a tremendous snowstorm. When the train stopped at the first little station, the grownups jumped out and searched for wood to light the stoves in the cars.

Arriving at Chelyabinsk, the train was stopped and the Swans were told that they could proceed no further since this was now the center of all army movements. Furthermore, all passenger service westward had been suspended. Appeals in big letters were posted on all the bulletin boards and telegraph poles along the tracks. They urged the soldiers to fight on and declared the policy of Kolchak's government to be theirs. They faithfully promised land to the peasants and the convocation of a Constituent Assembly. These posters made it obvious that Kolchak's position was not as assured as the Omsk government had painted it to Dr. Scudder. In fact, such appeals always appeared when Kolchak's troops were failing at the front. The cars were put on side tracks, squeezed in between a long train of sick war prisoners and the main platform where soldiers were embarking on the trains for the front.

Then began the long days of waiting. There were sporadic riots, and drunken soldiers hung around the cars where the older girls were. The soldiers would spent their last night before battle on the platform celebrating. Some of the girls managed to get out and had to be persuaded to come back into their cars. The military governor did all he could to protect them, but he was virtually helpless. All the talk along the tracks was about General Kappel, commander of the forces under the Constituent Assembly, and hopes seemed to be pinned on him. There were rumors floating around that he was planning an attack on the Bolsheviks who were evidently somewhere very near, though no one knew exactly where.

Finally one afternoon, after another of his innumerable visits to the military commander of the station, Alia came into their boxcar and began freshening up. Turning to Katia he said, "I'm going to Kappel. The commander is going to take me to see him soon."

All afternoon and evening Katia waited for news—then, long after dark, she saw scores of lanterns moving around the long train. Men were tapping wheels, and inspecting the cars.

Alia rushed in, "Kappel is going to let the commander switch our train to his. He's leaving in a few minutes."

He then told Katia the details. Kappel's train had not pulled in until midnight, and immediately after that Alia and the military commander entered his car. Kappel was a small man with very dark hair and eyes. He was surrounded by his military staff, and they were poring over reports and a large map of Siberia, deliberating on plans for a coming battle.

At this moment Alia made his request for the children. Kappel looked at him in blank amazement.

"What children? I'm taking a train loaded with shells and dynamite to the front—I can't have children around! If something happens—."

Alia said he would take full responsibility for the children's lives upon himself, because in their position it made little difference whether the dynamite blew up or the rioting soldiers killed them all. Kappel still said it was impossible, but again Alia pressed his argument saying that it was impossible for the children to stay and there was no other way to get out. The commander entered the argument, assuring the General that the children were doomed if they stayed.

Kappel demurred with, "I cannot be detained."

The commander replied, "It will take six minutes to switch them on."

Kappel rolled his eyes upward and said, "All right," as he waved them out. Within half an hour the entire cavalcade departed.

The rest of the night was spent wondering if the train would or would not blow up. They were fully aware that a wheel box on one of the children's cars was damaged, and if the wheel got loose or dropped off, or if it should start a fire, the whole train could blow up.

On the morning of May 3rd they arrived safely at Myass. They were unhitched there, and watched gratefully as General Kappel's train disappeared into the distance. Mamasha and the Czech Colonel Blajak met them at the station, and there was great excitement among the children. The weather had turned warmer, although there were still blocks of ice on the lake. The children all decided to walk the seventeen versts[1] to Turgayak and they set off singing at the top of their lungs. Vanya Semenov, one of the original big and uncontrolled boys at Petropavlosk, had undergone an amazing change when responsibility was placed on him. He walked with Alia and they began discussing music. He shyly told Alia that he could play the mandolin, balalaika, and guitar. He also knew and could sing Russian folk songs. Alia started to sing and Vanya harmonized with a rather pure voice. This impressed Alia who told him to work seriously with music. In the ensuing weeks they had many musical conversations.

Before the train left Chelyabinsk, Alia had dispatched Duvalensky, one of the most trustworthy of the older boys, to Troitsk with money and letters containing a proposal for the colony to join the other two at Turgayak for the summer. The plan was to return everybody to Petrograd in the fall. He was instructed to relate the whole story of the packing and moving of Uiskaya Stanitsa and Petropavlosk. Shortly after the Swans arrived at Turgayak, Duvalensky got there bearing a letter from Mrs. Boydanova, the manageress, which said that she would come at once and the colony would follow. On June 1st, as soon as the colony arrived, she announced her decision to retire. The strain of her position, and the capable and energetic way she had fulfilled it, had taken its toll on her health. This was unsettling news for the Swans, for of all the workers in the colonies she was one of the very best and the most popular.

Spring was just approaching Turgayak in June. The rugged mountains on the opposite banks of the lake were criss-crossed with patches of green and the still remaining snow and ice. Dark pines rose in sharp contrast to the background. There were chunks of ice remaining in the lake, but the water was very clear. In fact, it was possible to see right down to the bottom and distinguish all kinds of pebbles from the porch of one of the houses.

By the end of June, the whole community was on an organized working basis. The colony was spread out among fourteen cottages. None of the teachers lived in the houses with the children, who were totally responsible for the running and upkeep of each house. One group of older girls assumed responsibility for the little children. Each group had certain duties, such as cleaning the houses, setting tables, and washing dishes.

Boys had to bring water up the hill from the lake in a big keg on a cart pulled by a little horse. So heavy was the water that the boys had to help push the cart. Vanya Semenov mastered the art of harnessing and unharnessing the little horse and was so proud of it that he claimed to be a born stableman and bragged inordinately about his achievements.

The Red Cross had negotiated successfully for permission to use the whole summer resort and its twenty acres with the local Zemstvo (government). And Dr. Scudder had asked the government to furnish horses, carts, and feed as their part of the enterprise which was to be cooperative.

The center of the colony was the headquarters building where the general staff lived and where a social club was formed. Next door was a cottage with store rooms, a main office, and, upstairs, a dental office. In the yard were carpenter and shoe shops, a bakery, and the main kitchen. To the left of this central point were dormitories, a school house, laundry, hospital, sewing rooms, and the stable. On the right were other dormitories, a second kitchen, and three bath houses.

The hospital treated not only the colony, but all the village children as well, many of whom had never seen a doctor or dentist before. Its staff consisted of one doctor, one dentist, four nurses, and two order-lies. The domestic staff of the colony was equally adequate—seven cooks, three cobblers, four matrons, six attendants, five teachers, three seamstresses, two bakers, two chefs, two drivers, one secretary, one clothes warden, one provisioner, and one stableman—not Vanya.

Discipline was invested in a board of house presidents who were elected by the children. It made all the rules for the entire colony, guided the affairs of the houses, and assigned the daily tasks. Every evening a chief of girls and a chief of boys designated the tasks for the orderlies to carry out the following day. These orderlies had to sweep the floors, tend the yards, clean, serve in the kitchen, and do other similar tasks. Those who were not orderlies were known as free persons and had heavier duties such as gardening, fetching wood, carting water, repairing the roads, and taking care of any needed repairs for the houses. The girls took turns working in the laundry and sewing.

The colony now had fourteen horses and worked about forty-seven acres which were about twenty-five versts away in a Cossack section called Karsi. The land had been planted with potatoes, oats, beets, onions, carrots, and turnips, which would be enough to feed the colony the following winter if they should have to stay there. In the back of Alia's mind was the fear that a return to Petrograd was still very questionable—although he voiced this opinion to no one but Katia.

Money ceased to be used as a medium of exchange with the peasants for they could do nothing with it. Their chief need was for clothes, so an agreement was reached with the local cooperative whereby the Red Cross supplied cloth to the store and the store in turn got the necessary supplies from the peasants in exchange for the cloth. This worked out so successfully that the president of the cooperative made a long speech of thanks at a town party in the middle of June for the benefits the colony had bestowed on the community.

One of the first things organized were regular school classes for all the children. They were held in the morning, every day except Sun-day, from eight to one o'clock. There were one primary and six older classes. Both English and Russian were taught, and several teachers from Myass were brought in to aid in the work.

As soon as they could, a number of the children began to give musical performances. A trio was formed by Leo Nevolsky and two brothers, Nicholas and Serge Matveev. Their repertoire included famous Russian folk songs. Soon a chorus of girls joined in, and the musical group found themselves much in demand for evening dances. Vanya could hardly contain himself, because he had no instrument to play. But one day the Matveev brothers found a contrabass in Myass and somehow got it back to Turgayak. Although it had only three strings, and Vanya had no bow to play it with, he promptly tuned it like a guitar and learned to play it well enough to join the musical ensemble.

Some of the boys organized football teams, and a peasant living nearby loaned them his field to play on. Several lively games were put on for the benefit of the whole colony. By late June, the water was warm enough for swimming in the lake—the beauty and clarity of the water was a temptation for young and old alike.

The island in the lake aroused the curiosity of some of the older girls, so one day Katia organized an expedition to explore it. Embarking in a flat bottom boat, it took the girls several hours of hard rowing to reach the island. There they entered an inviting cove—the water was a bluish-green and extremely deep. Huge spruce trees lined the shore giving a wonderful pine smell to the air. The whole island had a mysteriously quiet atmosphere so that no one spoke above a whisper. Discovering a shack, they entered and saw an open prayer book on a stand in the middle of the room. There were prayers in praise of St. Vera inscribed on beams, mentioning the island of St. Vera. Back of the shack was a narrow path leading to a large flat stone. Behind the stone was an entrance to an underground passage. Along this passage were tiny rooms which looked like nuns' cells. A larger room was at the far end, probably an assembly hall. At one time it would have been pitch dark, but now light came through the partially caved-in ceilings. Coming out of the passage at the opposite end, they found a small beach, beyond which they could see the inaccessibly steep mountains separated from the island only by a very narrow strip of water.

On returning to Turgayak, Katia made inquiries in the village concerning the island. She was told that it was the sacred place of the district. The island of St. Vera had been chosen by the Old Believers as a hiding place before there had been any human habitation in that spot. In the 16th century, the Patriarch Nikon undertook to correct many mistakes in the church books which had been made by ignorant copyists. He also tried to abolish a few Russian church customs which had crept into the ritual and differed from the Byzantine Mother Church. This aroused great opposition among the strict

Orthodox people. Nikon's violent character, and the fact that his nearest assistants were South Russian theologians known for their close connection with the Catholic West, made the situation even worse. Soon the "old belief" was opposed to the "new Latin belief," so that the "Old Believers" ultimately refused to follow their priests. In 1667 the Old Believers were expelled from the All Russian Orthodox Church and persecuted. Many of them fled to the wilderness of the Ural Mountains and settled there. A young woman of saintly character and way of life lived on the island with a group of these worshippers. After her death she was called St. Vera, and the peasants of Turgayak, descendents of the Old Believers, still kept up the island and went there to pray on special days.

The days flowed peacefully by and the beauty of the countryside, surrounded by the forests and mountains, made the perfect background for a wonderful summer vacation. Some fifty-five years later, Vanya Semenov was able to recall the time in vivid detail, especially the food and shelter. He likened the whole ambience to the Krylov fable "The Grasshopper and the Ant," where beneath every leaf, there was a meal and security.

The boys wandered around the outskirts of Turgayak and discovered several abandoned mines. Dreams of finding gold filled their heads, but exhaustive searches produced only pretty pebbles, sometimes with shining specks of granite in them.

When the colony was being organized, plans were made to try to bring the colonies of Kurgan, Tyumen, and, if possible, Shadrinsk and Irbit, to Turgayak for the remainder of the summer.

One day Dr. Scudder arrived to see how the colony was working. He was quite overwhelmed by the efficient way it was established and functioning. He was shown the whole colony—sat in at the school, ate meals with the children, and was even taken on a picnic to the island. That evening the children decided to give an impromptu concert for him. Part of the chorus was on the porch overlooking the lake, and the other part was in the garden. They sang Czech and Russian folk songs such as the legend of Stenka Razin who sacrificed his beautiful Persian princess to the fast-flowing Volga to prove that he was still in command of his passions, and old church chants and prayers. Tales of birds and flowers, snow being melted by a maiden's tears, as well as some comic verses describing Vanya sitting on a sofa— these were all recounted against the background of Turgayak and the civil war. Dr. Scudder was so amazed that it was then he wrote a complete report in blank verse to the Red Cross, dated April, May, June 1919.

All these peaceful activities went on without too much thought about the continuing civil war. At first they heard only vague rumors that things were not going so well. Soon a few details leaked through—Kappel was evidently in grave trouble through some mysterious mixup.

He had been surrounded by Bolsheviks and, just as he was about to surrender, they began to break lines and turn back. It turned out that they were being attacked from the rear by more of Kappel's troops. This second batch of Kappel's men seemed on the point of saving the battle, when a new contingent of Bolsheviks hit them from the rear. People described it as a "sloyony perog," which means a pastry made of criss-crossed dough. However, since all the fighting was about one thousand versts away, and even though Kolchak was not advancing, there seemed to be no reason to panic. Unfortunately this rationalized optimism could not last very long. Word came to them that the confusion at the front was so great, and the Bolshevik forces so numerous, that Kappel had to retreat. By the beginning of July, it became obvious that Kappel had completely lost the whole front line.

The administrators now spent many tortured hours worrying about the next move for the children. The Whites were known to be retreating along the entire Siberian front, and it seemed more than likely that the whole Turgayak region would soon be uncomfortably close to the battle front. If the area should be taken over by the Bolsheviks, would the children be dispatched back to their parents and homes in Petrograd? Or would it be better to avoid the risk of violence and bodily harm by evacuating them deeper into Siberia? In the midst of these discussions a letter arrived from Alia's mother with the first news from home since the outbreak of the civil war. The letter was simply addressed, "Care of the American Red Cross, Siberia," and had come from England.

The news was that Alia's father was gravely ill, that their home in Petrograd had been broken up, and that some of the family had returned to England. Two days later a second message arrived which Dr. Scudder received and then passed along. Mr. Swan had died.

As Dr. Scudder was preparing to leave the colony, he suddenly asked the Swans if they would like to leave Russia. It was evident by then that the political situation was becoming very grave. But more important to Alia was the increasingly noticeable strained mental condition of Katia who was pushing herself beyond human limits and obviously could not go on much longer. The offer of Dr. Scudder, to send them anywhere they wanted to go under the repatriation plan for all Red Cross workers, came at a crucial moment and had to be accepted. Nevertheless they delayed their departure for several weeks, loath to leave the children in a situation fraught with uncertainties.

The control of the colony was turned over to Gregory Welsh, an English Quaker. He had been working with them ever since the children had been brought to Turgayak. He had been particularly efficient in bartering manufactured Red Cross goods with local peasants who, in exchange, brought in food and grain on their spacious Siberian carts. But pedigogically, Welsh was a harmful influence. He flattered and pampered the older boys and girls, and instilled in them a slippery set of values. He had no idea of what was going on in Russia and measured it all by the optimistic standards of a Britisher. His laudable Quaker philosophy of non-violence took on the form of non-resistance to any kind of evil, and soon the evil was viewed as something quite acceptable. The results of some of his teaching made considerable trouble later on.

One day a telegram for the Swans arrived from Omsk—"Your passage arranged—you can leave any time."

Even though the word had seeped through that the Bolsheviks were already crossing the Urals, the Swans could not tear themselves away from the children.

Then one day the colony's doctor approached them and said, "You must leave at once—the teacher, Streschkovsky, from Uiskaya Stanitsa whom you discharged in the spring, turned out to be a trouble maker. He was arrested for his Bolshevik speeches. Now he's out again. He's furious and telling everyone that you were the cause of his arrest. He's never forgotten his discharge and, being unscrupulous, is shouting everywhere that the first persons to be shot when the Bolsheviks come will be you. Beware of him and leave at once!"

This at last pushed the Swans toward departure, but they decided to take a group of fifteen children with them and leave them with their older brothers and sisters as they passed through Kurgan.

All the way to Myass the children sang and frolicked, but on arrival at the station things were in a state of chaos. Complete disorder reigned on the platform—trunks, boxes, and wooden cases were piled all over. The station resembled a military camp, with the train of the commanding general and his staff on the main track, along with their private car. The platform was jammed with panic stricken people all vainly hoping to leave. Women were shrieking, babies crying, while old people just sat on bundles staring out of hopeless eyes. Hurrying to their car which had been standing idle for several months, they learned that the general had given orders to confiscate it. In despair, the Swans told the children to go back to Turgayak without them. They would stay at Myass to see what could be done. Luckily the drivers were still around, so the children sadly agreed, realizing that the Swans might also be returning to the colony.

One gloomy old man came over to them and explained, "There are no trains anyhow—there's no way out of this trap, so what's the use? The Bolsheviks crossed the mountains long ago, and they're marching along the highway to Chelyabinsk already—so we're doomed. Our world is finished."

Suddenly a trumpet blew and the people made way for General Kappel and his suite to pass. All eyes turned anxiously to him, but he only looked dejectedly to the ground and went on. Troops lined up and gave a vague disheartened salute. These troops consisted primarily of young peasant boys who had just been conscripted and knew nothing about fighting. The fact that the short review was held right on the tracks convinced Alia that there would be no more trains.

Stunned and almost hysterical, Katia grabbed Alia's hand and said, "I can't stand these shrieking women any more! Let's get away to the woods."

They began climbing a steep slope into thick pine woods where the ground was covered with bluebells and white daisies. It started to rain lightly. Neither one had a coat—they had been burned in the car fire months before.

Suddenly Alia came to himself—"Are you mad? What are we doing here?"

Without another word he rushed down the slope, but Katia still did not move. After several minutes she saw Alia through the mist gesticulating violently, and at last she followed him down the hill.

Their only hope was to get their car back, since it was still under Red Cross protection and they were Red Cross representatives. Katia, in a flash, remembered that Dr. Scudder had given her a beautiful piece of cloth for a suit. It was made of pure wool from America, and was priceless under present circumstances. They rushed to the station master, whom they had been quite friendly with earlier. Offering him the cloth, they asked for help. His eyes popped out at the sight of the cloth and, in great excitement, he told them to go back to their car and not leave it. He would be on the lookout for the first chance to switch it onto the general's train, but under no circumstances were they to leave their car.

Hour after hour went by and they paced up and down the car

distractedly. Without warning, the local village school teacher came in. As they talked, the tense and frightening atmosphere made them immediate friends. Desperately, he expressed doubts about what to do next. His father, a priest, had been shot by the Bolsheviks just before Kolchak had come through. Although he had escaped by hiding, he knew that he probably could not get away again. His wife did not want them to become homeless refugees with no money. After listening to his tale, the Swans pressed him again and again to go with them. When he left without making a decision, they insisted on giving him most of their remaining money. But hours later he showed up again, only to repeat his goodbyes and to try to return the money because he knew his death was imminent. The Swans refused to take it back and he finally left, still despondent and arguing with himself. He disappeared into the night and was never heard from nor seen again.

A few minutes later, the station master poked his head in, "Are you still here? Good! There's a chance—don't leave! A troop train's coming through. The front's completely collapsed and everyone's fleeing. I'll switch you onto it."

The train pulled in and they heard the clicking of switches. The rusty wheels of their car started to move with hideous shrieks, and the train pulled out. They traveled until daybreak, when the light showed that they were moving through endless camps of refugees all along the line, all waiting. That day they passed through the junction at Polatayevo and reached Chelyabinsk. The train finally pulled into Omsk.

Knowing that they had at last slipped through the trap, they knelt and, thanking the Lord for their escape, prayed for the safety of the children, believing they would never see them again.

[1]Verst—approximately ⅔ mile

89

CHAPTER TEN

In Omsk the Red Cross workers lived in a lovely spacious house in the suburbs, but by this time it was overflowing with retreating Red Cross personnel. Fortunately, the weather was still warm and the sky almost cloudless, so a tent was pitched in the garden and, for almost two weeks, the Swans slept in it. Dr. Scudder had returned to Hawaii and was temporarily replaced by a Miss Matthew. During those two weeks, while waiting for a train for Vladivostok, Alia was writing full reports of the work that had been accomplished. He also turned over the eleven thousand rubles he had wrested from Mrs. Vosnesensky. This involved going over the Petropavlosk ledger books once more to show how the thefts had been covered.

He was greatly concerned about his own financial affairs, having only the equivalent of $100.00 left after giving all his money to the school teacher at Myass. Alia had been taking his salary out of the money allotted for all the colony's expenses, but he paid no attention to the tremendous drop in the value of the ruble. Consequently, he continued to take only the same amount each month as usual. Fortunately, the treasurer of the Red Cross, going over all the accounts, realized the situation and came to the rescue. He informed Alia that $400.00 more was owing to him. At the time it seemed like a princely amount.

One morning at six o'clock, Miss Matthew came to their tent and told them that a Red Cross train was coming through and their car was to be attached to it. Katia jumped up, remembering that all their laundry, which was all the clothing they possessed, was at a Chinese laundry. She hastened to town but found that all the streets were deserted, and when she came to the door of the laundry it was locked. Energetically pounding on the door, it was opened a crack at last by a frightened little Chinese boy.

"Where is the proprietor?"

"Sorry Miss, he's in jail."

"Since when?"

The door slammed in her face and was locked. Again she knocked and knocked but there was no sign of life within. Thinking of the impossibility of leaving for Vladivostok with only the clothes on their backs, Katia rushed straight to the jail and demanded to see the proprietor of the laundry at #3 Kataiskaya (Chinese) Street.

The stupefied warden threw up his hands and said, "But he is arrested! You don't know what you're talking about. A Chinaman's been murdered in the Chinese quarter and since they all look alike we had to arrest every man in the district so that the actual culprit couldn't escape. I don't know who your laundry man is."

Katia kept pleading until the warden, warning her of the unsavory conditions in the jail, picked up his keys and took her in. After unlocking several doors, they entered a big square room. Behind a row of heavy iron bars there was a mob of terrified whispering Chinese.

The warden, teasing her, said, "See, you're frightened—how can you possibly find your Chinaman?"

Pulling herself together, she shouted, "Is the laundry man on Kataiskaya Street here? Please come forward—I need you!"

There was a deep silence then a stirring in one corner—whispering—pulling—and a forlorn looking little man crept out of the group of prisoners.

The warden said, "Wait! Stop! You can't upset all the prisoners and raise such a ruckus here. Besides, I can't let any of the prisoners out, anyway!"

Undaunted, Katia chided him, "Come on! Have a sense of humor! This Chinaman has all the underclothes we own and we're leaving for America today. Please let him come with me so he can give me my washing. There's only a trembling little boy in his shop, and he knows nothing about the business."

"What am I going to do with you?" He turned a little sullen.

But Katia, knowing the Russian habit of cajoling and nagging, continued to try to charm and amuse him by her request. At last, giving in to her good humored pleading, the warden unlocked the cell and let the little Chinaman out. He called a guard to go with the prisoner, and the strange trio left the jail. The Chinaman, dazed by the whole procedure, quietly trotted along. When Katia tried to speak to the guard, he only frowned and looked at her severely. On such serious military duty, one does not indulge in light conversation.

At the laundry things were even worse. The Chinaman led Katia to a basement and showed her a heap of wet clothes piled up to the ceiling.

"Your wash is somewhere in here, but it'll take a whole day to pick it out of this heap."

Visions of a puffing train pulling out of Omsk without them made her go at the pile of wet clothes energetically. She made the Chinaman work, and even prevailed on the guard to put down his rifle and wring out dripping clothing. All three worked frantically for several hours and actually found all of the water-soaked drawers, undershirts, camisoles, and stockings.

She then went out and called a driver and, putting the clothes into a hamper, started driving along the busy street to the station. To her horror, people began staring and pointing at her carriage. She leaned out and, looking back, saw a stream of water running onto the road. Urging the driver to go faster only made the water splash all over pedestrians who proceeded to shake their fists and curse at the strange carriage.

The train was in the station, and she dragged her hamper to their car, only to be told that it would not leave for several hours. Deciding to try to get the laundry dry while waiting, she borrowed a line from an American canteen and strung it up on two poles right in front of the carriage where their seats were. She sat down to watch so that it wouldn't be stolen, but grabbed it off the line twice as the train made false alarm puffing noises. She then had to put it back each time.

After a little while, a messenger came from the canteen, begging her to come over and help translate for a rather desperate Czech soldier. Without thinking, she left her purse on the log where she had been sitting and went to the canteen. When the Czech's needs for some dressings and drugs were attended to, she returned to find the purse gone but the wash still there. Alia arrived a little later with all their documents and visas, and taking the laundry off the line they boarded the luxurious train.

Unbelievably, at almost the same moment, a train pulled in carrying the entire Turgayak colony. It was a happy and noisy meeting on the tracks at Omsk with all the children clamoring to tell them his or her tale. In the excitement Katia forgot all about her stolen purse which, after all, contained only money, and they could manage without that.

Just after the Swans had left Turgayak, and before any decision had been made as to whether or not to evacuate the children, Gregory Welsh had been called back to the American Red Cross headquarters at Omsk. His absence caused a great deal of uneasiness among those children whom the Swans had sent back from Myass to Turgayak when they were unable to take them along.

Even the local villagers were upset. Kolchak's army was definitely retreating and the war front was approaching the Urals. Many of the children became fearful, particularly remembering the chaos they had witnessed at the railroad station at Myass. A few days later, a Colonel Manget of the Red Cross had come to the colony at Turgayak and stayed for several days. He took long walks with the children, visited their cottages and became acquainted with many of them.

One clear warm evening the children gave a concert in his honor, and Vanya performed with his musical ensemble. He was now playing the important part of lower bass voice on his makeshift instrument and was terribly proud of his performance. The girls' choir joined and sang Russian folk songs. A particularly effective rendering of "Evening Bells" brought the audience to its feet. At the end of the concert everyone danced.

When the festivities were over, Colonel Manget asked if all the representatives of the different groups, (each house had its own representative), would meet in his headquarters immediately. There he told them that they would have to leave Turgayak the next day by twelve noon and go to the station at Myass. A sense of relief followed this announcement, for the children realized that someone was making decisions for their well-being. The unspoken, nagging fear lifted as soon as the message was delivered in the various cottages.

Early the next morning, carts were provided to take their modest luggage ahead to the station, while the children all followed on foot. Some time later communist provocateurs attempted to use this occurrence in their harassment campaign against the Red Cross when the children reached the United States. But the scene was actually a peaceful romp and lark along the way while playing impromptu games, singing songs, and telling jokes. Of course, the children had no idea that as the train left Turgayak, they were literally in view of the advancing army.

On the way to Omsk, the train stopped long enough to pick up the colony at Kurgan. It was there that a sad incident occurred. One of the boys, twelve-year-old Solomon Abel, looking for a friend in the Kurgan colony, ran up the platform while the cars were still moving. He slipped and fell between the train and the platform. Both his legs were crushed, and, although they rushed him to the hospital at Petropavlosk, he soon died from gangrene and shock.

For some time cars were pushed and shoved around the tracks, until three sections of the train were organized. Each was made up of twenty-two cars, and contained all the children and their possessions. The Swans' car was switched onto the first section.

Among the colonies on the trains headed for Vladivostok was the one from Irbit. It had a somewhat different history, which was recorded by Maria Gorbochova in her diary. She was the young teacher who had been involved in helping to get the young colonists through the awful fall and winter of 1918–19 at Kuraii-Tyumen. She had originally been trained at the famous Bestushevsky Teachers' Training College in St. Petersburg and had become a governess-teacher to the orphanage of the Imperial Humanitarian Society. When the food and military situation became so critical in 1917, the Society sent her to Irbit to find suitable quarters for the orphanage. The Soviet government had already taken over but gave permission for her trip. She had found and rented a large two-story merchant's house owned by a widow named Denisov. She then returned to Petrograd and helped the school move to Irbit, bringing with them her young sister, Alexandra Medvedeva Gorbochova.

The fifty-two girls from the orphanage arrived on October 25, 1917, with the headmistress Maria Victorovna Chitchegova in charge. In addition there were three teachers, Paula Prohofievna Zmolnikova, her sister Maria, and Lydia Ivanovna Yevaskinova. A nanny, Fedechka, and a cook completed the entourage. They journeyed from the Nicholas terminal in Petrograd in a whole car, taking pies, cakes, and bread, as well as all their own supplies from the orphanage.

The house on Alexandroff Street in Irbit was very large. Maria Victorovna had a first floor apartment, and there was a living room, hallway, and a dining room that also served as a classroom. The school was particularly interested in training girls for singing and dancing, but also trained seamstresses, taught painting, and provided a general education as well. Irbit, with a market second only to Novgorod, was untouched for quite a while and classes went on without interruption. The girls put on plays and enjoyed other diversions. Provisions continued to come from Petrograd, for the school had many wealthy patrons. But eventually conditions worsened and supplies stopped, so the older girls started looking for work or took in sewing. Then Irbit itself came under attack.

Maria Gorbochova had returned to Petrograd and joined the children's exodus in May 1918, leaving her sister in Irbit. Just as conditions became critical, Red Cross supplies started coming in under the guidance of Charley Colles, who was responsible for this northern colony. They remained in Irbit, never joining the others at Turgayak, and only meeting them at Omsk in July of 1919 when they were being evacuated.

When their car was finally attached to the Red Cross train and they were ready to leave, the Swans were puzzled and disturbed by a curious request made by Miss Matthew. She asked them not to see the children again. Later developments showed that this had been instigated by Miss Brown, who was in charge of the children during the railroad trip and had worked with them for a short while before the Swans had left Turgayak. During the trip it was impossible to obey the strange request, since the children continually disobeyed Miss Brown and came to the Swan's compartment anyway.

From Omsk, the train, carrying the children and the Swans, made straight for Tomsk to pick up groups from the three northern colonies originally under Charley Colles. Life had improved tremendously since that cold winter day when he gave his speech to the children in Tyumen, assuring them that they would be taken care of. Supplies got through to them regularly and they were able to get back to their school work. Although there had been tentative plans to move the colony to Turgayak the following summer, political events moved too fast. Charley was called back to Red Cross headquarters to discuss the increasingly grave military situation and, before anything could be decided, the front began collapsing. Peter Vasilivitch de George, one of the original teachers who started out with the children in May 1918, had remained with the group. He was the one who had located the first stopping place at Kuraii outside Ekaterinburg when the train route to their intended destination, Petropavlosk, had been blocked by the Austrian and Czech prisoners who had united with Kolchak's army and started westward. He remained in charge when they made the dramatic and desperate flight to Tyumen during the dreadful fall and winter.

Although the entrance of the Red Cross into the picture saved the situation for the time being, by the second summer panic was rife once more. Fearing that the older boys would be conscripted into the now retreating Kolchak forces, de George decided on the daring plan of spiriting them to Tomsk by boat and there meeting up with the Red Cross train.

Misha Denisov, one of these boys, kept a detailed diary of the event. On July 20th, a hot Sunday, they all went swimming, and afterwards, while they were lying around resting on the banks of the river, de George quietly told them they were going to board a boat the next day bound for Tomsk. Without frightening them he explained the need for the hasty departure, but the boys quickly grasped the gravity of the situation. On July 21st they boarded the *"Asia"* and left. The boat travelled about 15 versts an hour and twice got stuck on sand bars. Once all the passengers had to get off and walk until the boat got into deeper water. The weather remained very warm and they slept on deck under the open sky. On the 24th the boat stopped for a day at Tobolsk. Deciding to visit the city, they all went off to see the house where Czar Nicholas II and his family had been imprisoned for several months before being taken to Ekaterinburg and executed. Then when they returned to their boat, they had trouble getting back on because it was so crowded. In true Russian fashion, de George banged his fist and yelled until all the children were on board in second class. Since there were no seats, they tried to settle in the stern but were chased by sparks from the smoke stack and forced to rest uncomfortably on any unoccupied spot on the deck they could find. Young Misha noted that July 24th was just fourteen months after they had left home, and he was so very homesick!

On July 27th they met another boat, and twenty-seven passengers moved over to it, easing the crowded conditions somewhat. The following day they left the Irtish River and entered the Ob where the water was cleaner but the swampy shores had no villages. They made a stop at the town of Surgut which was situated among great cedar trees. Here they were obliged to keep night guard over their possessions because of increasing thievery. One charming remark in the diary tells of Misha's delight in having a meal with iced soup and meat. But that was countered by his reaction on July 31st to watching a child, dead from dysentery, being taken from the ship when they stopped to take on some wood. At the next stop he saw another dead person removed, but the closeness of death by this time seemed to have dulled his emotions and he simply recorded the facts without comment.

On August 1st they stopped at Kolpeshevo and bought enough bread for all the children. Constant references in Misha's diary to food being bought by the colony or himself points up the lurking fear of hunger remaining from the memories, still fresh, of the famine in Petrograd and, more recently, Tyumen before Red Cross aid had arrived. The same day they entered the River Tom and, at 1:30 P.M. reached Tomsk. Here they went to a city school where they stayed until the Red Cross train arrived to take them to Vladivostok.

When not on duty, the children were allowed to visit the city. Misha's entry a few days later mentioned happily his going to the baths for the first time since leaving Tyumen. Some of them enjoyed the favorite Russian occupation of picking mushrooms in the forest. They also visited other friends who had arrived with another group of girls. He made reference to dancing and singing parties with de George in charge, and to sneaking out to a cinema with Oleg and Vanya, a forbidden and rare pleasure.

But by August 11th, the Red Cross train had arrived and the rest of the month would be taken up with the hard and hectic work of preparing the five cars assigned to them for the trip to Vladivostok. Entries in the diary about these preparations were quite detailed, including an emotional account of several serious and upsetting events, such as the conscription of all men between the ages of 18 and 40 into Kolchak's troops. He also described an exciting parade of Czech troops on Sunday, August 17th. Most revealing was a note expressing his amazement that he, Misha, was given his own sheet and a brand NEW towel for the journey. From August 20th on, the diary deals with the buying of sugar, butter, and rice by the barrel, going to the bazaar to buy shoes and a trunk for general use, and another visit to the baths. During these preparations, Charley Colles and Xenia Jukova arrived, bringing with them a small homesick boy from Omsk. Misha had to take him to the market to buy shoes.

Then in late August the ship *Fortuna* arrived bringing the rest of the Tyumen colony. The boys from the *Asia* rushed over to visit the Fortuna children and took them bread, which was received with shouts of joy. There were still a few errands left before their departure, and Misha recorded that on different days he bought a pair of trousers, went to the market to buy dishes, and had all his clothes washed. On August 30th they had no dinner, much to Misha's chagrin, but by midnight the final boarding and packing was finished and they left. The train stood in the nearby station #1 of Tomsk for over an hour, and then the journey to Vladivostok commenced.

The voyage of the *Fortuna* with the girls of the Tyumen colony had been equally exciting. Eugenia Andreyevna Mazun, the director, who had been left in charge, made a quick decision to flee with the colony in the same way that de George had done. This was the only thing that saved them.

Finding one of the last boats which formerly carried salt from Tyumen to Tomsk, she got the children on it. Beneath the roar of approaching cannons and flames flickering in the distance, the girls were transported on the River Tur to the Tobol River and thence to Tobolsk. Here the memoirs of Vera Schmidt describe a short stop there, where they also visited the house where Nicholas II had been a prisoner. She had bought a newspaper which referred to him as an "ex-Emperor" on the ration card which had been issued to him, but she was confused by the article. At Tobolsk the river seemed coffee-colored to Vera and not very attractive. All things contributed to her uneasiness and dismay on the trip. The older children had to sleep on deck through lack of space, but the younger ones were put with the crew.

Frequent stops were made at various islands where the older girls would find swimming holes and take the younger ones to bathe. They continued down the Irtish until it joined the Ob. Along the shores was the taiga where little grew except brush, berries, and mosquitoes. When the boat would stop, the older girls searched in the taiga for berries and nuts which became their only source of food. The berries were mixed with a little flour and baked and they all lived on berry pies. Going up the Ob against the current made the ship travel very slowly. When at last they arrived at Tomsk, they found the special train awaiting. It had bunk beds, and best of all, regular food and hot baths. Vera's voice was one of the most happy and vociferous, cheering at the gift of bread from Misha and his group.

Now they were joined to all the other colonist groups and together they moved across the taiga toward Vladivostok and further away from home.

CHAPTER ELEVEN

For those in charge, the early part of the trip to Vladivostok was far from pleasant. Bands of Bolsheviks tried to stop the train at several places and even the tracks were torn up. They passed through stations which were burning, and beyond each smouldering building, they would see the bodies of station officials hanging from the trees.

Just before arriving at the Manchurian border the children's train stopped and the Swans noticed another train on an adjacent track with a long line of sleeping cars, supply cars, and kitchens. But the most remarkable one was the dining car with a huge open platform fitted with railings and a roof. On the platform was a big table covered with white linen and set with silver trays, tea services, and other elegant furnishings. Underneath this strange dining car were two cages. In one of them was a young bear, and in the other a fox. These wretched animals must have been shaken unbearably while the train was in motion, but evidently served as a distraction to the bored marauders. This train belonged to a band of guerilla troops who were terrorizing all Eastern Siberia under the leadership of the notorious Ataman Semenov. Although they seemed to recognize no authority but their own, they were, in fact, essentially Japanese puppets.

Ataman Semenov had financed his career by stopping and searching all passing trains. The peasants at first refused to support his demands for food, but were quickly punished by having their villages put on fire. He would then line up all the men of the village along the tracks and simply shoot every third man. The survivors of course, heeded his wants after that, and word of his butchery brought other villages quickly to heel.

The Swans soon learned that Semenov's guerillas had held up the train looking for gold. But after a fruitless search, they were persuaded by the Red Cross officials to let it go through. The children apparently knew nothing about the ordeal, and only remembered seeing Semenov's private train and the fascinating dining car with caged animals.

99

The trans-Siberian railroad passed over the many high rivers flowing south to north in Siberia, and through a countryside studded with wild flowers framed by white birch trees. Delicious wild strawberries were plentiful and peasants sold them at every station.

But in the far distance they could always see the bluish virgin wood of the taiga with its threatening icy appearance, reminding everyone of the coming winter. One day when the train was moving forward at a snail's pace, a startling apparition appeared to a few girls who were sitting in an open doorway dangling their legs. There against a forest background stood one of the girls, Maria Nikolayeva, in her bra and petticoat, obviously confused, and holding a large wet flannel rag in one hand! The other girls began to scream wildly, and all the other cars joined the chorus. Fortunately, in one of the next cars, a male military guard was able to pull her back in while the train was in motion. It seems that Maria was washing the floor of her car and stumbled. She quietly tumbled out of the car onto the wet grass and didn't even hurt herself when she hit the ground!

The train stopped at Krasnoyanzk and they all went sightseeing. To everyone's surprise the city was filled with Italian troops, almost giving a comic opera aspect to the inept assistance of Allied help at the end of the war. While Kolchak's forces were collapsing thousands of miles away, the beautifully and elaborately uniformed Italians were parading in the streets of Krasnoyanzk. Misha Denisov remembered a group of people coming from the village of Technica just outside of Krasnoyanzk and begging to be taken into the colony. But Charley Colles was forced to refuse for lack of space and no Red Cross authorization.

Their next stop was Irkutsk where the Swans witnessed another human tragedy. They were on their way into town, crossing the bridge over the powerful Angara River, when they saw crowds of people rushing to the river side. The bluish water of the Angara was icy and the racing current was fearfully swift at this part of the river. Soon they could see a big log raft being swept downstream. Two women and a boy were shouting and screaming frantically for help, while a man tried desperately to steer the craft away from dangerous rocks or the bridge. A number of people ran madly along the banks trying to throw ropes to the unfortunate passengers of the raft, but to no avail. Within seconds they disappeared, swept away by the greedy river.

When they arrived at Lake Baikal there was great excitement among the children who, for the first time, saw American soldiers along the tracks. The railroad around Baikal was a high point for all the colonists. Vera Schmidt wrote of the fifty short tunnels the train had to go through, as well as the one long tunnel of three versts which was one of the great engineering miracles of the whole trans-Siberian railroad. She and an older boy were in the very front part of the train on a little bridge between the cars. She spoke of eight minutes of intense darkness in the long tunnel and feeling water dripping from the roof of the tunnel onto the train and their heads. She felt a child-like relief from fear when they came out into the sunlight once more.

When the train arrived at Chita, there was a prolonged stop, and Misha's car, which had already broken a coupling and had been hitched to the end of the train, was repaired. The boys took all their possessions out of the car and cleaned the inside completely while mechanics worked on the couplings. On September 13th, they arrived at the border of Manchuria and all the cars were inspected.

One of the more dangerous aspects of the three week trip was the loss of several children, – fortunately they were always found.

The train would sometimes stop for long periods, and it was the custom of the children to get out and play during these intervals. There were occasions when the train would start up unexpectedly, leaving some behind. Misha recorded one instance in his diary: two girls, Larissa Vorodieva and Elizabeth Nivenskaya, who were having their picture taken by Americans at the Manchurian border, were inadvertently left behind. The following day three more girls disappeared just outside of Harbin where the train had stopped. Vanya Semenov's notes explained how these problems were handled. As soon as a child realized that he or she was left behind, he would go to the station and report to the station master that he was under the protection of the American Red Cross. So powerful was the reputation and name of the Red Cross that everyone knew and respected it. The station master would put the child on the next passenger train that came through. Since all passenger and military trains had the right of way, they would catch up and pass the Red Cross train while it was shunted onto a siding. In this way all lost children were reunited with the colonists by the time they reached Vladivostok.

There were times when the train would stop in the middle of nowhere. For example, it was once held up a whole day when the tracks were torn up just beyond Chita, possibly by Semenov's band. At other times it simply ran out of wood for fuel. It was impossible to burn green wood, so long negotiations had to be made with peasants for seasoned fences. By now the peasants were leary of all money—Romanov, Kerensky, or Soviet—and would only barter. The Red Cross quickly adjusted to the new situation and, when assembling the train to transport the children, had included a number of bolts of yard goods. When the train stopped, Carl Myers, who was the Red Cross representative in charge, would cut off a few yards and send the train crew out to negotiate. Sometimes it took an hour and sometimes a whole day, but they always returned with wood in the end and the train continued.

The Ashela station at Harbin was completely Chinese in style and made a great impression on the children. The train pulled in on September 16th, and there was great concern among the adults because cholera was rampant and special precautions had to be taken promptly. Every child had to drink a glass of saline solution before each meal, wear a cheesecloth mask, and wash hands in a disinfectant. These measures paid off, and not one child became ill, in spite of the fact, according to Vanya, that many children took great risks by secretly buying and eating the fresh fruits sold at the station. The children were constantly starved for sweet things and so many of them remembered those occasions when they could get some special bit of candy or fruit.

The last two cars of the train were filled with French soldiers all armed and with mounted machine guns. Although the cars were clearly marked with large red crosses, this had not saved other Red Cross trains from attacks, mainly on the Chinese section of the railroad, by bands of marauders who waited for any passing train. Many of the children spoke French and soon became acquainted with the soldiers. Before long, buckets full of compote made from large round French plums began arriving from their kitchen for the "little ones"—an unheard-of treat for the children. In 1974, when Vanya Semenov was 74 years old, he still happily rolled his eyes over that memory.

On September 19th at 10 P.M. the last section of the train pulled into Vladivostok and was switched over to a quarantine track. As with the other sections, they had to wait several days for clearance because of the threat of cholera. Of course, the children could not realize that circumstances would force them to remain for the better part of the year in that far outpost of Russia, still not knowing how or when they would see their families again.

CHAPTER TWELVE

As a result of the incredible patchwork of strident political demands, humanitarian drives, and new conflicting ideologies, the American Red Cross had been called into Siberia simultaneously with the Allied military intervention. The crux of the matter centered around the necessity of keeping Vladivostok out of Bolshevik hands.

In 1917–18, Vladivostok, and most of northern Siberia, were controlled by a variety of White regimes which were unable to attract the support of the people. They were equally unable to form a unified and vigorous government among themselves. In the meantime, the Bolsheviks had gradually unified their hold on the western part of Russia, forcing thousands of Czech troops to come together and to start their exodus to the East in a desperate attempt to get home, even though it meant travelling around the world in the opposite direction.

The trans-Siberian railroad, therefore, became the center of all military and political activity. The line was being cut more and more and the only hope of saving it seemed to be more intervention. The Allies had recognized Thomas Masaryk's proclamation of a Czechoslovakian regime, and promised, in any post-war settlement, to honor the nation's independence. So they now believed themselves to be honor bound to aid the Czech warriors who were battling their way home. More than that, each nation had her own private reasons. The exhausted French would do anything to have the vigorous Czech fighters replenish their too-thinly held trenches in the West. The British openly pushed for intervention with an almost simplistic view of Lenin as the destroyer of property and class, not just in Russia, but in the whole world. With the defeat of the Hun, an even greater menace was rising in the East, and the British War Office felt that it must be smashed.

Japan was more demanding of intervention than any other country. Taking a page from communist tactics, she hoped that Siberia would become such a mixture of nationalities and ideologies that it could result in a power vacuum—and she was quite prepared, actually anxious, to fill it. Aiding the Czechs in their cause could only increase the chaos and improve the Japanese chance of including the mainland in her empire.

The most confusing reasons, however, came from Washington. President Wilson, who entered the war for only the highest principles, now had to undergo agonizing reappraisals as he found his own principles attacked. He believed so strongly in self-determination of people, that he had committed himself to this principle in the famous fourteen points for the peace negotiations. He knew that military intervention would certainly only aid the confusion in Russia rather than cure it. But how to get the Czechs out so they could fight for their newly created state? Should the Slav Czechs, perhaps, help their Slav Russian kinsmen to cooperate among themselves and work out a form of government which could be accepted by the Russian people as a whole? Wilson did not see Bolshevik power as the British did, but rather as an attempt to right undeniable wrongs that the Russians had suffered from their own rulers. He believed optimistically that, if a new government righted these past errors, class hatreds and exported revolutionary ideas of Bolshevism would die down. But in a Department of State memo issued in July 1918, he assured the other governments associated with the United States that his country would not even contemplate interference of any kind with the political sovereignty of Russia, her internal affairs, or territorial integrity. This document was contradictory to a telegram of June 1918, to the Japanese chapter of the American Red Cross received by Dr. Russell M. Story, the Field Director stationed in Siberia:

"Will Red Cross work among Czech troops? Need is serious. Czech organization is prepared to furnish full cooperation and bear expenses not usually assumed by Red Cross."

This would, and did, of course, produce interference in Russia's internal affairs and, certainly, impairment of her territorial integrity. To this day, the influence of the Allied military debacle colors U.S. relations with the Soviet Union.

At the time that Dr. Rudolph Bolling Teusler replaced Bishop Tucker, he was given the rank of Commanding Officer and Commissioner of the newly designated American Red Cross Siberian Commission. He arrived to make a first-hand inspection of conditions in Vladivostok right after the first Czech units came in. They had just invaded and captured the city, then immediately turned it over to a White Russian civilian government.

The city began filling up quickly with more and more wounded Czech soldiers arriving from the West where the main body of Czech refugees were still thousands of miles away, fighting as they came. A few were being treated on the *U.S. Brooklyn* at anchor in the harbor, but most were being taken care of inadequately in old warehouses along the waterfront where almost no attention was being paid to them. Each day more trains arrived with boxcars filled with refugees. The shortage of local food and medical supplies was a deepening crisis. Epidemics threatened and made no distinction between nationality or ideology. All this was reported back to Washington and the Red Cross there accepted the responsibility.

Then there appeared on the scene at Vladivostok the man who was to become one of the most influential leaders of the last part of the children's odyssey, Riley Allen. Allen was a thirty-four-year-old editor of the Honolulu Star Bulletin. In October 1918, just as the Great War was grinding to a halt, he informed the general business manager, Wallace Farrington, that he was giving up his job to go to Siberia. Friends and business colleagues alike tried to dissuade him. Peace, they said, would bring new problems; there was a great change coming with the return of millions of men to peace time economic conditions; unemployment was bound to come, and editors' jobs would not grow on trees. "Why the Red Cross? You'll only end up pounding a typewriter for the Red Cross!"

But Allen was set on his path. By background and education he was a liberal Republican, Protestant but tolerant, seemingly without personal ambition but imbued with great energy. In appearance he had a young boyish face belying his thirty-four years, and he always seemed about to break out in a grin. But behind his innocent expression was a great stubbornness, and the courage to make difficult decisions without fanfare. Realizing that nothing would deter Allen's plans, Farrington gave in and grudgingly promised him his job back, whether he wanted it or not.

A man of Riley's character was just what was needed, since circumstances were to require a tremendous amount of tact and talent for quietly solving problems and stopping explosive situations from becoming public issues. As he took hold, time and time again he prevented incidents from being blown out of all proportion, which might have overshadowed the main goal of returning the children to their parents. And it was the mutual respect and affection of his associates that enabled him to carry out his decisions without internecine struggles.

On November 18th, 1918, the Japanese ship, *Shingo Maru*, steamed out of Pearl Harbor bound for Vladivostok. Among the passengers were 20 Red Cross volunteers—doctors, nurses, sanitary engineers, railroad specialists, and Riley Allen, wearing the bars of a captain in the American Red Cross. The uniforms of the Red Cross were copied from those of the United States Army, with puttees, Sam Brown belts, and high stiff collars. The women wore brown, flat-brimmed sailor hats with a Red Cross pin attached to the grosgrain ribbon around the crown of the hat. Skirts were modestly ankle-length, but some women had four inch patent leather belts around their waists to give the khaki-colored jacket a jaunty touch. As the ship pulled out, a native band on shore played "Aloha" and friends and relatives waved goodbye. Vladivostok was four thousand miles away.

The *Shingo Maru* arrived at Vladivostok on November 30th. Vladivostok was a huge congested city primarily consisting of four or five massive stone and brick buildings. It was protected by two great arms of land encircling one of the finest harbors in the world, the Bay of the Golden Horn. For many years it was the chief naval base for Czarist Russia's eastern fleet and the massive stone buildings were built that way to withstand the wild Siberian winters. Seemingly a drab city at first sight, at dawn the golden onion domes of the Orthodox Churches would pick up the rising sun and insinuate an oriental atmosphere to the gray bleakness.

When Allen arrived, the Czarist fleet was gone, and the Allied powers had each established their own compound and flew their own flags. French, British, Italian, Canadian, Rumanian, Serbian, American, Polish, Czech, and Japanese were coming in with men and supplies. As the ship docked carrying Allen and his colleagues, a dozen Red Cross volunteers who had arrived earlier greeted the rather awestruck and lonely newcomers from the United States. Dr. Teusler, wearing eagles on his uniform, welcomed Allen with an outstretched hand, but his thin, aristocratic face remained wrapped in a tight smile. Asking Allen to settle in as quickly as possible, he made an appointment to meet with him. Since all the Red Cross personnel and officers were in Barracks #7, it took Allen little time to accomplish this. The building was an old Russian military barracks, two blocks long and three stories high, extremely solid and ugly, with its thirty-six inch walls and double-paned windows stuffed with sawdust to keep out the severe winter frost. Heating, although somewhat primitive, worked by means of coal stoves built into the side walls which funneled heat through pipes threaded inside the walls. This same system is still used in many parts of the world.

When Allen arrived, the building was still being prepared for the Red Cross, and complete confusion reigned, with Korean, Russian, and Chinese laborers noisily putting up wooden partitions. The first floor was to have the administrative offices, a recreation hall, kitchen, and dining room. The women's dormitory was on the second floor, and the men's on the third. Allen found the third floor being converted into a warren of rooms with partitions, each small room holding eight cots and footlockers. Obviously, a great influx of Red Cross workers were expected from America.

Unpacking quickly, Allen made his way to Dr. Teusler's ascetic office containing one old desk, six straight chairs, and a large map of Siberia.

Teusler, with no preliminary small talk said, "We need a good press officer."

With that, Allen's forebodings were fulfilled—he had not come to Vladivostok to pound a typewriter. But Teusler, understanding intuitively, explained quickly, "Most of us can organize relief trains, distribute food and medicines, and nurse the sick, but to explain what we're doing, to interpret our policy, not just to the rest of the world, but to the various military commanders right here in Vladivostok, that's a special skill!"

Brushing aside Allen's simplistic argument that Red Cross policy, as everyone knew, was to give relief to the military and civilians in need, irrespective of nationality or politics, Teusler continued, "Not in Vladivostok. There are dark suspicions here. It's thought that we have secret Machiavellian plans to intervene in Russia's civil war. The Whites suspect us of aiding the Reds, and Reds are convinced that we are an arm of the American military occupation. Even General Graves, commander of the American military forces here views us with some hostility."

As they talked, Teusler filled in the background of the Red Cross Commission in Vladivostok, stemming from the Czech troops' plight and the reluctance of President Wilson to make a definite decision, until at last the Red Cross assumed responsibility on its own. Somewhat chastened, and quite favorably impressed with Teusler's quiet control, Allen began to tackle his new job.

He started out tramping the streets of Vladivostok every day, interviewing the various military commanders, and meeting and talking to people. He soon found quite a different picture of events than was known in Washington. The city was jammed with refugees from all over Russia; fear, poverty, and crime stalked the streets. Swarms of underpaid coolie labor of all nationalities vied for menial jobs. Although not known at the time, within six months thousands of foreign soldiers would be brought in, with 68,000 Japanese leading the count, closely followed by 55,000 Czechs and about 25,000 from other countries, including 8000 Americans.

Necessities of life such as shoes, candles, and eyeglasses were quickly disappearing. On the day Allen arrived, Admiral Alexander Vasilivitch Kolchak, with British and Japanese approval, had optimistically proclaimed himself Supreme Ruler of Russia, which changed the atmosphere completely. It was hoped that this would rally all anti-Bolshevik forces in Russia and he would sweep westward from his Siberian base and push the Bolsheviks into the Baltic Sea. Vladivostok became the center of White Russian political terror. Men were arrested without charges, executed without trial, and the unholy whims of the so-called White Cossack chiefs such as Ataman Gregory Semenov and Ivan Kalnukov, clearly puppets of the Japanese, kept the country surrounding Vladivostok in a frightened and paralyzed grip through their control of the trans-Siberian railroad.

The more Allen listened, the more he realized that the Russian masses were not rallying to Kolchak. Kolchak's most effective troops, the Czechs, under the Czech General Gaida, had gotten just beyond the Urals and were now retreating. There simply was no organized groundswell to stop the triumphant march of the Bolsheviks. Kolchak was seen as a continuing symbol of the weak but oppressive Czarist regime. Supported primarily by old propertied classes, he could not really promise the land to the peasants. He could only offer them a vague declaration of a future plan for a Constituent Assembly to revise the government once the civil war was over. Allen reported all this to Teusler in many talks, and Teusler depended on him when setting Red Cross policy. Soon Allen became secretary to the Red Cross Commission, and then Assistant Commissioner, second only to Teusler in command of the entire operation.

The load of work for the Red Cross during the winter of 1918–19 grew by leaps and bounds. The need for military, medical, and civilian relief was extraordinary. Its activities stretched over 4000 miles from Vladivostok to the Ural Mountains. Statistics may help to provide an understanding of the situation:

At their height the Red Cross Personnel operated 18 hospitals with 6,596 beds. There were 56 American doctors, 34 non-American doctors, 182 Red Cross nurses, and 13 Chinese nurses. The Red Cross relief trains would leave Vladivostok and start westward, distributing supplies of clothing, food, and medicine as they travelled. Thirty ships from America and ninety-two from Allied countries went back and forth supplying the trains.

It was one of these which had become an impromptu hospital and cleaned up the typhus epidemic in Petropavlosk in November 1918, when the Swans had first gone to the colony there to try to straighten out its affairs. The entire operation had been specifically designed by Dr. Teusler, even to the planning of the details of the typhus hospital trains. The military relief activities of the Red Cross consisted of supplying sweaters, socks, helmets, pajamas, toilet articles, athletic equipment, etc. These and countless other items were needed by 8,000 men of the American Expeditionary force, 13,330 officers and men of the Army Engineers, warship and transport crews when they were in port, as well as railroad dispatchers and engineers of the Russian Rail Service corps. But the relief operation had to grow larger each month as the Czech casualties mounted, and Red Cross hospitals were set up as close to the front as possible. Most Czech clothing wore out quickly, and only the warm clothes from the Red Cross protected them from the deep freeze of the Siberian winter.

Allen continued his investigation of life in Vladivostok by interviewing the stream of Russian refugees, wounded Czechs, and the flotsam and jetsam of various nationalities. He kept hearing strange rumors about starving children who were seen in the early fall and winter of 1918. They were dressed in rags, and travelled in packs. Czech officers reported that they had tried to talk with them, but at their first advance the children would turn and run toward the woods, though staying together. They ranged from small children to teenagers and did not seem like ordinary war orphans.

Fascinated and horrified by the tales, Allen made an appointment to see Admiral Kolchak's so-called Minister of the Interior. The Minister, although greeting him cordially, was obviously ill at ease, for it was common knowledge that his main job was to shield Kolchak from bad news. Since most of the news from the front was bad, his task became more difficult each day. Allen, now a major, knew full well the precariousness of Kolchak's position. He went straight to the point, asking the Minister if he had heard the rumors about the children, and did Kolchak know? He said that he had, but that the Admiral's burdens were too heavy to add to. Besides, he could not possibly undertake the care of an unknown number of children when he was having difficulty supplying his own troops. Since the Russian

Admiral Alexander Vasilivitch Kolchak, a Czarist-era holdout, maintained tenuous control over parts of Siberia and fervently opposed the Bolsheviks. Kolchak was a force to be dealt with as the children passed through territory under his control. (National Archives)

Red Cross had ceased to function, the "great and good American Red Cross" would have to do what it could. Grimly replying that he thought as much, Allen wasted no time but went to see Teusler that same afternoon, prepared with maps and logistics to support his case to the Commissioner.

Both men agreed that they had no concrete proof that the children existed, but that there was every probability. Carefully, they marked the map showing Tyumen, Chelyabinsk, and Petropavlosk on the eastern slopes of the Ural Mountains, all well within the battle area. Obviously, to penetrate that deeply toward Western Siberia meant that military guards would have to be on the relief trains. This brought up a very serious problem in connection with General William S. Graves, Commander of the American Expeditionary Force in Siberia.

General Graves had only agreed to take the assignment at the direct urging of General Newton B. Baker, Secretary of War, because he was considered the sole military commander who would not panic, would not permit American intervention to become a military adventure, and above all, would interpret President Wilson's intentions, as strictly as possible, not to damage relations with our more militant allies. He felt strongly that the World War was over, and the slightest involvement with any military activities was direct intervention in Russia's internal affairs. He and Teusler had clashed head on already, with Teusler's insistence on giving succor, particularly to the Czech soldiers. Both men, more alike in personality than either would admit, stood firm. Teusler announced that the Red Cross would take all wounded soldiers, Red or White, into their hospitals, would use its relief supplies to feed the starving, regardless of political beliefs. It would also maintain its long-held tradition of non-partisan aid. If the Czech soldiers were supporting an "adventure" of the Allies, it was not for the Red Cross to judge, and to withhold food and medicine from anyone was both inhumane and contrary to all principles upon which the Red Cross was founded. But when confronted by the fate of the starving children, General Graves did not hesitate to agree with the plan of assigning armed military guards to relief trains headed for the Ural Mountains—"If the children were located, and if the Red Cross decided to assume their responsibility."

Members of the Siberian Commission of the American Red Cross. Burle Bramhall is fourth from the right. (American Red Cross Photo)

Major General William S. Graves, Commander of the American Expeditionary Force in Siberia, at his headquarters in Vladivostok in 1918. (National Archives)

CHAPTER THIRTEEN

When Teusler was given the green light by General Graves, he sent out word to the field directors to be on the alert for these children. For that reason, in the fall of 1918, Alfred Swan was miraculously able to get through so quickly to the directors of the Red Cross when he urgently telegraphed all across Siberia for help with the children, while they had been trying to ascertain whether the rumors of the lost children were true.

Putting Alfred Swan in charge of the operation, the American Red Cross had supplied and funded the colonies all through the winter and spring of 1918-19. And Swan worked at gathering the children together from Petropavlosk, Kurgan, Troitsk, and Uiskaya Stanitsa, while Charley Colles was in charge of Tyumen, Schadrinsk, and Irbit. As the colonies became better organized, plans were made to locate them all at Turgayak for the final summer before returning them home. But the collapse of the White armies changed all plans. By July 1919, even though final orders had not been sent to Turgayak, it was obvious that emergency steps must be taken or the Bolsheviks would take over, and there was no guarantee for the safety of the children. The die was cast and the American compound in Vladivostok became a center of beehive activity to take in hundreds of children, in a city itself torn by strife, hunger, and endless outside interference.

One of the people Allen came to depend on more and more was a woman named Hannah Campbell, whose early history had already contained enough adventure to last a lifetime. Mamasha Campbell, as she later became known to every homesick Russian child, was a strong, fresh-faced, giving woman in her middle thirties. Laughter came easily to her, and many a tight situation was relaxed when she would break out into great whoops, throwing her head back and shaking with mirth. It was impossible to resist her natural good humor, and both adults and children responded with released tension and a refreshed outlook.

Hannah and Charles Campbell had originally been chicken farmers in New Jersey, but with little success. Packing their few belongings plus Elizabeth, age eight, and Charles Jr., age three, they decided to go gold hunting in Alaska. Here too success eluded them, but rumors of rich deposits east of Lake Baikal in Siberia drew them on. A cousin of Charles joined them and in the autumn of 1917 they built a cabin by the side of a stream in Siberia. After negotiating a mineral lease with a farmer named Karpoff, the owner of the land, they began digging.

From the beginning they faced tremendous problems. The earth was frozen to a rock-like hardness ten months of the year and muscles and pickaxes had no effect. Heavy equipment had to be brought in laboriously by horse and sled. A wood-fired boiler was obtained to which long hoses with iron stemmed points on the end were attached. These points, made of perforated hollow tubes, were forced into the frozen earth, and through the night steam from the boiler would soften the ground. By morning they could take it to the stream where it could be panned for gold.

During the winter of 1917–18 they worked through the long, bitter cold, Siberian nights, and gradually their little bags of gold grew. Back in Petrograd the events of war and revolution continued, but none of that reached their ears until March of 1918. Charles Campbell was shoveling chunks of earth into a wheelbarrow, and Hannah was taking ashes out of the fire box of the steam boiler to start a new fire, when they saw a half dozen villagers approaching. There was no menace in their arrival, but a certain cocky self-consciousness. At first the leader, the village barber, greeted them, and then, becoming very formal, informed them that the land and its gold now belonged to all the people. The ensuing conversation almost defied description. The Campbells asked, "How many people? Did the village want a new lease? How could it be shared?" The barber replied that it had to be shared with one hundred million Russians. Lenin was totally misquoted, socialism referred to, but the conversation led absolutely nowhere. Finally Hannah, perceiving the futility of it all, said, "It's no use, Dad. We'll go. Er—You'll allow us to take out our possessions, of course?"

But apparently these also had to be shared with the whole population. So with just their clothes and personal items, they reluctantly started the journey south and eastward.

The trip back took several weeks. At one point, joining with a dozen other refugees, they built a flat bottom scow and floated down a wide stream. After a week they arrived at one of the most remote towns, Blagoveshchensk, where there was a single track that connected with the trans-Siberian railroad. The next few weeks they slept on the floor of a boxcar being shunted from train to train, but always hoping to get to Vladivostok. Each new change of train would seem to make the passage slower, side trackings longer, and there were days when the train did not move at all. There was no fare charge, no one owned the trains, but the railroad continued to move, evidently just from habit. Engineers and conductors knew nothing except their jobs and so they kept right on doing them. Refugees without a destination jammed into the boxcars carrying their pitiful possessions—a book of photographs, a broken samovar, a bit of jewelry, or a closely guarded sack of food.

Eventually their train met up with a Czech military train, and when the Czechs stopped and searched, they recognized the Campbells as American. Hannah was never able to explain how young Charles Jr. was holding a tiny American flag in his fist when the Czechs boarded. She said later that she had never seen it before, but the Czechs waved them back on the train and allowed them to proceed. Late that night, two and a half months after beginning their journey, they rolled into Vladivostok.

The next morning, when a brakeman pounded on the boxcar and told everyone to get out, they heard the sound of a bugle. There below, in the harbor, was the great battleship, the *U.S. Brooklyn*. The sailors were just beginning to hoist the flag and, as it waved in the wind, they saw that it was the stars and stripes. The Campbells had had no idea that there were any Americans within several thousand miles, and this welcome sight made Hannah Campbell weep happily. While they were trying to arrange passage home, they came upon the American Red Cross headquarters at the harbor and promptly volunteered their services. Charles was placed in charge of the warehouse, and Hannah was assigned responsibility for Barracks #7.

The second colleague whom Riley Allen came to depend upon, and the man who would become an integral part of the children's lives until they returned to Petrograd, was Burle Bramhall. He was a tall, slender, rather silent man who did everything in an organized, measured way. He would enter into all activities, take a drink, joke, even dance, but at all times his mind seemed to be quietly ticking away on some problem or piece of work, concentrating and patiently awaiting a solution. His inner drive was work, and when he approached it he was unflappable. His sense of responsibility and duty never left him, and he made a perfect assistant to the more extroverted Allen. An accountant by training, he had come from Seattle with other volunteer Red Cross workers in 1918 as a personnel officer of the Red Cross Siberian Commission. He proved his value almost immediately.

Soon after Bramhall's arrival, another sudden financial crisis developed because of seesawing political events. Most of the Red Cross money which paid for supplies and services in Siberia was in Kerensky rubles which Admiral Kolchak had adopted for his own regime's use. With the rapid deterioration of the White forces in the Urals, the Kerensky ruble fell from 300 to 3000 per dollar in one week's time. To save the investment, the Red Cross had to find a way of converting its Russian money to another currency without too much loss, and the only suitable one seemed to be the Chinese max which had to be negotiated via Harbin, Manchuria. This was the heart of all money changing for the area. Such a trip was fraught with tremendous danger, and the slightly academic-looking Bramhall was chosen for the job. A small boxcar was quietly requisitioned, loaded with a stove, food, and a Hungarian POW who spoke Chinese. Bramhall had $250,000 in Kerensky rubles hidden in a small briefcase. The trip to Harbin was uneventful, but once there, the situation changed.

All the money changers sat on one long street. They would only exchange 10,000 rubles at a time, and endless bargaining was necessary, with trips to other changers, negotiating deals back and forth, while every bill was inspected through a huge magnifying glass. For three days Bramhall and Stephen, the POW, slept and ate in the car on top of the money. When at last they left Manchuria and arrived at the border town of Grodekovo, they found that the Japanese were in full control of the railroad.

The train arrived in midmorning and was stopped unaccountably— no freight was unloaded, no other trains blocked the way, and yet for several hours it did not move. As the minutes wore on, Bramhall told Stephen to go to the train official at the station and demand an explanation. No sooner had he left than Bramhall saw several soldiers follow him and then heard angry shouts and sounds of fighting. Throwing caution to the wind, Bramhall jumped out and, running into the station, found Stephen being beaten by several soldiers. He waded into the melee and, with his greater height, bowled over two of the soldiers, grabbed Stephen, and they both bolted back to the boxcar. Breathlessly, the POW explained that the soldiers wanted to know if they had any money—but he swore he had told them nothing.

Looking out, Bramhall saw that the boxcar was surrounded by excited Japanese soldiers just on the verge of charging. Quickly he grabbed his side-arm and strapped it to his belt, then returned to the open door of the boxcar. One soldier grabbed the iron rung of the ladder to climb up, and, as his head appeared, Bramhall kicked him square in the face with his heavy army boot. The man screamed and fell backward moaning as the rest of the soldiers looked on, suddenly motionless. Bramhall sensed that the whole atmosphere had changed. The soldiers began smiling and scraping. They were so sorry, but they had not realized that the gentleman was a representative of the American Red Cross—they would not dream of disturbing him. Picking up their comrade, they quietly disappeared and the train slowly pulled out a few minutes later. By that evening Bramhall and the money were safely back in Vladivostok.

Riley Allen had a number of difficult decisions to face, but one of the first and most important was where to house the children.

His search led him to a rocky barren island in the middle of the Bay of the Golden Horn in Vladivostok. Early in the 19th century massive barracks had been built for the sailors of Russia's eastern fleet. But since the overthrow of the Czar, the barracks were now empty. Many political and quasi-legal groups claimed them, but Allen saw the place as a perfect solution to the problem, away from the chaos and violence of the city itself. With his usual tenacity and one-track energy, he obtained a lease from the faltering city government and energetically sent an army of carpenters, plumbers, and cleaners to restore the massive buildings and make them a livable place.

Mother Campbell became the unofficial boss of the job and was instrumental in rearranging the rooms, partitioning off classrooms, dormitories, and recreation rooms, and making the kitchens into a workable area. It was she who directed the collecting of books and supplies for schooling, toys for the younger children, and some usable sports equipment. All this was undertaken while she remained in charge of barracks #7. It was also her self-imposed task to provide a warm welcome for incoming homesick Red Cross personnel, even scouring the local markets for turkeys and cranberries for an "American" dinner. No one could resist her infectious and zesty energy. Even strong men on the verge of fighting each other over a bed in the dormitory or a dislike of some food, were reduced to children, and abashedly dragged their feet like naughty school boys when she scolded them. Under her capable direction the barracks began to take shape.

On August 20th, the section of the train carrying the Swans arrived at Vladivostok. They were assigned a room at the Red Cross barracks #7, while the children with their teachers were taken to the barracks at Second River, a suburb of Vladivostok. They were still under the watchful eye of Miss Brown. While the Swans were waiting for the boat to take them to America, they decided, order or no order, that they had to see the children and went to Second River. As soon as they arrived they were surrounded and greeted with a barrage of happy chatter as the children tried to tell them of their experiences and all the things they were doing.

When Miss Brown learned of their visit, she became so excited that she denounced the Swans to the Red Cross officials on the charge of inciting the children against the Red Cross. Alfred Swan was highly incensed at this absurd accusation and went immediately to Dr. William H. Gutelius, in charge of the refugee division, asking him to investigate the whole business.

The investigation proved fatal to Miss Brown. Uncovering some of her intrigues, it exonerated the Swans. But aside from knowing that she was a very neurotic woman, there was no explanation for her peculiar behavior. So many strange facts were uncovered that the Red Cross felt it had to discharge her. Miss Brown, hearing of her coming disgrace, and before any action could be taken, quietly packed up and shipped off on an English boat under the protection of the departing British consul.

Only one final tragedy marred the triumphant farewell which the children had prepared for the Swans. Marya Goriakova, one of the older girls, had fallen ill during the trip to Vladivostok—the harsh climate and hardships of freight car existence took their toll, and it was obvious that she was dying from tuberculosis. She was taken straight from the train to the hospital and asked to see Katia. Marya had been one of the girls Katia had befriended back on her first dreadful trip to Petropavlosk. Katia found her in bed in a sunny corner of a big room occupied by a few recuperating typhus patients. Pulling Katia's head down to her mouth she tried to speak, but her voice was gone—all she whispered was, "I knew you would come." With that, she closed her big grey eyes and gently slipped away.

The Swans were finally instructed to embark on the transport *S.S.*

Logan to America. They were also told that their hair and clothes would be inspected so as not to carry typhus infected insects to the ship.

Katia later wrote: "This terrified me because, in spite of the many cans of disinfectant I had used, along with endless washing and combing my long hair, I felt that there were still a number of undesirable inhabitants there. As I ascended the gangplank, I became positively ill at the thought of the shame awaiting me when my hair would be inspected. But the doctor simply looked at me and said: 'This is all right!' I uttered a silent prayer of thanksgiving."

On September 10th, they watched the city of Vladivostok disappear into the bluish haze of the far horizon as the tiny transport left the harbor and headed into the boundless sea.

Chapter Fourteen

The colony trains arrived in three different sections, the last on September 19th. Misha Denisov wrote a detailed account in his diary. His train was taken straight to a quarantine area and all the children were given a cholera shot. From there they went to Second River where the other two trains had preceded them. Americans met them and gave them all candy. Alexandra Gorbochova was given a hot chocolate and sandwiches by a beautiful young woman named Gladys Gorman, and an instant friendship developed that went on for years across two continents.

For several days the children had to stay on the train, although they were allowed to take long walks around the area. The boys enjoyed learning how to catch crabs and starfish in the river. They also went into town, and Misha wrote about having a two-course meal for 16 rubles and also buying 125 tomatoes to take back to the train. After six days of washing clothes and cleaning cars, as well as making sure that no child had come down with cholera, they were moved into the barracks at Second River and began to set up their own pattern of life. Much against his wishes, Misha was elected prefect again, which meant he had several responsibilities and could not roam as much as he would have liked. Self-discipline did not seem to be one of his priorities.

A dance was arranged on the first Sunday night there. It was so successful that it became a weekly event. Their director, Charley Colles, left them after two days and went over to inspect Russian Island. When he returned, he announced that the smaller boys and girls would live at Russian Island, but the bigger children would remain at Second River and start lessons again. Later, on a surprise visit to the older boys' section, he detected and confiscated tobacco which some of them had managed to smuggle in. Thereupon he announced that life from then on would have to be better organized and disciplined.

Barracks #10 was filled with bedbugs, so while the girls scrubbed all the beds with kerosene, the boys painted the walls and floors. When both the girls' and boys' sections of the barracks were ready, they were all taken to the local school for two exams to evaluate their scholastic standing. One exam was in mathematics and the other in Russian. Each child had to write a theme—"Impressions of Life in the Colony." Then classes were scheduled to begin on November 10th in the Zebonaya school, with religious services in the gymnasium.

By now the cold weather set in and the children were given warm sweaters and wool socks. Some sort of black market activity must have begun, for Misha tells delightedly how he sold a pair of his socks for 25 rubles. Several days later he wryly described a meeting for fifth graders (older boys) about selling public property.

Attendance at school entailed a certain amount of danger. Only one week after the school opened on November 17th, it closed because of an uprising in the town. The sounds of shelling continued for two days. Apparently it was a thwarted attempt of local Bolsheviks to take over, but school opened again soon after.

After that, the weeks went by without incident and students were allowed to walk around town. Misha found and explored an old abandoned fort on the First River. Since the old style calendar was still observed for religious holidays, Christmas was celebrated on January 6th. Misha and two other boys were given the job of getting a Christmas tree. When they came back at the end of the afternoon, they found a sumptuous meal of fried goose and cabbage. In the evening, bags of gifts were given to each child containing candy, nuts, an apple, a tangerine, a toilet kit, soap, handkerchief, wool cap, and a Turkish towel. The next day all of barracks #10 was invited to Russian Island where the festivities continued. Although Russian Island welcomed their guests warmly with more food and candy, and even performed Chekhov's *The Wedding*, Misha felt the whole place was cold, dirty, and ugly.

But Misha's general disgruntlement was not shared by other children. From early in the month of December, the girls on Russian Island had been preparing for the event in defiance of the violent weather out of doors. Snow covered the roofs of the barracks and sharp stinging blasts of wind made it impossible to stay out more than a few minutes. Rough white ice, heaped by the action of wind and water, covered the harbor of the Golden Horn, and clouded daylight was seen just a few hours each day. The girls, undaunted by the depressing weather and surroundings, made a frenzied search through the Red Cross warehouse where they turned up a big case of many-hued crinkly crepe paper which some impractical soul had sent from America.

The Christmas party was planned around a costume ball and a play. The dining room was cleaned and made usable. Old brick Russian stoves were put into working order, and homemade wooden candelabra, with candles, were hung from the ceiling for light. Several war prisoners fell eagerly into the plan and went to work to construct a stage, dressing rooms, and even scenery. Hand-decorated programs were lovingly made in the art class, and invitations sent out to other Red Cross personnel on the island and in Vladivostok.

At last Christmas Eve came, and 860 children and personnel had a simple supper crowned by a surprise of canned fruit with soda crackers. The kindly old resident priest began the meal by praying that this might be the last Christmas the children would be separated from their parents. He also gave a special prayer of thanks for Red Cross aid. After supper everybody disappeared to their rooms to dress in their best bib and tucker, and then to return at a given moment. In their absence, a beautifully hand painted curtain had been put up in front of the stage by a clever Austrian war prisoner. On the curtain was the well known Golden Horn harbor and in the harbor was a great white ship with a Red Cross flag waiting at anchor to take the children home. How they cheered and applauded, for they all hoped and believed that the ship would come and they would go home at last.

The show went on as the curtains parted to reveal the cast in a spirited dance followed by a series of skits, and tableaus based on Russian folk stories all familiar to the children. At 9 o'clock the curtain closed and the children rushed back to their rooms to don their costumes. Then the fun began.

The orchestra started to play for the Grand March which was led by Red Cross personnel, teachers, invited guests, and all the children from five to eighteen in their costumes. This was followed by dancing, and they all whirled round and round in one direction to fast waltzes until they were exhausted. Then they formed a large circle on the edge of the room, and exhibition dances were given by some of the children.

The older children performed Cossack dances with mad leaps, ballet, and Russian folk dances and received tremendous applause from the enthusiastic audience. When a committee of judges gave their reports, the first prize went to Olga Kondratyevna who was so skillfully dressed as a polar bear that no one had guessed who she was all evening. A group of boys, dressed in feathers and red paint, and emitting endless war whoops in front of a homemade wigwam, were also singled out. As the evening drew to a close, a group of the older boys seized Dr. Herbert Coulter, the popular medic of the colony, and making a net of their hands, bounced him into the air three times by way of saying goodnight.

The difficulties of getting the children to school increased daily. Sometimes they would have to be taken in trucks because of the frequent strikes of trolleys and every other kind of transportation. In order to simplify the problem, a decision was made to move the girls from #10 barracks over to Russian Island where the Russian teachers, who had remained with the colonists from the beginning, were schooling the younger children. Extra teachers were hired at Russian Island to teach any subjects the girls were expected to have. The move became inevitable when a bad typhoon hit the city on January 11th and 12th, which made transportation even more difficult for some time. When the girls left Second River they were given a farewell dance, and even a dancing bear performed. By January 17th, only twenty-six older boys remained at Second River, including Misha, much to his disgust. Although the girls promised to write, he sourly confided to his diary that they would probably expect him to write back.

Eight of the older girls who were training to be nurses, including Katia Kozlova, remained together as a group in the city going to the hospital each day. They were housed in a small officers' dormitory on Peter the Great Street. Their apartment had five rooms, two of which were used by the girls and one by their housekeeper, Mrs. Repin. They shared meals with the American officers. Katia was so impressed that her accounts of the wonderful food the Americans had for breakfast and lunch took up several pages in her diary. Their life was very restricted and they were allowed out for walks only with Mrs. Repin. The only time they walked to the center of town, they got mixed up with a protest march, but Katia couldn't remember what the protest was about. In spite of the good food, they became homesick for Russian Island, and Katia's happiest moment came when she could go back for a big celebration for St. Katherine's day on the island. There were three Katherines in her group and, using white muslin, each girl had a new dress made. One of the teachers had bought a pair of high heel shoes in Omsk which were too tight for her, so she gave them to Katia on her name day. "That night," Katia wrote, "never had the boys' orchestra played more beautifully nor the children danced so well, for everyone saw how beautiful I was in my new high heels." Even the canned food on Russian Island tasted good.

After graduation all eight girls returned to Russian Island in time to welcome the first signs of spring. Many of the children learned how to catch crabs and, building fires on the beach, cooked them in tin cans. This was a great enrichment for their dull diet.

Back at the barracks a feeling of nervous boredom and restlessness set in. There wasn't enough to do except for school work, and school was repeatedly canceled because of the chaotic conditions in town.

Then another abortive uprising took place on January 26th. Trains again went on strike. Word came through that Kolchak and his chief minister, Perpolatev, had been captured at Irkutsk by the Bolseviks. Rumors were rife that the Bolsheviks were victorious everywhere, and the Americans were going to evacuate. On January 28th, Nikolsk and Surish fell, and Vladivostok was declared under siege. The newspapers were heavily censored. But in spite of all the trouble and confusion, somehow a box of musical instruments arrived at #10 barracks for the boys' orchestra.

Notations in Misha's diary for the next few weeks range from the fearful to the most mundane. He described among other things weather conditions, studies, playing with friends, unsettling rumors, letters from girls and grumbled because he knew that he'd have to answer them. Then, with no more emphasis, he told about an armored train arriving at the station at Second River filled with armed Bolshevik soldiers, and later going to the First River Station to watch other soldiers leave while the crowd cheered.

One Sunday trains began running again and the town returned to normal. Several days after school reopened, barracks #10 had a scare when Fedya Petersky came down with smallpox and was rushed to the hospital. The children's quarters had to be cleansed and sterilized, and, for fear of contagion, they were kept out of school for several weeks until Fedya had recovered and returned.

With the Bolsheviks in charge, the children were organized into boy and girl scout groups, which later were called Red Scouts. They became the prototype of the Pioneers to which all Russian children today must belong. They were proud to take part in a scout parade led by Popov, the new Bolshevik Governor of Vladivostok. After the parade, there were songs, speeches, and fireworks, followed by a masquerade. Misha even mentioned that he actually fell asleep and remembered little of what went on.

So, regardless of all the explosive things happening around them, life for the children quietly drifted on.

But behind the scenes, the Red Cross people and Russian teachers saw affairs in a much graver light. Every week they had to hold a staff meeting to deal with constant crises. The city was becoming more and more chaotic, with supplies gradually being used up. Food was a continuing source of problems. The expense of operating the colony was estimated to be $20,000 a month. Personnel included 112 American doctors, nurses, and specialists in child welfare and institutional work. They also had to pay 151 Russian matrons, teachers, and interpreters, as well as German and Austrian military prisoners who did all the manual labor such as cooking, cleaning, carpentry, and shoe repairing.

Clothing and feeding children at an age when their activities were hard on their clothes and produced healthy appetites, called for careful planning. Connected with the colony was a sewing room for making and repairing girls' clothes, a tailor shop for boys' clothing, a cobbler shop which repaired and made boots and shoes, and a carpenter's shop, which not only kept the barracks in good repair, but also gave carpentry lessons to many of the boys.

Three meals were served daily, requiring a month's allotment per child of 3½ pounds of sugar, 7 pounds of fresh meat, 6½ pounds of fresh fish, 8 pounds of dried milk, 1 pound of jam, 8¼ pounds of salt meat, 22½ pounds of bread, 22¼ pounds of potatoes, 8 pounds of cabbage, 2½ pounds of butter, 2½ pounds of lard, and as much rice, macaroni, vermicelli, oatmeal, cornmeal, flour, dried fruit, tea and coffee as was needed. Special diets were prepared for anemic children which included nourishing foods such as broth, eggs, and malted milk. Red Cross figures show that the colony personnel and children were consuming a total of two tons of food a day. The difficulty of obtaining the food in that troubled period was heightened by problems of getting it there when the harbor was frozen. For that reason, four months' supplies had to be purchased in advance and transferred to the colony's warehouse on the island. Similar problems arose over heating supplies—coal and wood had to be brought in from Japan for the colony's winter needs because labor troubles had closed the Siberian coal mines and wood had become correspondingly scarce.

But the larger problem of how to return the children to their homes remained as baffling as ever. Allen was asked constantly, "When can we return? What are the plans?"

The trans-Siberian lines had become worse and worse, and by February, all lines west of Chita were cut. No equipment was available, and no new tracks could be laid. The teachers' only hope was Allen's pledge that the children would be returned to their parents as soon as possible, whatever that meant. But no solution was in sight.

Morale was slowly breaking down at the top level, when somebody came up with the idea to have the children write letters to their parents and let the "good Red Cross" get them through. They had been away for over a year and a half, and if only a small message could reach home, it would at least reassure both parents in Petrograd and the children in Vladivostok.

For Allen it seemed an impossible task. No mail could go westward across Russia, and the other way meant crossing two oceans and getting through the complications of a Europe still tied up in fighting wars, euphemistically called "Wars of Liberation." How to send the childrens' letters through a world torn by suspicion, hatred, and chaos? Again Allen's controlled patience refused to admit defeat. Nagging, harassing, leading, he set the snail-like apparatus of diplomacy in motion at last. The children's mail was shipped across the Pacific to the United States, then across the Atlantic through the North Sea to Stockholm. The Swedish government had somehow stayed neutral throughout the holocaust, and used its good offices to get the mail to the International Red Cross in Tallinn, Estonia. From there it travelled the 200 miles to Petrograd, and from then on there was a steady stream of messages between Vladivostok and Petrograd.

Petrograd, Gorochovaia Street, 334, apt. #49
Elizaveta Aleseivna Tsvetkova

Dear Mama, Grandmother, Misha, Katia, Verashka
and all the others:
I am greeting you. How are you? We are all right. Just at the time when we have to go to school, we are told to write letters. Americans are taking care of us. They teach us and furnish us with clothing and supply us with food. Can you imagine that they are giving shelter to more than 800 children? Everyone has been well treated. It is only a pity to say that many of the boys are spoiled and therefore Americans

have to resort to discipline. I am very glad that Misha and Katia did not come with me, otherwise who knows what would have happened to them?

The Superintendent of our colony, Mr. Coulter, a well known American, is taking care of our living and tries to do his best in keeping us entertained. Miss Shermer and Elena Ivanova are also well inclined towards us. The Red Cross is trying to furnish us with shoes so that we do not have to go barefooted. Many soldiers came to the town but nobody knows who they are. Some people say that they are Bolsheviks. But it is hard to believe all the rumors, because many people do not always tell the truth. We enjoyed the holidays very cheerfully.

> Your daughter,
> Lidia Tsevtkova

Petrograd, Geslirovsky 50, apt. #65
Mrs. V. M. Yacobson   February 3, 1920

Dear Mama:

I am writing to you in a hurry because the letters must be turned in immediately. We all—God be praised—are safe and sound—we are wishing the same for you.

We are clothed and fed very well; all of us have three blankets, warm trousers, linen, and so forth. We are hoping to come home soon. Also all of us are attending the higher elementary school at Vladivostok. I am in the fourth form. Sergei is in the fifth and Kostia in the second class.

We have our own club and are making up dances and literary evenings and in general are living very happily.

We are kissing strongly, very strongly, you, Nadia, Lidia, and Grandmother. Our greetings to our relatives and acquaintances. In the meantime good bye for the present. We shall see each other before long.

> Sergei, Kostia, Lidia Yacobson

Petrograd, Tarasoff House 326
To the Janitor Alexandra Aleseivna Burmistrova

I'm greeting you my sweet and dear Mama. How do you do? How is your health? Sweet Mama, we are sound and safe. We are living at Vladivostok on Russian Island under the auspices of the American Red Cross.

We are living very well. The Americans are furnishing us with clothing, supplying us with food and arranging entertainments and we are all very attached to them. They expect to leave in January for America and we are very sorry to part with them. Dear Mama, they are endeavoring to do all the best for us.

We are all very satisfied, dear Mama, the Americans are very hospitable, kind, and hard-working. Dear Mama, they want to transport us in May to Petrograd.

Next Christmas we shall celebrate at home together with you. We are praying to God that He will help us to make all ready for our journey. God keep you safe. We kiss you strongly.

Lisa and Lena Burmistrova

But things did not go smoothly. Before long the new Bolshevik government began reading all letters. The happiness of the children, their stories of good food, warm clothing, continuing studies, were in marked contrast to the desperate conditions of life in Petrograd.

Peter Azaroff's father wrote about how delighted he was to hear from his son, for he knew the Red Cross had taken the children to Vladivostok. He was very happy to know that his son was not hungry or sick, and then he told about having to spend 500 rubles a month to buy grain and dried herring. But this amount of money bought so little food that the family was starving. He mentioned friends who had died, and said that the family was losing weight month by month. Thank God, Peter was in good hands and had enough to eat and warm clothes.

So many letters of this type went back and forth that the Bolshevik government, fearful of its image abroad, decided to act in a fashion which has since become a pattern — throw enough mud and some is bound to stick.

The Russian news service came out with the following report on November 29, 1919, and it was picked up in London, then relayed to

Washington, D.C. "The People's Commissar for Education, Lunacharsky, published in Izvestia a telegram he received, reporting the
fate of the former Petrograd Children's Colony, which was transferred
from Petrograd in 1917 by the Union of Towns, and was by Kolchak's
Minister for Home Affairs under the uncontrolled administration of
the American Red Cross. According to the statement of the priest of
Turgayak and of the local inhabitants, the children lived under the
most disgraceful conditions, both physically and morally. The children had to beg to earn some means of existence. The Americans
made the children work as assistants to their shops. In the end of
May, just before the arrival of the Reds, the Americans removed the
children to an unknown destination. Their departure took place at
night. The children were given two hours to get ready. During their
journey, one small girl was drowned, and many of the children
contracted serious illnesses. At the station at Kurgan, boys over 15
were mobilized . . ." Lunacharsky then went into a diatribe about this
cruel treatment by the American Red Cross, which was typical of
what people could expect from any representatives of uncivilized
imperialist governments, and if any Russians were wavering in their
political beliefs, this is what they could expect from outsiders.

This report was forwarded to Riley Allen with a letter from the
State Department, and he was asked to make a statement to the press
about the matter. When he shared the contents of the document with
his staff, there was an uproar, for they all knew the real facts about
the flight from Turgayak, and several had actually been involved in it.
For a while there was a great deal of heated discussion, but Allen
finally decided to write a calm and detailed report of the situation to
the State Department, rather than engage in a verbal battle with the
Soviets.

From: Acting Chairman, Executive Committee
      Siberian Commission, Vladivostok   January 28, 1920
To: Dr. Livingston Farrand, Chairman, Executive Committee,
      American Red Cross
Subject: *Return of Petrograd Children*
In your cable no. 1257 you ask for additional details about the
children of Petrograd. Former correspondence about these children
has acquainted you with the conditions under which their care was
assumed by the American Red Cross, and it is the opinion of the
Commissioner and the Executive Committee of the Siberian Com-

mission that the Red Cross cannot do less than return them to Petrograd where most of their parents were living at the time they were sent across the Urals for safety.

The care of these children and the continuance of their education has been one of the most significant works the Red Cross has undertaken in Siberia; and the fact that they are healthy and vigorous looking, with a very small percentage of sickness is commented upon favorably by visitors of different nationalities who have seen them.

The total number of these children in round numbers is eight hundred. There are teachers who have been with them all the time and whom we consider part of the colony.

The total number of people to be returned will approximate eight hundred and thirty. Supervising, nursing, and medical personnel make the total number for whom transportation must be secured, eight hundred and fifty-five.

The situation politically seems to be clearing. Recent events give rise to the belief that within two months we will be able to send these children through to Petrograd. This does not take into consideration the physical condition of the trans-Siberian railroad. If trains can be sent through, it will require about four trains, but up to this time we have not been able to get definite data about the cost of sending the children through. We estimate it would take four trains with sleeping, dining, kitchen, and medical equipment to accommodate the children and the attendant personnel. Before we can offer a definite recommendation, it will be necessary to complete these estimates. As soon as they are secured we will cable you.

In addition to the investigation of the rail route, we are asking the various steamship agencies represented at this port to give us figures. It is possible that we will find it more feasible to send them home through the Suez or Panama Canal than to ship them by rail. Our request for estimates are based upon second and third class accommodations with, not to exceed, twenty-five first class.

In this connection, may we ask your attention to the possibility of securing an army transport for the movement of the Petrograd children, either through the Panama or the Suez Canal. It appears to us here that the Suez route would be preferable, inasmuch as we would touch at a much larger number of ports, and the problem of food supplies and any needed relief in case of an emergency, could be more easily met.

If this matter of securing an army transport can be taken up by you and advices sent to us, it would assist us in reaching a decision on the most feasible plan.

We are not committed to, and at this time cannot make, definite recommendations as to the most adaptable plan of sending these children to Petrograd. When the estimates are received and the entire situation properly investigated, we will cable. It was never contemplated to take the children to the United States or home by way of America. Besides the expense, there would be the likelihood of being accused of attempting propaganda if we sought to send the children home by that route.

R. H. Allen
Acting Chairman, Executive Committee
Major, A.R.C.

But the more effort the Red Cross officials put into their plan to return the children home by train, the more outside political events thwarted them. By November, Allen had faced the fact that the Bolsheviks would soon be in charge of the entire eastern part of Russia. The French and English were already deep in preparations to pull out of Siberia totally, and the Allied intervention there was being written off as a total failure. While Allen and his staff were organizing the trains and having them fitted out with the usual kitchens, dormitories, dining and medical cars, the United States was following the French and English plan to pull out.

As the vacuum of power in the immediate environs of Vladivostok widened, the Japanese quickly took advantage of the situation and began moving in with more and more forces. By March, no trains could enter or leave the city without Japanese permission, and such permission would not be given for children of the Bolsheviks to be returned to their parents.

In spite of all the discouraging facts, Allen continued to hope and to plan, counting on American persuasion to its supposed ally, Japan, to let the children through for humanitarian purposes. Certainly his contacts with the Japanese Civilian Commissioner, Matsu Daria, had been extremely cordial right along.

CHAPTER FIFTEEN

On April 1, 1920, American troops withdrew from Vladivostok under the command of General Graves, and an ominous quiet descended on the city. But life went on for the children, as classes in arithmetic, physics, history, Russian, English, French, and natural science continued; clubs met, and the dentist on Russian Island saw eight small mouths, including Misha Denisov's whose tooth hurt again.

On Palm Sunday, April 9th, an armed revolt of the Japanese against the Bolsheviks took place in Vladivostok. The center of the battle was directly under the bedroom windows of the Red Cross personnel. Bramhall was awakened by the din and ran to warn Mother Campbell to keep the girls down low, only to find she already had everyone lying on the floor. Looking out the window, Allen and Bramhall just had time to see the Japanese flag flying over a government building before they, too, hit the floor as a wild bullet smashed the window and flew past their heads to the wall behind.

Order was soon restored as the Japanese took over. The next day Misha Denisov and some of the older boys ventured into the center part of the town after tea. Japanese watchmen were everywhere, and all the stores were closed, but a great deal of damage had been done. Wires were down, windows broken, no trains or telephones were working. At the station, Russian soldiers were locked in railroad buildings which had been changed into makeshift prisons. Only Japanese cars were on the streets. Misha and one of his friends dragged a spent artillery shell back to their dormitory. But, in spite of all the changes, school reopened much to their disgust.

Even though the delivery of all supplies had been stopped, every child attended the celebration of Easter Sunday with the midnight church service and the breaking of the Lenten fast at the early morning supper from 2 to 4 A.M. Monday and Tuesday of Easter week were holidays spent hiking, having scout drills, orchestra concerts, dances, and other amusements. Life seemed not to have changed after all.

But soon a sinister feeling became evident in the town, and the colony began to feel the lack of the presence and protection of American troops. Brutal and unjust incidents took place, frequently witnessed by the children living in town. Some of the boys began teasing the soldiers and calling them baboons. Without warning, several of the soldiers turned and threatened the boys with bayonettes. They ran, but the soldiers followed them into the dormitory building. Only the strong intervention of two Red Cross officials, throwing themselves around the boys, saved the situation from a tragic ending.

At the end of May, classes were finished. In spite of the tension, ceremonies were held for the awarding of diplomas. Report cards were handed out, and even several silver medals were given to those who distinguished themselves. About eighty percent of the children passed the regular accredited zemstvos exams given throughout the Russian Empire. For those unable to pass, special classes were planned for the summer to give the slower children a chance to pass their subjects later and be ready for the next school year.

In an extensive report, Dr. Herbert Coulter, Superintendent of the Children's Colony, sketched the work and accomplishments of the colony during their stay on Russian Island. He provided detailed information on their studies, living quarters, duties, and the schedules for both work and play. The role of the doctors, dentists, nurses, kitchen aides, and others was carefully annotated. Special problems of children who were backward, physically or mentally ill, recalcitrant, or charged with stealing and bullying, were taken into account. And then, of course, there were the inevitable personality conflicts among the staff. It is evident that, in spite of the unique circumstances of life, the world of the children on Russian Island was amazingly normal and secure.

With the Japanese attitude becoming more and more implacable, Allen realized that the children would not be permitted to leave Vladivostok by land, and yet the very idea of leaving them as hostages under Japanese control was unthinkable.

The days of civilian control by the Japanese could easily be numbered if fighting broke out again—and what chance would the children have under their military control? He had already sent a feeler in the direction of removing the children by sea in a January letter to Dr. Livingston Ferrand, Executive Committee Chairman of the A.R.C., but, of course, the problems were enormous. Where could they sail?

On whose ships? Would it be feasible to circumnavigate the globe with 800 children and staff to be housed and fed? Should there be extended stops? Would other countries provide temporary shelter? These, and a hundred other questions, were urgently considered.

Although there were many ships of all nations in the area, most of them were already fully occupied with removing the allied intervention forces or returning prisoners to their own countries. Allen's first try was to turn to one of the numerous White Russian passenger ships cruising around the Sea of Japan—but as soon as the owners found that the children were to be returned to Bolshevik Russia, negotiations broke off. As usual, politics overruled human considerations. In one instance, negotiations with the Russian Volunteer Fleet, a company from the days of the old regime, headquartered in Shanghai, seemed to promise success. Three ships were chartered, and the *Simbersk* actually arrived at Vladivostok to pick up the children. The new Communist government promptly took over the ship, announcing that it belonged to the people and not to a shipping firm of private owners. In other words, a hundred million people owned it. This effectively deterred any more privately owned Russian vessels from coming near Vladivostok for any purpose.

In vain, Allen checked other ships in the area, but none proved adequate for the job, so he began to bombard the American government with calls for help. At first he thought that it would be comparatively simple, because there were many ships around operated by the Army Transport Command, the War Shipping Board, the Navy, and even several private lines. To his astonishment, after two months of waiting, the War Department, which had the authority to assign a ship, refused. The United States was committed to take out all Czech soldiers and return them to the new state of Czechoslovakia but refused to aid the children, whose only crime was their lack of political importance. Allen wrote letter after letter to anyone he thought might be willing to help, including Dr. Teusler, who was back in Japan.

Finally, at the end of May, the Red Cross was able to charter the *Yomei Maru*, owned by the Katsuda Steamship Co. of Japan. She was a 10,000 ton freighter deadweight who had just made her maiden voyage with an average cruising speed of ten knots per hour. On the surface she seemed to be a good ship, capable of transporting all the children. Dr. Teusler signed the charter for the Siberian Commission of the ARC. In an effort to explain the choice of a Japanese ship, Charles R. Barge, special Red Cross Commissioner to Siberia, wrote the following, which was obviously part explanation and part reproach to the War Department:

Mr. T. P. Keppel
Vice Chairman, Executive Committee
ARC National Headquarters
Washington, D.C., U.S.A.
Dear Mr. Keppel:

We have signed the charter for the *Yomei Maru* to take the children to Petrograd, and we expect to get them off the latter part of this month.

From our experience with the various people who claim to be officials of the Russian Volunteer Fleet, we are convinced that we can have nothing to do with the boats of that fleet. Notwithstanding the good intentions of the Russian Ambassadors at Washington and perhaps in other places, one cannot safely use the boats of that fleet. There are too many groups claiming control and exercising some control. The captains of some of the ships seem to be acting upon their own initiative and pay no attention to orders of any of the groups who contend that they control things.

I think we would be making a serious mistake if we put any freight or passengers on any of these boats.

The Czechs have many tons of freight in excess of the boats which have been chartered by them or which are to be sent for their use. It is, therefore, absolutely impossible to get any help from them. It will be many months before they get all their freight away.

We are exceedingly sorry that our War Department could not be induced to furnish us a boat to take the children home. Aside from the Red Cross, I think it would have been good advertising for both the War Department and the State Department. . . .

Again I express regret that the War Department was not able to help us. When we hear of the frequency with which transports are diverted from one purpose to another, it makes me feel that the department might have assisted us in this case. . . .

Once the decision was made, Allen determined that he would organize the whole expedition. He would sail with her as well, and remain with the children until they had been reunited with their parents. His dependence on Japanese fairness and honor was based mostly on hope and prayer, but somehow the mutual arrangement between Japanese business instincts on the one hand, and humanitarian instincts on the side of the Red Cross, found a mutual meeting ground.

The first tour of the ship was not inspiring. She was a new steamer owned by the Katsuda Steamship Company of Japan, which had built her for dry cargo freighting. She carried a crew of sixty-eight officers and men. Only the quarters for the crew had been constructed, and the cargo hold had no ventilation, lights, or plumbing.

Ward Walker was made instant engineering officer and was sent to Japan to oversee refitting of the ship to Allen's specifications. There was no time for large structural changes. Five hatches were utilized which led to between-deck space and divided the area into sleeping quarters containing 1020 bunks, or steel cots, stacked three high and fitted into wooden frames. These were for everybody—children, personnel, and staff. Both the sleeping and living quarters were ventilated by a newly installed electric blower system which completely changed the air every six minutes, in order to make these quarters below cool and comfortable. A large galley was constructed on the starboard deck. It was capable of serving three meals a day to children, teachers, and the war prisoners who acted as attendants, as well as to all the Red Cross personnel. It included a bakery, which was almost in constant use, since bread was the favorite food of Russian children. The bakery and kitchen were so constructed that they would be pushed overboard if fire should break out in the kitchen. Huge vegetable bins, and ice chests for hundreds of pounds of meat and fish, were fitted into the hold.

A well-equipped hospital and dispensary were added, with twenty-four beds for general cases, as well as twenty-four beds in an isolation ward which would serve in case of contagious or infectious diseases. Fortunately none developed during the entire trip.

Walker's concerns included anticipating contingencies and planning health related routines. One of the major problems was special feeding for some children who had been severely undernourished from the first rigorous winter. Also cuts, sprains, bruises, and stomach troubles could bring up to 60 children a day to the dispensary. The medical staff would have to inspect all sleeping and living quarters twice a day, and also provide emergency dental care in a well-equipped laboratory. The plans for the medical and sanitation staff were so well organized and efficient that no major problems developed during the entire time the children were aboard the Yomei Maru.

The newly refurbished *Yomei Maru* arrived in Vladivostok on Friday, July 9th. Then began unnecessary delays. The Port doctor, customs, passport, and police officials were late, although Allen had cleared all arrangements through President Medoedioff of the Provisional Government. When at last formalities were over, the ship proceeded up the bay to the Red Cross headquarters where the provisions had already been loaded on barges. Again delays were encountered when it was discovered that the ship's hatches would not open and cargo booms had to be rigged. Later in the day loading began, but at a snail's pace, so the sailing was postponed until Saturday night. This was pushed up twice more as it became apparent that more construction was needed to enlarge and correct defects of the icebox and bins for meat and vegetable storage. Carpenters of dubious value were hired for day and night shifts.

The problems of loading were compounded by inadequate facilities, incompetent gangs without bosses, and the mixed cargo of supplies, equipment, luggage, and everything needed for the long voyage—all in different size cases. Allen's frustrations and worries were apparent in his account of these problems recorded in the ship's log.

The original figures, which were estimated by Fred Winfrey, controller of the Siberian Commission, reveal that the charter hire was $4,500 per day. This did not include the $100,000 cost of alterations to the boat, or the salaries for the Russian teachers, POWs, and equipment for ARC personnel, nor spending money for the children—from 50 cents to $1.50 a month depending on age. Ultimately his estimates of the total cost proved to be far too low, as the voyage took much longer than expected.

Twice word was sent to Russian Island and barracks #10 that the children were to be taken to the ship by city steamer and barge on specific days, and twice the order was cancelled as the work proceeded inefficiently and at a maddeningly slow pace. Finally, on Monday morning, July 12th, the American flag was run up on the *Yomei Maru.* The remainder of the colony was then transferred to barges and shipped to barracks #10. At the same time, all the Russian Island Colony's equipment and supplies were presented to the City Municipal Board for use by a large new orphanage for homeless children.

The hospital patients were the first to be loaded in the early afternoon, followed by the rest of the children. Keeping track of the children seemed an impossible task until Berle Bramhall worked out a numbering device. Each child was given an aluminum tag with his or her number, and throughout the voyage, whether boarding or disembarking at a port of call, they came and went in sequence up and down the gangplank.

The passenger list of the ship's log showed:

Boys	428		
Girls	370		
		798	
American personnel — male	13		
female	4		
		17	
Russian personnel — male	10		
female	75		
		85	
Prisoners of War — male	78		
TOTAL		978	

As the children from barracks #10 were boarding, many visitors came aboard to wish the strange ark and its passengers bon voyage. The Commander of the Czech army forces, Cecek, heavily involved in his own problems of moving the fleeing Czechs around the world to their homeland, wished Allen well, as did many representatives of the City and Provisional governments.

We know from the increasingly emotional entries in Misha Denisov's diary that he was aware of the impending trip as early as the middle of June and shared the general excitement with the other children.

With the end of the school term, plans were set into motion to outfit all the children for the long voyage, and, as always, all new shoes had to be purchased. The children had little to do except go on long organized walks and nature studies, and were becoming aware of the worsening political situation. A kind of demoralization took hold, which was heightened by the theft of several sewing machines late one night. The next night guards were posted around the storage area and, much to the children's excitement, chased away a number of thieves.

Although nobody knew the exact time of sailing, supplies were rapidly being collected. Toward the end of June the bigger boys, including Misha, were organized into work squads and shuttled between Russian Island and barracks #10 carrying mattresses and beds loaded on automobiles over to the barracks. As more and more older children transferred to the barracks, meals were served there. A good deal of grumbling occurred over the quality of the food and condition of the bathrooms. To relieve the boredom, the geography teacher began to give nightly lectures on the Panama Canal and other places they would visit on the trip.

On July 5th, all children at the barracks were quarantined and no one was permitted to leave the area except with the express permission of Dr. Leperowsky. Then around 3 P.M. on July 9th, the *Yomei Maru* arrived and docked. To Misha and Kotya the ship seemed enormous. It had a huge American Red Cross sign painted on the side. Kotya hired a small rowboat to take Misha and him out to the ship, but bad weather forced them to cancel that idea. The next day the children spent staring at the ship and excitedly discussing their hope that it would finally bring them to their homes and families. The only ones who went on board were Misha and 19 other big boys. They went out to put sheets and blankets into the girls' quarters. That night it was decided that the boys should move onto the ship to help with the work. Then poor Misha fell and bruised his knee badly, so he had to return to land. The following morning, he complained incessantly while stuck in his chair watching the final stripping of the beds in barracks #10 and the younger group of children being taken to the ship.

During lunch he and the children who remained were given aluminum tags with their numbers on them. Then toward evening, all the rest were transferred to the ship. Katia Kozlova was frightened at the narrow gangplank, in fact so many children were, that sailors individually led each child up holding their hands and reassuring them.

The first impression was scary. The weather was extremely hot and foggy. The dining hall was under the hatch and so small that the children had to be fed in shifts. There were no cabin windows or lights at first. The deck available for exercise or walking was very small, and the sleeping niches in the hold seemed terribly confining. In the center of the sleeping quarters were tables and chairs, and daylight only came in down the exit stairs to the deck.

Unknown to the children, Allen was facing another crisis. Part of the ship's papers had been left at the Custom House for registering, including bills of lading and the British Bill of Health. When the Lang and Company agent was sent back, he was informed that they were mislaid and could not be found. The Captain of the *Yomei Maru* and Allen agreed to sail without them if his company and San Francisco were notified of the facts, for the boat was due to make its first stop there. Apparently the papers were never found. All that day and into the evening, with the aid of an extra gang of coolies, loading continued, and it was not until 3 A.M. that the hatches were covered.

At 4:30 A.M. on the morning of Tuesday, July 13th, Captain Kayahara finally gave the order to sail and, as if by a miracle, all the passengers appeared on deck to wave farewell to Vladivostok which was still wreathed in heavy fog. The pilot was dropped off at Russian Island.

As soon as breakfast was over, sailors, colonists, and personnel went to work clearing away the refuse and storing their hand baggage. Preliminary inspection showed that many of the children had already changed bunks. This had to be stopped and corrected so that record keeping and personnel checking would not become confused. When the children were given the reasons they quietly returned to their original bunks.

Later that morning more serious problems developed — meat and vegetables were spoiling having been left on the dock too long while waiting to be loaded. They also found the emergency rations were disappearing from lifeboats and rafts, particularly cans of chocolate. Allen, realizing the seriousness of the situation, tactfully went to the hatch where the older boys were staying and gave a short talk on the necessity of keeping the supplies intact. He appealed to the guilty parties to come to him before 5 P.M. to discuss the matter. The results were gratifying. Before the deadline, eleven boys reported that they had taken one or two cans but had eaten most of the contents. They all expressed repentance — and one half-eaten can was returned. Allen concluded that only boyish pranks were responsible, and made them all promise to see that the rations were never raided again. His account in the ship's log is filled with true warmth and understanding, and clearly indicates the man's own basic integrity.

A great part of the early success of the trip was due to the organization and tender care of Mother Campbell. She had been approached by Riley Allen early that spring with the following: "Mother Campbell, how would you like to join the ARC to be matron in repatriating the children's colony this summer? I just learned that Dad is going to Manila for a few months for the YMCA and, with the children in California, I can't see any reason why you shouldn't add another star to your crown!"

Discussing the matter with Charles (Dad), they decided she should not miss the opportunity, and when the trip ended, the family could return to China and wait until Russia settled down. As Mother Campbell wrote later in her memoirs, "We are still waiting!" Mother Campbell was in charge of feeding a family of over nine hundred, and the whole spring and early summer were spent in gathering supplies. Until just before sailing, she was the center of a whirlwind of activities, but several days before departure, she and many others began to falter. Riley Allen, trying to revive their spirits, wrote a little note to all those who were involved:

"If Noah stood it, I reckon we can. It will be remembered that Noah took into his famous Ark two of every kind of creature. Two-footed, four-footed, sesquipedalian, and otherwise. Two of every kind of beasts of the earth and fowls of the air. Jones, who stocked our ship in Japan, has wired that our ship has plenty of cockroaches. The common garden variety of cockroach comes under almost any or all of these classifications. Hence we may safely assume that there were cockroaches on the Ark.

Noah stood it for forty days and forty nights, and turned up smiling, with enough faith in the goodness of God to send out over the dark, subsiding waters, through the murk and gloom of a drowned world, a dove of hope which presently brought to him the green twig which spelled the resurgence of life and a second chance for the human race to make good.

The Ark was three hundred cubits long, fifty broad, and thirty deep. Her tonnage wasn't anything near that of the *Yomei Maru*. Noah not only had none of the modern facilities for getting comfortable, but he didn't have much personnel on his ship.

That's just where our Ark has it forty ways over Noah's, and where, by good luck and good fortune, I'll have old Noah lashed to the mast. Picked out for the *Yomei Maru* is a group of personnel that can't be beat. They came through the game out here in Siberia with flying colors and smiling. We've worked long enough together to be acquainted. We've had a few tests in adaptation—of making the best of conditions—of making shift with lots of discomforts.

It's up to us to make or mar this great enterprise. I consider that the pace set on this trip will be, and must be, set by the American personnel. We'll be judged by our discipline, our courage, our cheerfulness, our willingness, our morale. The whole ship will take its tone from us. If we're grouchy, the whole ship will be grouchy. If we're up in the morning with a smile, carry a grin all day long, and go to bed with enough smile left to take into the next day, the

The S. S. *Yomei Maru*, chartered by the Siberian Commission of the American Red Cross to transport the children across two oceans to reach their home again. (American Red Cross Photo)

whole ship will feel the invigoration. We are going to sail for three months, with a shipful of the most impressionable and perhaps the most sensitive children in the world, and with grown-ups, almost as quick to sense that intangible atmosphere which is optimistic and wholesome or the reverse.

I'm not writing this because I have any special apprehension that we aren't going to pull it off all right, I merely mention these things en passant, as the society writers say, to indicate that the *Yomei Maru* trip isn't so bad after all, and that Noah bucked a lot harder job single-handed, and goes down to posterity as the man who sailed the dark waters with a faith, a hope, and a vision so big, with a backbone so stiff, and with his crammed, jammed, and packed Ark so well impregnated with his spirit, that the whole expedition remains as a sublime example to the rest of us.

In closing, I say that we can show teamwork, and ability to operate the *Yomei Maru* which will throw old Noah's sea-excursion into the shade and cause future historians to cut him down to a paragraph and give the Petrograd Children's Colony Homeward Bound Expedition a whole chapter!"

CHAPTER SIXTEEN

It was a sad leave-taking for many of the personnel who left friends behind in Vladivostok, having no idea when they would meet again. Mother Campbell wept at the parting from Dad and, as the ship pulled out, went to her cabin to have a good cry.

She didn't have much time to dwell on her sad thoughts, for a sudden loud commotion alerted her to some kind of trouble on deck and she dashed up the ladder to see what was happening. It seems that, just before sailing, a kind friend of hers heard that there were no steamer chairs on board. He was surprised.

"Look!" he said. "I've got a lot of bentwood chairs that are strong and no use to me. I'll have them aboard before you sail." He did and twenty-four chairs arrived right on time.

When the children came on deck, they gleefully pounced on the chairs, spread them over the railing, and were swinging back and forth over the water.

Mother Campbell, shocked, called out sharply, "Everyone of you hop down off those chairs and bring them to the deck!"

They gave up their game reluctantly at her stern command. Just then Riley Allen walked by.

"Trouble already?" he asked.

She muttered, "If we get half these kids to San Francisco, I'll be very thankful!"

Under Mother Campbell, a regular routine was set up for meals. The POWs were primarily cooks, bakers, and all-around helpers. In return for their work they were paid a small salary, and were to be repatriated to Germany, Austria, and Hungary as soon as the children were delivered to their parents. Mother Campbell had taught them to cook during her efforts of the previous three months to get organized for the trip, and the training was successful.

Also, the entire personnel had to help by cleaning their own quarters and serving their own food. This even included Riley Allen.

Regular lifeboat drills were held, and countless hygienic and preventive measures were adopted to keep the ship clean and free of diseases.

But in spite of careful checks on mechanical equipment, it took only one day to discover that the drainage arrangement for the deck toilets was not working properly. The weight of the cargo had shifted the center of gravity of the boat toward the stern, making it lower than the bow, so that the toilets, which were constructed to drain to the center and out the vents, kept refuse in the troughs. Also an error in pipe joints had connected the showers and wash rooms to the fresh water supply instead of the salt water. That brought an alarming drop in the fresh water tanks within only two days.

A stop in the nearest port in Japan, Muroran, was inevitable, and Allen sent a wire to the ship's agent to have men and materials ready for immediate work. In spite of the setback, a group of older girls gave an informal concert that evening in the small personnel dining room to try to give a lift to everyone's spirits.

At dawn on July 15th, the *Yomei Maru* dropped anchor about a mile and a half off shore in the harbor of Muroran because the harbor was too shallow for docking. Tugs arrived carrying police officials, contractors, and the agent. A spirited argument rose between the two contractors who both demanded to do the work, and Captain Kayahara had to intervene. He settled the matter by hiring all of their men on the condition that the work be completed by late afternoon.

The deep tanks were prepared to take on fresh food. In the meantime, Allen gave orders that the food on board be given to Muroran officials to be used for orphanages or other purposes. It was not rotten but had been exposed to normal temperatures too long to be safe for a long while at sea.

Of course, the children started getting into everything, so Allen, realizing that they would undoubtedly be in the way and interfere with the work on the ship, went with Captain Kayahara to the waterfront police to request permission for the children and POWs to be allowed ashore for the day. As usual, this required several hours of intense discussion and delay, plus a complete inspection of the ship, to convince the Japanese that there were no contagious diseases on board. At last they had permission for everybody to go on shore until 6 P.M.

Allen and Chief Surgeon Eversole called formally on the Vice Mayor of the city and also contacted two schools. To their surprise, all doors opened when they learned that the head of a boys' secondary school turned out to be a former pupil of one of Allen's old friends who had founded Normal Schools in Japan a generation earlier.

The children were taken aboard four large barges. On shore they were lined up in two columns and marched through town to the boys' school. There for an hour they saw Japanese children demonstrate Judo, much to the delight of the Russian boys. Allen made a note in the ship's log of the "sight of the 650 fair haired and blue-eyed Russian children lined up in the courtyard (some remained on the ship by preference) ringed by the darker skinned Japanese children with coal-black hair."

From the boys' school they went to a girls' elementary school where the Japanese girls sang a number of songs, and then some of the Russian girls responded with a selection of their own.

Later they all returned to the ship, but to Allen's distress, the work was nowhere near finished. He saw nothing but problems. The workers were untrained, sloppy in their jobs, and badly directed. The new supplies were not stored away, the beef had not arrived, and most of the deck space was covered with coal needed for the trip to San Francisco. Everything was filthy.

In a letter to Commissioner Teusler in Tokyo, Allen advised that the repairs should be charged to the Osaka Iron Works Company which did the original refitting and had done the work poorly. The bills presented that evening were ridiculously high, and overcharging was evident everywhere, so Allen simply deducted amounts at his own discretion when paying them. But during the evening, tension relaxed when the Mayor of Muroran sent 300 packages of Japanese sweets for the young children, and the girls' school sent packets of postcard views of Muroran to the girls.

It was not until 1 P.M. the following day that the *Yomei Maru* up-anchored. Even then some of the work was not finished, but Allen felt the ship's POWs could cope with whatever was left undone. Immediately after leaving Muroran, a cleanup of the ship was organized. Luggage had to be arranged in the deep tanks, and hand luggage, which had been removed during repairs, had to be replaced in the hatches. The new equipment was given a trial test, particularly the water circulating system, and although numerous leaks developed, mostly at the joints and fittings, it was deemed adequate.

The children responded beautifully; in fact, by evening a semblance of cleanliness and order had returned to the ship. This, of course, provided another excuse for them to arrange a concert for that evening and a Russian dance for the following night.

The ship's log showed that the 10 knots per hour achieved on the Vladivostok-Muroran run was maintained consistently all the way to San Francisco. Approximately 240 miles were covered every 24 hours. From the beginning Allen's log was concerned with the life belt situation and drills were called every day at different times. Repeated reprimands, lectures, even mild punishments for persistent offenders, at last produced more or less satisfactory results, and even the laziest children promptly obeyed. The log gives many accounts of the roles that Allen had to assume in a single day—mentor, teacher, judge, administrator, friend, policeman, and pacifier. All kinds of problems were inevitable in a situation where hundreds of young spirited souls were confined in extremely limited spaces for an extended period of time. It was only natural that troubles should burst out in different ways—and they did.

A group of boys from Hatch #5 had proved almost incorrigible from the outset. Life had forced them to steal and lie long before they came into the colony, and no amount of lecturing or persuasion changed them. Open rebellion occurred on several occasions, always justified by the youthful excuses that they were stealing to give to their starving parents at home, or the teachers were thieves, or everything belonged to the people, or any other possible pretense. Somewhat in desperation, Dr. Hal Davison was assigned to them, for their Russian teachers had lost control. Dr. Davison was a small, mild mannered man who wore steel-rimmed glasses. He had been in Siberia for some time as a surgeon doing relief work and, while there, met and married a Russian Red Cross worker, Natalia Alexayevna Beklimesheva. But his unassuming manner belied his inner strength, by which he was able to enforce strict discipline over his recalcitrant charges and, at the same time, gain their respect.

Another problem of discipline, a little more amusing, came about because of the girls' habit of washing clothes and draping them all over the ship to dry. So ubiquitous was the laundry, that Allen referred to the ship as Hogan's Alley and restricted clothes drying to one area. But this order was also repeatedly disobeyed.

In spite of all attempts at supervision, one of the most confusing problems was meal serving—until a unique solution offered itself. As in most societies, there are some people who are unable to stand around and prefer to get involved, to organize and to help. To Allen's delight, Dimitry Vorolioff, one of the older boys, came to Bramhall, the business manager, and said he had organized 24 boys who would volunteer to do any work on the ship. He promptly placed them in charge of the smaller boys to supervise mealtimes. Within three days, instead of rushing to the table in a rough and unmannerly way, they were marching in quietly and eating in a more orderly fashion.

Some of the boys were put into hatches to aid the teachers in maintaining discipline. For example, Hatch #1 alone contained 120 small boys all sleeping together. The sheer quantity of young animal spirits would inevitably lead to explosions.

On one occasion, Mother Campbell saw one of the boys high up on the rigging. Fearful of frightening him, she whistled and spoke softly. Slowly he clambered down.

"Why in the world did you climb up there, Boris?" she asked. "Especially in this kind of sea?"

"Oh, I just wanted to see if the waves were any higher further out than they are right around the ship," was the reply.

By the second day out of Muroran, a regular daily schedule was instituted. At 5:30 A.M. the first rising bell was rung, and the regulated day continued until 9:30 P.M. when the lights out signal was sounded. Reveille was at 6 A.M. and breakfast at 7 and 8, with some quarters having three sittings in the more crowded hatches due to lack of space for tables and chairs. At 9 A.M. there was a general inspection and all beds had to be made, dining rooms cleaned, floors swept, and everything tidy. School began at 10 except on Sunday. There were two hours of school each morning and one in the afternoon.

At the beginning of the trip, Allen called all teachers together and set up a daily round of classes to which various children were assigned. In spite of the limited space, a great deal of serious work was done and classes were conducted in Algebra, Geometry, Physics, Russian, Arithmetic, French, German, History, Geography, and Natural History. The average number in each group was 16 to 18 students. When a call went out to find out who might want to study English, over 200 children signed up. Even Mother Campbell was dragooned into teaching conversation, since the tremendous demand was more than the regular teachers could handle. Classes in arts and handicrafts were also given.

While groups of children studied below decks, others were assigned recreation and exercise above. Mr. Woods of the original YMCA group took all the older boys in hand with gymnastic exercises and games. Space was extremely limited, but when all else failed he would run around the deck and make them keep up with him.

Leonty Duebner, who had been appointed to "big boy" status in

Vladivostok, was paid five dollars a month plus a double food ration to act as a leader of the older boys. But he, too, had great difficulty trying to cope with those in Hatch #5. When Dr. Davison took over, they both referred to their charges as "pigs," but Leonty felt that their problems were caused by the tremendous overcrowding on board and the inability to work off steam. He also thought that much of the trouble was due to the stringent regulations of the day's regime, along with the ever-present fog and the motion of the sea. Fortunately, there were not too many incidents of seasickness on board, for which both Mother Campbell and Riley Allen were devoutly thankful.

Most of the children had one particular complaint—that was having to wash in salt water. Of course, it was unavoidable on account of the small space available for fresh water storage.

Lunch was served at 12:30 P.M., and the second period of school started at 3:00. There was a second inspection at 4:15 and then after 5:00 the decks were cleared for drills by Boy and Girl Scouts. These movements were very popular in Russia and Siberia, and every town had troops. The Children's Colony had two popular troops which were active all through the journey. Groups of children were rotated for participation in various activities, including bathing. In the evening, movies, some taken at Russian Island, were often shown—on deck if the weather permitted. And no Sunday night was complete without a dance, when the hour for retiring was pushed up to 10:30.

One of the small but irritating problems for Allen was seeing that the children got enough rest. He was puzzled by observing that the Russian children would not settle down to sleep at night as readily as American children. Actually they were more excited with play, music, dancing, and other kinds of recreation, and would lie awake in their bunks talking for hours. He evidently did not realize that a room with about 120 children could hardly be as restful as an American nursery. However, lack of sleep sent many a child to his bunk for a nap after lunch, and school was not as well attended in the afternoon as in the morning.

Many of the older boys and girls were very much interested in music and organized orchestras, bands, and choruses to entertain the entire ship. On most Sunday nights the air would be filled with the sounds of Russian melodies. And the laughter was infectious as forty or fifty young people would gaily dance their national dances or sing in beautiful harmonies. Even Japanese seamen would stop work and stand quietly on deck when a hundred girls would raise their pure sweet voices in song. Many a POW openly wept with thoughts of his family and homeland.

The word "prasdnik" means holiday, and there is no more important prasdnik for Russians than a Saint's name day for all those named after that saint. July 24th was the Saint's day for Olga, and there were thirty-two girls named Olga in the colony. The celebration and dance that night, given in their honor, took place in the personnel dining room and was attended by all the children. Riley Allen said later, "We were packed in there like sardines!" After that they decided that no more big parties would be held in that room, so all Saint's days, which came along frequently enough, were held on deck.

On July 27th, Burle Bramhall was 27 and a special dinner was given in his honor, which even Captain Kayahara attended. The personnel dining room was decorated with flags and bunting. One enthusiastic young revolutionary of 12 put up the Red flag and there was a moment of general uneasiness. Burle Bramhall good-naturedly clapped the boy on the shoulder and said, "Well done, son!" The tension dissolved in laughter and cheers.

July 31st began happily enough with thoughts of their arrival at San Francisco the next day. Pay day was announced for the colony children, and they all lined up in three groups according to age. They showed tremendous delight over the new American one dollar bills and shining change. The nearer the ship got to San Francisco, the greater their excitement grew.

Previous arrangements had been made with the Captain that all music on that Saturday night would stop at ten o'clock and the decks cleared by 10:30. Special lights were strung up on deck so the musicians could see their music, and the POWs, as well as the Russian and American staff, were all invited. Never had the music been so gay. Everyone took part, dancing whatever way they wished. Czech, Hungarian, German, and Russian folk steps were tried—when suddenly, a little before ten o'clock, the First Officer came out of his cabin and angrily complained that he couldn't sleep. Allen immediately said to him that the music would stop promptly at ten and the decks cleared as quickly as possible. But the Captain appeared shortly afterwards and angrily asked how long the boys would play. Allen gave him the answer, without reminding him of the agreement. Then, not realizing the seriousness of the situation, he went to the poop deck for a few minutes of relaxation, when Dr. Eversole came along and told him that the Captain was extremely angry and was threatening to call the whole trip off in San Francisco. He was going to insist that the Red Cross get an American ship for the rest of the voyage.

When Allen went back to try to calm the Captain, he declared that he was going to get a tin can and beat it outside Allen's door. Just at that moment they saw a five gallon kerosene can being carried to the Captain's stateroom. Allen gave immediate instructions to stop the music and clear the decks, but realizing that the anger of the Captain and the First Officer was so great, they decided not to discuss it further that night. For several hours the Captain prowled around the deck, but did not accost anyone further.

Vladivostok 1919 Christmas costume party.

CHAPTER SEVENTEEN

The next morning, Sunday, August 1st, dawned bright and clear. Somehow the high emotions of the night before seemed to dim in the warm sunlight. As they neared San Francisco during the day, the excitement of everyone on board kept mounting. But the ship arrived shortly after six in the evening, too late to dock, and so they had to wait until morning to get to land. That night it took powerful persuasion to get the children to bed and to sleep. Even the Japanese crew showed great enthusiasm, although they were not allowed ashore.

There were several wirelesses awaiting Allen. Much to his surprise, he learned that his earlier detailed letters requesting assistance in taking care of the children had gone astray. Something had to be done with them while the boat was being refurbished and repaired during their brief stay. Also a cargo of sugar bound for New York had to be loaded to serve as ballast and to help defray some of the expenses of the trip, since the Red Cross was being charged $5000 per day for the steamer. Only the cables sent a few days earlier had arrived.

However, the enthusiasm and excitement in San Francisco about the news story of the travelling ark had galvanized even the bureaucracy. Fort Scott, unused for over a year, was opened up. Leave was cancelled for all army personnel, and from Friday to Monday, when the children arrived, an entire regiment worked day and night.

The grounds, overgrown with grass and weeds, were cleaned. Bunks for 800 children were installed. The kitchens were refitted with stoves, ice chests, dishes, and all the necessities for housing and feeding the whole colony.

The coast artillery regiment sent their cooks and waiters whose leaves were all cancelled. The street car company furnished two cars solely for the use of the children. The city offered its auditorium for shows, and the musicians' union gave the free use of a band. Private firms donated food, fruit, candy, ice, and all sorts of good things. And the Junior Red Cross took on the responsibility of providing various kinds of entertainment and enormous gifts of toys.

But all this was unknown to Allen when he learned by cable before the ship docked that his original letters had never arrived. One wireless brought greetings from the San Francisco *Chronicle* to the children, so Allen promptly composed a reply which was printed in the *Chronicle* on Monday morning.

While the ship was slowly docking, Allen completed a lot of necessary paper work, but the children hung over the railing for hours. Their exhilaration at the prospect of setting foot on land again knew no bounds.

As the children disembarked, they were met by members of the Junior Red Cross who gave each one an orange, a pack of gum, a Junior Red Cross button, and a toy. They were then taken to Fort Scott.

Amid the excitement of disembarking, Vera Mihailova, a young teenager, absorbed in looking up at the tall buildings, walked off the dock and fell into the water. A San Francisco policeman dove in and rescued her to the loud cheers of the crowd. When the children left a few days later, the same officer came to bid them farewell, having adopted a proprietary air for the whole group. The incident received great notices in all the local newspapers, and the officer became an instant public hero. But Vera was teased unceasingly from then on.

Misha Denisov's account of San Francisco was somewhat different from the general opinion of the others. He was dreadfully disappointed because there were no really tall skyscrapers. But his description of Fort Scott and its grounds was most vivid—there were lovely wild flowers and grass lawns but, strangely enough, no cows! He was also very favorably impressed by the evening meal which had three courses, and, even better, he had two cups of delicious coffee.

The first evening they were entertained by a movie at the army post and a recital by child dancers from the Casino Theater.

The next morning the boys were taken by twenty-five U.S. Army trucks and the girls via the Municipal Railroad to the Civic Center for a welcoming ceremony by the Junior Red Cross. Later, they were taken by car to the San Francisco City Hall. Much to Misha's delight, the car he was in hit a trolley and damaged it slightly. Great excitement prevailed, with the police taking evidence from witnesses. A series of warm speeches were delivered by Mayor Rolph and other local dignitaries, and telegrams from the Governors of California, Nevada, and Arizona were read; following that, Miss Estelle Carpenter led a community sing.

Afterwards, they crossed over to the City Auditorium where a cold supper was served by the Pacific Division of the Red Cross, and an organist gave a recital during the meal on "the biggest organ in the world."

Then the doors were opened to the public, allowing about 8000 people to enter. Three brass bands marched around, with a group of old veterans in ancient uniforms bringing up the rear. Father Sakovitch of the Greek Orthodox Church explained to the children that these were veterans from both the North and the South sides of the Civil War who only marched on special occasions. There were singers and acrobatic acts and rousing Cossack and folk dances. Then the Colony's orchestra and girls' chorus gave musical selections. The bands played again, starting with several hymns, and later switching to dance music to which the children began to dance. By 10:30 the whole lot of very tired colonists piled onto the army trucks and fell into their beds at Fort Scott.

They were only there a few days, and the children were continually delighted by the city's extraordinary hospitality, for each day was filled with different entertainments. For instance, they went to Golden Gate Park where they were given free use of all the thrilling rides and other amusement concessions. They had an afternoon of fun at a small zoo where they were treated to rides on carousels, swings, and some animals. For lunches they were fed things like hot dogs, ice cream, and other indigestible delicacies.

The *Yomei Maru* was scheduled to leave San Francisco Thursday morning, August 5th. At 8:10 A.M. the last visitors left the ship, among them Chief Executive Riley Allen. It had become obvious that detailed planning would be needed to receive the children in New York and prepare them for the final leg of their journey. He decided, therefore, to go by train to Washington so that he would have plenty of time to make all the arrangements while the ship was sailing there via the Panama Canal. He had turned over the command of the colony to Dr. Eversole for the voyage. As he left the ship, there was much shouting and waving by the children on deck, with the general gaiety enhanced by a brass band playing on the dock for everyone's amusement.

All in all, the children's memories of San Francisco were very happy ones, and quite different from the experiences they would have when they reached New York.

The ship passed through the Golden Gate by 9:30 A.M., and, as they passed Fort Scott, the children, recognizing it, waved and shouted good-bye to their happy home of the last three days.

Immediate housekeeping chores had to be attended to, including the sorting of 11,000 pieces of laundry. Telegrams of farewell were posted, and an unexpected one from Laura Schirmer, who had been one of the teachers on Russian Island, arrived from Chicago. By the evening of the next day, the ship was back to its regular routine.

On August 7th, Burle Bramhall, with the help of several assistants, distributed the hundreds of toys and books given to the colonists by the children of San Francisco's Red Cross. It was a scene straight out of Christmas. Some of the children jumped for joy, while others quietly showed their appreciation in their eyes and faces. Many photographs of the event, taken by the ship's photographer, became treasured possessions of the colonists for years to come.

By August 8th, the weather became increasingly hot. Even out under the canvas awnings, the temperature rose to 105° Fahrenheit. Several of the active boys who could not be kept quiet had slight sunstrokes. Ice tea and lemonade were provided on deck at all times, and for a few days, only cold meals were served. With everybody suffering from the excessive heat, classes had to be cancelled.

Two of the boys were badly affected and became delirious. They were placed on the port side of the poop deck under constant surveillance. One of them, Vladimir Malizin, repeatedly tried to throw himself overboard. The boys in Hatch #5 were called upon for help and, as a result, two of them were assigned, along with a nurse, to hold him down when he became violent.

In the afternoon and early evening during the worst spell, the motor and lights of the ship had to be turned off to cool down. This made the ship even hotter, for no breeze passed through the hatches. Most of the children remained quietly in their bunks, dozing every afternoon, though some protested that they were all right and were given permission to stay out on deck. At night many of them tried to come on deck to sleep, but were soon chased by the night patrols. The whole schedule of sleeping and eating was moved ahead by one hour to allow the children to sleep later in the cooler early morning, which also gave the hatches an hour longer to cool off in the evening before the children went to bed. No matter what the outside temperature, Dr. Eversole recorded that the sleeping temperature in the hatches was never below 85° nor above 88°.

Something unpleasant happened on August 10th. At about 8:30 in the morning one of the Japanese sailors, on his way to the motor room, was walking through the hatch occupied by the older girls. He put his hands on the shoulder of Natasha Lebedova, frightening her, of course. When Dr. Eversole heard the complaint, he went straight to the Captain who promised that his men would stop going through the hatch.

Suddenly that evening, a strong breeze came up, followed quickly by a heavy downpour. Everyone rejoiced at the promise of relief. Some even stood out in the rain, faces upturned, enjoying the fresh cool drenching rain. Within minutes the temperature dropped to comfortable levels.

But the Japanese sailors ignored the Captain's commands, and the following morning walked through the aisles between the bigger girls' bunks again. This time they turned their flashlights directly on the girls, some of whom screamed and ducked under the covers. The same man who had bothered Natasha the day before, put his arms around her and began caressing her. Unfortunately, she had a weak heart and became hysterical, after which she became quite ill.

This time Dr. Eversole went directly to the Captain and spoke in no uncertain terms.

"Look here, Captain Kayahara! We will not countenance such things on this ship. You'll have to call together all your men on night duty and talk to them in a manner they'll understand. If you can't control them, we'll have to put them under surveillance ourselves."

The Captain was furious that he had been disobeyed and sent for them at once. The very threat of passenger surveillance was startling and, if carried through, would clearly prove to everyone that he was not in control. His anger, pride, and loss of face must have turned the tide, because from then on there were no more of those incidents. But Natasha suffered for weeks from nightmares and shortness of breath.

The rain relieved the oppressive heat only for a brief time. Once again it was relentless and began to tell on their frayed nerves. An almost mutinous attitude developed among those with work to do, including teachers, POWs, and nurses. No amount of cajoling by Mother Campbell could induce them to do their jobs or even to join in social affairs. Luckily, a few days later rains came again, and this time the temperature broke and so did tempers.

An ongoing and seemingly insoluble problem was the stealing of food by all the children, and no one seemed to be able to come up with a workable way to put a stop to it. For some reason different kinds of food, from fruits to cereals, were squirreled away in bunks, always "to take home to my family who are starving." No amount of vigilance was effective, and the hatches began to smell like garbage pails. Also, in spite of their promise to Allen, the older boys kept on stealing chocolate from the life rafts.

One suggestion was to build a brig, but Eversole turned that down for fear of antagonizing the whole ship's company. At last he hit on a new scheme. Summoning several offenders who had been caught red-handed, he announced that he did not believe they would do the things they were doing unless they were ill.

"As a doctor, it's my duty to treat you as sick children," he said. "So I'm afraid I'll have to have you stay in bed. You'll only be able to go to the toilet with a nurse. And when we get to New York, we'll have to report you to the immigration officers as incorrigible. Of course, that means that you'll be confined under military guard in military hospitals."

To some extent, the tactic had the desired effect and the situation improved considerably.

On August 18th a few islands came into view, and they sighted the first flying fish. All they could think and talk about was the prospect of going through the Panama Canal the next day. They had already been given some lectures on the construction of the Canal and the complications and dangers involved.

Eversole telegraphed the Captain of the Port of Balboa that afternoon to tell him that the ship would be arriving in about six hours. He described her overcrowded condition and asked for quick clearance through the canal. He also ordered a variety of fruits, meat, bread, and other food supplies. When the *Yomei Maru* arrived, she was met by a pilot, the Port Captain himself, along with the American Red Cross Representative, Payne Wardlaw, and the quarantine officer. Normally they never admitted ships at such an hour, but, due to the *Yomei Maru's* unique situation, they waived all rules and took it directly into Pier 6.

Not only was there a large reception of Red Cross personnel awaiting them at the pier, but also representatives of the United States Government. Supplies were already on the dock, and a large corps of workmen began loading them, giving their time freely to the Red Cross. The ladies of the Canal Zone Red Cross Chapter came with 50 gallons of ice cream, fibre plates and spoons, boxes of oranges, pineapples, and other fruits as gifts. There were trucks and autos waiting to take the children on a tour around the city, but because of the late hour, that idea had to be cancelled.

The American personnel and a group of the older children were given permission to go ashore to see Panama City. Before leaving San Francisco, Allen had asked Mother Campbell to go ashore at Panama as chaperone if any of the older boys and girls went, and to stay with them. He warned her of low dives and unscrupulous men lying in wait for new "suckers." With Dr. Eversole's permission, she kept her word and off they went. At 4:30 in the morning she succeeded in shepherding the brood back to the ship intact.

Later she told Eversole, "We visited every joint in the place! We saw Spanish dancers galore, and discouraged fancy dames flirting with the young blades. Wherever we went, everyone ate sandwiches and danced miles." She had obviously enjoyed the excursion, and went on, "In one of the toughest dives, all of a sudden I heard a voice shout, 'Mother Campbell! Of all people! What are *you* doing here?' It was a young American captain I had met in Vladivostok. He teased me unmercifully for being in a place like that!"

Just before the *Yomei Maru* left Balboa, a wealthy Russian family came on board and asked if they could do anything for the children. They talked with a number of them, and all the children explained that they needed nothing.

One little girl spoke up. "Won't you pray for the American Red Cross to keep on being kind, and thank God for the wonderful care they've given us all?"

The story was repeated around Panama and made a tremendous impression there.

The *Yomei Maru* entered the Panama Canal at 7:30 A.M. on August 19th. The weather was cool and cloudy, and the children were all over the deck. At Balboa pamphlets had been sent aboard for the children, giving the history of the canal and some of the details.

At nine o'clock they started through the Miraflores locks, and at 10:45 they arrived at the Padre Miguel locks. There, and at the next three locks, people were lined up on shore to see the "children's ark." They pelted the ship with mangoes, bananas, limes, cakes, candy, and flowers, and the children responded with enthusiastic shouts of "SPACEBA" (thank you)! They were also very excited when they passed a submarine in one of the locks.

At the end of the canal they were lowered 88 feet to the level of the Caribbean Sea, proceeding to Colón, which they reached in the late afternoon. Here the balance of their food supplies were waiting, along with quantities of magazines for the children. They sailed out of Colón about an hour and a half later and soon encountered rough seas, but everybody was looking forward to their next destination, New York City.

CHAPTER EIGHTEEN

That evening Dr. Eversole wrote thank you letters to the Port Captain and the Red Cross Chapter in Panama for their aid and attention. He then opened a telegram which had just arrived from Washington, D.C. It was the beginning of a long and unhappy period for both the Red Cross and the colonists. It read as follows:

Owing to the international situation, also critical food situation in Petrograd, necessary land entire colony in France, repatriating thence by individuals or groups if possible. Red Cross making every effort early delivery children to parents. Present plans France necessitate retention entire American and Russian personnel in order to operate colony along lines Russian Island. Authorize you announce the foregoing. Assure colony stay in France merely preliminary to getting home. Emphasize impossibility direct entrance Yomei Maru Petrograd on account military international situation. Received your cable from Santa Cruz deeply regret heat stroke cases. Keep us clearly advised about conditions of ship. Have good location New York. Entertainment plans progressing. Warmest regards to all colony.   Allen-Ferrand.

Eversole telegraphed back at once that either he or Dr. Hal Davison would be willing to go to France, and he would speak to the other personnel. But the brevity of his cable concealed the uneasiness he felt over the matter. However, more important things had happened to claim his immediate attention.

Going up for evening inspection, he found about fifty boys sleeping outside on deck. When he remonstrated, they told him they would no longer stay in the hatches because of the evil smell. He promised to rectify the situation, and persuaded them to go back down that night.

The next morning, the reasons became clear enough. In Hatches #2 and #5, there was enough breakfast food, rotting grapefruit, half-eaten mangoes, decaying meat sandwiches, and any other kind of food squirreled away in the bunks to feed the entire ship. It was easy to locate because of the terrible odor.

Eversole decided to stop giving fatherly talks about not hoarding food for starving families. Instead he organized a general cleanup—floors were swabbed down with disinfectant, and the order went out that if any food was found in any hatch, the entire group of that hatch would lose one day of privileges in New York City.

Even then the situation didn't improve immediately. Mother Campbell had bought 65 fresh pineapples for a surprise breakfast for the personnel and hid them back on the Captain's bridge. The next morning there were only a few left. In order to get to them, the boys would have had to shinny up a tall pole and swing across to the bridge. But somehow they managed to do it, and pineapple debris was found littered in Hatch #5.

At last Eversole was pushed into doing what he had fought against so long. One-half of the isolation ward which was not in use was converted into a "very sanitary" pen. The worst offenders were to be put in there. Between meals they were given knives and other kitchen implements to scour, and for exercise, they were taken up by Dr. Davison to scrub the decks for three hours a day. This punishment finally had the desired effect on the whole colony.

One Saturday evening, during a band concert, Eversole was hastily summoned to the deck by an excited teacher who said that a Japanese sailor had drawn a big knife on some of the boys. Rushing out on deck, he found the Captain, Mr. Woods, and Mr. Walker standing at the foot of the companionway leading to the Captain's quarters. They explained that there had been trouble between one of the teachers, Mr. Kotovsky, several of the boys, and several sailors. Eversole asked the Captain to send for the sailors involved for an immediate meeting in the Captain's dining salon.

At the meeting were the Captain, Bramhall, Walker, Kotovsky, and Eversole, plus the three boys—Boris Illyn, Peter Borarin, and Serge Yakovleff. Miss Helen Domerschikoff served as interpreter. Each person was asked to tell his version of the incident, and later the boys and Serge Kotovsky put their testimony in writing, which was duly recorded in the ship's log.

The incident was described in the following way: Borarin was on his way to the dance when he saw a crowd of boys gathered on the deck. He pushed through and saw Illyn wrestling with a sailor. At that moment, he saw Mr. Kotovsky take the sailor by the shoulder to try to make him let go his hold on Illyn. The sailor got mad and began striking at everyone, hitting some of the other boys, including Borarin. He then ran to the coal hatch, took up a board and threw it at the crowd, missing everyone. Yakovleff took hold of the sailor to try to quiet him; Borarin helped, and another fight was under way. Borarin hit the sailor on the head, and another sailor hit Borarin. Then all the sailors left the scene, but within a few minutes the wrestling sailor returned brandishing a knife. Other sailors surrounded and disarmed him. By then the crowd was so great that Kotovsky and Illyn had been pushed far toward the stern and apparently never saw the sailor return with the knife.

At this point Eversole asked the sailor to tell his story. He said that he had been wrestling with Illyn, Japanese fashion, when Kotovsky came along, pushed him away, and beat him with his fists. During his testimony he became quite excited, beating the table with clenched fists and shaking them at Kotovsky. He seemed to bear no ill feeling toward the boys, but held Kotovsky responsible for everything.

Serge Yakovleff's story was much the same as Borarin's. He had watched the wrestling match with the sailors, some POWs and other colonists for a few minutes. When the band struck up, he decided to stop the wrestling. At the same time Kotovsky stepped in, also to end the match. Evidently, the sailor didn't understand their intentions and began to strike out at everybody. He claimed that Borarin was only defending himself, and then described the sailor throwing the board at the crowd. He also gave his own description of the knife incident, and the way the other sailors interfered, trying to stop their comrade's threatening gestures.

Kotovsky's evidence threw little more light on the subject. He had been looking for one of the boys on deck when he saw a crowd of them clustered together, obviously interested in whatever they were watching. He pushed through and saw a sailor lying on the deck with Illyn sitting on top of him, trying to press his arms to the floor. Afraid that the wrestling match might get out of hand, he told them to stop.

The other boys shouted "Astopha! — astopha!" (stop!), but a second sailor kept egging the wrestler to keep going.

Someone shouted, "It's time to go to the dance!", at which Illyn jumped up and turned away. The sailor, freed, went after Illyn, and they both fell on the deck.

Kotovsky, thinking Illyn was being choked, shouted "STOP!"

When they were pulled apart, the sailor again rushed at the boys, and Kotovsky stepped in to stop him. Others seized him, but he jerked himself loose, ran to the coal hatch, grabbed a board and threw it at Kotovsky. As the crowd carried Kotovsky away, he heard voices shouting that the sailor was threatening the boys with a sword, but he didn't see it.

At this point Eversole explained to the Captain that obviously neither side understood the words of the other, and that Kotovsky thought he had to stop the match because it was getting too serious. The Captain objected to Kotovsky striking the sailor, but Eversole pointed out again that everyone was excited and that Kotovsky was only trying to stop the sailor from beating Illyn. The Captain talked to the sailor, who heatedly drummed the table, shook his fist at Kotovsky, but paid little attention to the Captain's words. Eversole interrupted the scene.

"Look," he said to the Captain, "Isn't it strange that this man didn't report the incident to you? Instead he seems to have gone back to his quarters to find a knife. Wasn't he taking over the discipline of the ship and usurping your authority?"

The Captain said nothing.

Eversole went on, "I would suggest that you take the knife from him and make all your men understand that you're in charge, and that you're the only one who has the right to discipline anyone on board. In fact, it might be a good idea to tell your sailors in no uncertain terms to forget the whole thing because it all happened on account of the language barrier. Remember that I'll have to report this to New York, and if any further settlement should become necessary, it could make unpleasant headlines in the American newspapers. Also, if it should become a court case, it could be even more unpleasant."

The Captain agreed quickly to that. Eversole then promised to instruct the Russian and American personnel and children to forget the whole incident. He also offered to have two of his doctors examine the sailor for any injuries, but this was met with a new fit of fury. So he left and went out on deck to think.

All of a sudden, he heard a shout. It was Bramhall on the other side of the deck. Eversole ran over and was told that Bramhall had just come upon another sailor drawing a knife on an older boy. They were still standing there. Eversole sent for the Captain again. When questioned, the sailor claimed that he was merely showing the boy how he himself would fight and how to carry a knife. Eversole patiently explained to the Captain again how misunderstandings in language could cause trouble, because the boy thought that the sailor was out to "get him," and even pantomime could lead to trouble. The rest of the night was quiet.

The following day, Eversole had the Allen-Ferrand telegram translated and read to the children. He quickly realized that it was causing a great undercurrent of tension, and so followed it up with a short talk. He emphasized that the American people and the American Red Cross would stand by them until the Russian government could receive them, but that the Red Cross, although totally supported by the people of America, was not an agency of the United States government. Half the Red Cross moneys were donations from poor people who were just as anxious to get the children home as the children were to get there. Although Americans had little money, it was only their unselfish spirit and pride in finishing the job that made them determined to repatriate the children regardless of the sacrifices to themselves.

He promised that he would go to France to arrange for their living quarters, but that stricter discipline would have to be enforced on the voyage over and during the stay in France. Rules were for their own protection and would have to be obeyed.

He then asked the children to support their teachers and the American Red Cross personnel with all their might so that they could all be one happy family. During that day many children came to Eversole and said they knew they had been spoiled and had gotten into bad habits, but they would try to be more cooperative from now on. But an underlying tension remained, and Eversole did not seem to realize the reason.

The rest of the day was pleasant enough until Eversole, walking by Hatch #5, saw Kotovsky sitting on it and reading. The sailor who had caused all the trouble the night before, went up and shook a broom at him. Kotovsky turned his head and looked the other way. The sailor walked around to get into his line of vision, pulled out a knife, and threatened him with it. Kotovsky didn't move but motioned him to go away. The sailor, looking around, suddenly saw Eversole and quickly darted off.

A few minutes later some of the little boys came running to Eversole and said that the same sailor had threatened to stab Borarin. Dashing out on deck, Eversole found groups of excited boys. He decided to go back to his office and lock the door to be able to think quietly for a few minutes. He then went to the Captain's quarters and told him about the incident, noting at the time that the Captain actually seemed to be afraid.

Taking matters into his own hands, he told the Captain to call all his officers together, along with the entire crew, and say that if any sailor molested any of the children, teachers, or other personnel without provocation again, or drew a knife on anyone, he would order the ship into the nearest port and take on a strong American guard, and this would all be put into writing. Also the expense of the whole operation would be charged to the owners of the ship. The Captain agreed at once. About an hour later he came to Eversole's cabin and said that he had assurances from his officers and men that there would be no further incidents.

The following afternoon the Captain invited Eversole to his office for a chat. He wanted to tell him that the guilty sailors had come and apologized to him, saying they were aware of the seriousness of their actions, and there would be no need to put into port for guards. On the contrary, they would work all the harder to speed up the voyage. That proved to be true. In the next 24 hours the ship covered 257 miles instead of the usual 240. Fortunately, as the Captain promised, there were no more unpleasant incidents.

The seriousness of the confrontations between the Japanese and the Russian children and personnel were certainly not all due to the close quarters and lengthy trip. Russia and Japan had a long history of hostility, beginning with the Russo-Japanese war in 1904 and never really ending. Again open hostility broke out at the end of World War I, and Japanese aggressive actions around Vladivostok and Siberia aroused world-wide concern. In the ensuing chaos of occupying forces and various revolutionary movements, no one could predict whether war might openly break out. Certainly the Japanese sailors must have wondered why they were taking so many Russian children around the world to get them back home in time to join the Russian forces, possibly to fight the Japanese.

The following day, August 24th, Eversole cabled Allen about the decisions of various personnel to continue with the children to France or to leave the voyage in New York. Then in one short sentence he expressed his real concern: "Russian personnel and big boys worried about France period fear of being interned stop." This was the first indication given to Allen of the new problem simmering on board.

In the meantime, cool breezes, pleasant weather, and the distribution of monthly allowances, made everyone's spirits rise. Every little girl was engaged in making a new blouse, and, to the surprise of Mother Campbell, all the material they were using had ARC stamped all over it. The girls explained that these were their new ARC sheets which were nice and fresh looking, whereas the sheets from Russian

Island looked old and yellow. The innocent delight of the children wanting to look pretty for "Fifth Avenue and Broadway" produced a small crisis. Finally, Mother Campbell, with permission from Dr. Eversole, worked out a trade with the old, yellow sheets being legally transferred to the Red Cross, and the new fresh-looking sheets becoming the property of the children. They looked absolutely splendid in their new finery.

About this time, Dr. Eversole was dealt another unpleasant problem. Peter de George, who had been a tower of strength and extremely resourceful during the stressful days of the colony's travels through war-torn territories, presented a protest to him demanding a higher salary or to be totally relieved of all his duties. Fortunately, Eversole had Major Allen's General Directives from June 14th back in Vladivostok, which had been agreed to by all the teachers. The Directive stated that the teachers and educators on the trip would be under the general manager of the boat for all necessary orders. He, therefore, refused to give in to de George's demands.

On August 26th, Eversole was awakened and called to the infirmary. Elena Alexandrova, who had a badly infected eye, apparently from a mosquito bite, had been ill ever since the Panama Canal passage. Her fever had shot up suddenly, and a partial operation was performed to enlarge the opening above the eye for irrigation. Her respiration improved somewhat, and the doctors were hopeful that she would live. As the day wore on there was a slight improvement, but, unhappily, it was only temporary.

Mrs. Davison, the Russian bride of Dr. Davison, reported that one of the teachers, Eugenia Mazun, told her that all the Russian personnel understood that the American Red Cross was cooperating with France and were going to turn the boys and men over to France to work as war prisoners inside a wire fence, and that the women and girls would be used as white slaves. At first, Eversole thought to call Mrs. Mazun up to his office and ask her authority for such statements but then decided to ignore the matter, at least for the time being, because discussion would probably only increase the rumors.

The same day two telegrams arrived from Allen about the New York plans. Fort Wadsworth on Staten Island was designated as their home in New York. It would be impossible to unload the cargo of sugar which had been taken on in Panama to help pay the expenses of the trip if the colony stayed on board while they were in New York. Also a new shipment of coal had to be loaded for the trip across the Atlantic. Eversole wired back about two critically ill children, and asked for transfer to a hospital for them.

The next day was spent packing, washing, and cleaning up the children and their quarters. Since they would land at New York on the morrow, their anticipation had lifted their spirits to a new high. Early in the morning of August 28th, the *Yomei Maru* docked at Pier G, Pennsylvania Piers, Jersey City. The count now stood at 428 boys, 352 girls, 12 male personnel, 4 female personnel, and 77 POWs—a total of 958 passengers, including 85 Russian personnel.

The boys of "Hatch 5" aboard the *Yomei Maru*.

CHAPTER NINETEEN

As the *Yomei Maru* sailed into New York harbor, there was great excitement on board. Everybody crowded the rails to get their first distant glimpse of the fabled city. The children were lighthearted and excited, impatient to get over the endless formalities, so that they could see this magical place with their own eyes. Their dreams did not include forebodings of conflicts, political maneuvering, and stark tragedy which would engrave the memory of their stay in their minds for the rest of their lives.

Of course, none of those on board the *Yomei Maru* could know the drama surrounding the plans to repatriate the children, nor could they know the reasons behind Riley Allen's decision to remain behind when their ship left San Francisco.

Allen had found disturbing letters from Washington awaiting him there. He was surprised to learn that plans to change the route of the colony were already well formulated. It seems that the children were to be taken to France first and kept there until their parents were located, rather than landing them at a Baltic port and returning them as a group to Russia. Knowing full well the tension that such a change of plans could cause in the colony, Allen decided to go overland to Washington, D.C., to speak directly with Dr. Livingston Ferrand, Chairman of the Red Cross Central Committee, and Frederick P. Keppel, Vice Chairman and Director of the Bureau of Foreign Operations. Unfortunately, one of the most unnerving circumstances for Allen at that time was the fact that the head of the American Red Cross, President Woodrow Wilson, had suffered another serious stroke and lay inert and uncommunicative. Allen realized that he must deal with Keppel and Ferrand to make his case, for there was no higher authority to whom he could appeal.

Arriving in Washington on August 11th, he spent the next couple of weeks shuttling back and forth between New York and Washington, alternately discussing plans with Keppel and Ferrand, and arranging for the reception and entertainment of the colony during their stay in New York.

Although the war was over, passions and tempers were still high. With the advent of the Bolshevik revolution, unsuccessful intervention of the allied expeditionary forces in Siberia, and the seemingly successful export of Bolshevism to Germany and Hungary, tremendous nervousness was felt by all segments of the political spectrum.

Poland, counting on Russian weakness from six years of war, revolution, civil war, and famine, attacked her from the west at the end of the war. Her excuse was to retake "lost Polish territory." To her surprise, although Russia was seemingly on her knees, she rallied enough to put up a strong fight, and not only defeated the Poles, but invaded part of the newly created Polish state. Only the immediate intervention of the French on the side of Poland saved the new state. But both pro and anti-Bolshevik Russians were highly incensed by the action of France. This was, of course, known to the children, because of endless rumors about Russian POWs and refugees being imprisoned or forced to work in France. It surely explained their fear and intense dislike of the French.

The instigator of the change in plans was Robert E. Olds, Commissioner of the Red Cross European Commission. When the children had left Vladivostok, it had been assumed that they could be repatriated directly from New York to Russia. But little was known at that time of the European political situation. Colonel Olds, in France, was asked early in July, to begin planning for the arrival of the children about the middle of August. He cabled back: "Who would be responsible? Where would financing come from?" And most important, "How and where would the children be repatriated?" Olds pointed out the general belief, later proved erroneous, that many of the parents were refugees in Europe and would not want their children sent back to Russia, fearing that the older boys would promptly be conscripted into military service.

Olds knew that whatever the Red Cross did, it would be criticized by both the Soviets and the western world, so he believed that it simply had to do whatever it thought best for the children. He felt that the so-called "Parents' Association" in Petrograd, used by the Soviets as their identifying agent, was merely a camouflage organization set up by the Soviet government.

The Red Cross was already having great difficulty trying to locate the parents of the children from the published lists. Beside the colonists, thousands of children had left Petrograd for the Ural District in

1917 and 1918. Most had never been heard from since.

But uppermost in Olds' mind was the need to find a safe and convenient location where the children could remain until definite contact could be made with individual parents. He feared that the children could become political pawns if held in the wrong place, and wanted to make sure that the location picked for a temporary camp would be carefully chosen. Also, that would give the Red Cross time to conduct a thorough investigation of conditions in Russia, as well as an up-to-date evaluation of the political climate before attempting to repatriate the children.

Olds felt that only France was strong enough to withstand the demands of Moscow and that, in France, the Red Cross could be more effective in controlling the delicate inquiries about the families. On the other hand, if sent to one of the smaller European countries, the children could be used as a political weapon in current sensitive peace negotiations. He sent long letters and cables to Washington expressing his concern on all kinds of issues to bolster his conviction that France was the logical country to use as a base—adequate financing, political and administrative conditions in France, versus the harsh climatic conditions of smaller northern European countries. He also cited radiograms emanating from Moscow claiming the children to be prisoners of war and the Soviets' right to insist on immediate delivery of them, demands which would be difficult for a small or new nation to withstand.

Commissioner Olds was a highly respected and experienced officer of the Red Cross, and his arguments were extremely logical—with one exception—they totally ignored the wishes and feelings of the children. This was basically the point which Riley Allen had to present to the Central Committee in Washington. When Allen arrived there, he found that the plan for temporary quartering had been definitely decided upon. A camp location near Bordeaux had been selected. Arrangements were already in work to prepare and stock the camp for occupancy. It seemed unlikely that anything could change them. Realizing the negative reaction the colony would surely display upon learning that they would not be going directly to a Baltic port, Allen insisted that a telegram be sent immediately to the *Yomei Maru* and the entire colony be informed. It was this telegram that Eversole read to the colony and then gave his somewhat tactless speech.

Eversole wired Allen to inform him of the anxiety of the Russian personnel and the older boys, as well as their need for an adequate dental outfit. Washington cabled Colonel Olds:

American Red Cross 13753
Considerable apprehension exists among Russians in America and older members Petrograd colony. Lewis has reported your assurance that attitude French Government entirely cooperative, but to allay feeling here need cable on subject from you. Children's colony needs complete dental outfit and full time dentist. Can you furnish or should we send one to Yomei Maru.

Keppel-Ferrand

Within five days, the following reply came:

September 2, 13753
We have excellent dentist here with equipment.

Olds

Needless to say, this was not the reassurance that Allen was looking for.

But complications were not caused by Red Cross decisions only — various government bureaus also helped to make things more difficult. The Commissioner General of Immigration, Caminetti, was as uncooperative as possible over arranging details for admission to the United States of several Russian children who were being claimed by relatives in America. Since the parents were no longer in Petrograd, Caminetti wanted proof that they did not exist. He was deathly afraid of any publicity on the matter. By this time the "Red Scare" in America had reached hysterical proportions. Government bureaucrats trembled at the very word, "Russian!" Mother Campbell, in her own picturesque fashion wrote, "We were as popular with the Immigration Department as a skunk at a lawn party!"

Allen boarded the *Yomei Maru* at New York after it had passed quarantine and was immediately showered with questions from the Russian personnel and children about whether they were going to France and not straight to Russia. He explained clearly that this was the plan, but that it was only temporary. Later he recorded that the general feeling on board was antagonistic, even though no protest was made at the time.

Riley Allen.

When Allen had first arrived in Washington, he set about arranging with the Red Cross for New York quarters for the colony, describing the successful housing at a military camp in San Francisco. After he had rejected several possibilities as unsuitable, Major General Bullard, Artillery Post Commander of the Department of the East, and a war hero of the war in France, stepped in and turned over Fort Wadsworth on Staten Island to house the colony in New York.

There the colony received the same happy and efficient care accorded them in San Francisco. Food, blankets, mosquito netting, and all other necessities were provided by the quartermaster's store, while scores of cooks, bakers, nurses, and a housekeeping staff supplemented the work of the POWs. There was no limitation by army authorities on visitors in and out of camp. The patience and good sense of the military guards and officers seemed endless, even at the unintentional and, at times, wilful disregard of the rules by the restless children and company personnel. Fortunately, the weather remained cool and pleasant, and the cleanliness of the camp contributed to the general improvement of minor health problems during the two week stay.

CHAPTER TWENTY

As the *Yomei Maru* docked at New York, an air of anticipation hung over the ship. The passengers, children, personnel, and POWs, were not disappointed when they were treated to a short ride on three U.S. Army boats to Fort Wadsworth on Staten Island.

Everything was ready for their arrival. Each child was assigned to a numbered bunk and was quickly settled in. A little while later, church services were given for them by the Russian Orthodox clergy and choir of St. Nicholas Cathedral.

Entertainment for their stay had been planned in advance under the auspices of the New York County, Bronx, and Richmond chapters of the American Red Cross, involving some of the most prestigious members of the New York business and social world, including Mrs. August Belmont.

That afternoon a "Russian Market" was presented at the camp by artists, painters, and actors of the "Russian Izba," a professional Russian entertainment group in New York City. Over 3000 visitors descended on Fort Wadsworth. They included Czarist supporters, pro and anti-Bolshevik sympathizers, and innumerable agitators of one persuasion or another. The entertainment was delightful, and all kinds of gifts such as candy, toys, and clothes, were presented to the children. Nevertheless, a great deal of harm was done.

Until 6 o'clock the children were surrounded by visitors, all giving their own misinformed and distorted versions of the Red Cross and the role of America in the saga of the colony. When they finally left, they left behind many unhappy and disturbed children and Russian teachers. One little girl sadly told Mother Campbell, "Mr. Karlieff told us that boys on the ship would be forced into the French army to fight against Russia, and we girls might be made white slaves if we landed in France!"

Mother Campbell tried to soothe the children by telling them that the Red Cross would never allow such things to happen, and they were being told lies just to confuse and frighten them, for the obvious purpose of causing trouble. But still the rumors persisted and the children remained upset. Fortunately, the daily entertainment that had been planned kept them fairly busy and diverted.

About two weeks before the children arrived in New York City, a campaign had been mounted to smear Red Cross activities in general and the handling of the children in particular. It was spearheaded by one Mr. L. Martins, head of the Russian Soviet Bureau, a self-appointed organization which acted as a go-between and spokesman in the United States for Lenin's government, since there were no diplomatic relations between the two countries. He had begun by telegraphing Keppel in Washington, who turned the matter over to Allen upon his arrival in New York.

Allen telephoned Martins, who demanded that he come to the Soviet Bureau office at once. Allen said he had too many appointments but would be glad to see anyone interested in the welfare of the children at the Red Cross office that morning. A man named Kenneth Durant came instead of Martins, and Allen outlined the whole history of the colony for him. He told him that Mr. Vilensky, the Soviet representative in Vladivostok, knew the Red Cross plans and had often visited Russian Island there. Durant demanded lists of the children and said he would locate their parents in Petrograd, to which Allen replied that lists were available to anyone. He then attacked the French plan and was told the reasons that the plan had been adopted. Durant argued vehemently against it. Further accusations followed.

He had heard that the children were ragged when they reached San Francisco. Allen's answer was that they deliberately wore old clothes on the ship because it was a freighter, and good clothes wore out too quickly—but in San Francisco all children were issued several changes of new clothes.

He attacked the American Red Cross for aiding Poles, and Allen patiently explained that the ARC had nothing to do with politics or factionalism.

He then asked Allen to take medical supplies into Russia with the children, to which Allen replied that each child had a first aid kit and that there was simply no more room on board for extra luggage.

But these attacks were only the beginning.

On August 23rd, Allen received a brief letter from Mr. Martins, a copy of which had been sent to Dr. Keppel and released to the New York press. The communication also enclosed some letters from Russians who purported to have talked with the children at the Russian

Market festivity and claimed that the children felt that they were prisoners of the Red Cross. Essentially Martins' letter was a protest about sending the children to France as tools of capitalist imperialism.

News of newspaper articles reached the children quickly from visitors and teachers, and they decided to form a committee to represent the colony to the ARC. One of the oldest boys, Leonty Duebner, was evidently well liked and trusted by the other children, so he was asked to compose a protest. He said later that he was chosen for his age, seriousness of purpose, and "savoir faire in Russian literary composition." The protest read:

The American Red Cross. The boys and girls of the Petrograd Children's Colony protest of the sending over of the colony to France. We boys and girls of the Petrograd Children's Colony declare to the American Red Cross that we will not go to France. We cannot go to a country, thanks to which the population of Russia died and is dying by the tens and hundreds of thousands from the consequence of the blockade which is sending to Poland weapons of war that take to their graves hundreds of thousands of best young Russian forces. We cannot live in a country where Russian soldiers who gave their blood during many years on the western front for the interest of France were shot or sent to hard labor in Africa. If the American Red Cross did not realize until now that between us is quite a big number of children who understand, we want by this protest to draw the attention of the American Red Cross to this fact and we demand that the American Red Cross should change its decision about the sending of the colony to France and would send us to Petrograd.

We wait for an answer from the American Red Cross at noon.
September 3, 1920

The protest was signed by 592 children of the colony, although Allen did not believe that it was actually written by the children, for it reached him on the evening of September 1st, only 48 hours after Martins' letter. Nonetheless, regardless of the sequence of events, he recognized the depth of the children's fear and decided to leave at once for Washington. The following morning he met with Dr. Keppel at his office.

It was obvious that the older boys were determined not to go to France, and only force could get them there. The ARC had neither the legal nor moral right to use it. Keppel was quite sympathetic and open to the viewpoint of the colony and suggested that they go to England first and send a small select group of boys to France to examine the proposed headquarters there and hopefully realize that France would not be an enemy to them.

With this in mind, they went to see the French Chargé d'Affaires to ask him to call on the British Consul at the Embassy with them to explain the predicament. To their surprise and discomfort, the Frenchman was cynically humorous about the whole affair.

"Well," he said, "it would seem to me to be merely an outburst of temper on the part of the children. In my opinion they ought to be spanked and put on the boat anyway. Or maybe it's just an exhibition of Bolshevism."

Allen quietly assured him that it was not temper on the part of the children but a real fear of military internment which, though wrong in its conception, was a sincere emotion. The Frenchman was still unconvinced and refused to go along, so Allen and Keppel went to the British Consul alone. He was far more understanding but had no constructive ideas to offer.

Still seeking some sound and helpful solution to the dilemma, they proceeded to the office of Mr. Bahmetief, the man who claimed to be the real Russian Ambassador and legal successor to the old Czarist Ambassador. He was strongly anti-Bolshevik but completely understood the children's fears. He even expressed the same feelings as the pro-Bolshevik Russians about sending the colony to France. Nevertheless, he advised that they talk quietly with the children and ignore their ultimatum. So far no one had come up with a practical solution to the problem.

In the meantime, all efforts to quietly quell the volume of protest failed. Newspapers continually carried stories about the children, their activities, the propaganda of diverse groups, and its effect upon the children. Letters kept pouring in to news editors, and Russian newspapers in New York thundered about Red Cross machinations. The colony representatives were deluged with written and verbal harassment and abuse which culminated in a near riot at Madison Square Garden a few days later.

Against this background of unrest, the children were being royally entertained by numerous private and public organizations. On August 30th they were taken sightseeing around the city, up and down Fifth Avenue and Broadway, stopping at Grant's Tomb and having a picnic lunch.

While most of the children took part in the excursion, one busload of older children, known as the Nepenina group, all friends of nine-year-old Elena Alexandrova, were taken to Mount Olivet Cemetery in a Russian section on Long Island for her burial. All her friends had expected her to recover rapidly after the emergency operation on the ship, but after landing in New York, her condition had worsened and she was taken to a hospital. Within two days she died of meningitis, believed to be caused by an insect bite in Panama. Many years later, her older brother, Sergei, recalled his grief on that beautiful clear day, and how he, Leonty, and many of the others wept uncontrollably as her body was committed to the earth during the emotionally charged Orthodox service.

On August 31st all the children boarded a big excursion steamer, the *Mandalay*, and were treated to a wonderful trip up the Hudson River. The boat had a large dance floor, and the children's orchestra alternated with the boat's orchestra for dancing. Lunch and dinner were served on board to the children and 100 visitors, including 40 Russian students from the New York public schools. They also landed at West Point and the children were given a tour through buildings.

The next day was supposed to be a day of rest, but so many visitors came, claiming to be friends or relatives, that there was little time for relaxation. By late afternoon, gifts and donations were heaped high in the Red Cross office at the Fort and distributed that day to the children. Then the following afternoon, they were all taken to a matinee at the Hippodrome, where the spectacle was so exciting that it was almost impossible to calm them down.

By September 3rd, the excessive publicity about the children began to have bad effects. A visit to the Bronx zoo that had been announced in the newspapers drew a mob of the curious, all of whom wanted to see and talk to the children. About 5000 people pushed and shoved, shouted and pointed, and tried to thrust gifts and food at them so that the children were unable to see the animals and had to be raced through several of the buildings—much to their disgust. The whole excursion was marred by the well-meaning but misguided actions of the populace.

Even before the children arrived, some 40 Russian organizations in New York had petitioned the New York County Red Cross organization to allow local Russians to do something for the children on their own. Permission was given, since at that time there was no hint of the coming attacks by Martins and the press as to Red Cross motives. As the time drew nearer, Allen considered cancelling the affair, as it was now obvious that it was becoming a propaganda circus. But he was disinclined to hurt or offend innocent Russian organizations and decided to take a chance and go ahead. He did take the precaution of quietly speaking to the older boys the night before, asking them not to provoke a riot or demonstrate in any way. The boys all promised.

At 2 o'clock in the afternoon of September 4th the children arrived at Madison Square Garden, and the Russian Symphony Orchestra began a musical program. All streets leading to the Garden were heavily patrolled by the police and were jammed with people, mostly Russians, who had waited for hours to get in. A big police squad had to push through the crowd outside to open a path for the children. As they entered the packed hall, 12,000 voices erupted in part cheers and part defiant screaming against the Red Cross. As group after group came in, the yells increased in volume. The ushers and police were hard pressed to keep the crowds from the children as people began pushing packages of food, candy, and cigarettes at them. Then some others started to pass hats around the crowd to collect money for the "urgent need of the colony." Needless to say, that money never got to the Red Cross, nor was it needed, but only served as a propaganda trick of implied criticism that the children were not really being taken care of.

The children were seated in front of the stage which was draped with a huge American flag. The Symphony Orchestra bravely continued its program, with the director constantly stopping to ask the crowd to be quiet. His efforts were useless. They finally quieted down when Alexander Brailovsky, the Chairman of the occasion got up to give his speech. He was editor of "Russian Voice" and a known radical agitator. He had shown a polite text to Mr. Burrall, chairman of the New York County Red Cross Chapter, who had O.K.'d it. But he promptly departed from the text and attacked the Red Cross connection with imperialist France. Next, he introduced Martins as the "Russian Ambassador," although he had promised Burrall that he would be the only speaker. Martins promptly proceeded to shout about "taking all measures to get the Petrograd children's colony out of the hands of the imperialist Red Cross. Cheering, clapping, and booing followed this tirade and Allen nervously feared a riot. But his talk with the older boys the night before had its effect. They kept their word, even when other people were screaming and pushing against the police barriers.

Suddenly Brailovsky led two older boys and a girl to the platform to make a speech. The crowd went wild for a moment and then quieted completely to hear these children. Fortunately, Allen's words had reached their hearts, for they each just thanked the Russian people in New York for their entertainment and interest in the colony. They were followed by Peter de George who also expressed thanks on behalf of everybody but made no criticism or protest against the Red Cross.

The noise in the auditorium proved too much for the Russian Symphony Orchestra, who walked off without attempting to complete their program. The Russian Izba Chorus next tried to sing but soon gave up when no one paid any attention to them, and the crowd again tried to force their way in among the children to press gifts and food upon them.

Although the ship's log faithfully recorded the facts of the afternoon's events, it was Mother Campbell's diary which gave a detailed account of her emotional reactions to the experience. Brailovsky's heated denunciations had already stirred up the crowd before Martins began to speak. Now he not only announced that certain measures would be taken to get the children out of the hands of the American Red Cross, but villified the organization and the American personnel connected with it. He questioned the motives of Riley Allen, Mother Campbell, and the rest of the American staff. Mother Campbell became highly upset, and Helen Domerschikoff, the Russian teacher, began to weep.

A Russian sitting beside Mother Campbell said, "Lady, don't pay any attention to this, it's just a publicity stunt."

She cried back, "Sure it is, and I'd like to tell him so!"

"Do you want me to take you around to talk to him?" the man offered.

"Indeed I do!" and with that she followed her new acquaintance to the entrance behind the speaker's platform and confronted Martins.

With tears still rolling down her face, she began speaking in her faulty Russian about how hard the Red Cross worked to keep the children well and happy and how tough it was to get clothes for them in Russia. She told him that his statements about American personnel spending the Red Cross money on themselves and keeping the youngsters in rags were out-and-out lies.

"Compared to New York children they look like beggars!" he shouted.

"Compared to the children we left behind in Vladivostok, they look like royalty!" she retorted snappily.

Her diary continued: "I was just going good in my argument, when I noticed newspaper reporters with pads and pencils, eager for a story. They pulled at my arm, asking, 'Who are you? Tell us what you're so angry about?' I told them, 'Shut up!' and went on cussing the speaker.

Out off nowhere popped Riley Allen. 'Good God, Mother—you can't do this!' and he pulled me away and back to the children."

Pandemonium was breaking out, so at a given signal, the children regrouped and marched out of the auditorium without too much confusion. Miraculously, when they got back to Fort Wadsworth, not one child was missing or left behind in the crowds.

Everybody welcomed the next day, Sunday, as a chance to rest and get over the unsettling experience of the Madison Square Garden disturbances. Except for a morning church service at the New York Cathedral, the remainder of the day was spent quietly at the fort.

CHAPTER TWENTY-ONE

Earlier, on August 21st, Allen had set in motion another plan to make the colony's visit a memorable one by asking the Red Cross to get in touch with Dr. Stockton Axson, a presidential intimate, to ask if he could get President and Mrs. Wilson to send greetings and signed pictures to the children. At this point President Wilson was very ill and incommunicado, but Mrs. Wilson was reached and did send the following letter, which unfortunately mentioned the trip to France, and so misfired:

The White House
Washington, D.C.

August 24, 1920

My Dear Mr. Rule:
Doctor Axson has shown to Mrs. Wilson and me your letter to him of August 24th, and I write to beg that you will convey to the colony of Petrograd children which has been in the care of the Red Cross Commission to Siberia during the past year, and is now being transported by the Commission to Brest, France, our warmest greeting. I am sure that you may say to them that the hearts of all the people in the United States go out in the tenderest sympathy and that they will always hope that their future will be happy enough to make some amends for the past.
Cordially and sincerely yours,
Edith Bolling Wilson and Woodrow Wilson

On September 6th, the children were invited to an affair for the presentation by Junior Red Cross officers of autographed photographs of President Wilson and Mrs. Wilson and a reading of the letter.

By now the stream of visitors overrunning the camp was becoming a disruptive and distracting element for all the children. When the presentation was held on the parade grounds at the fort, although many Russians and Americans attended, there was a notable shortage of colonists. The older boys completely boycotted the affair. And when the reference to France was read, there was a noticeable restlessness among those children present.

Along with the official programs there were also a number of slide illustrated lectures given at the fort on American history and geography, and many films were shown. But in spite of public and private entertainment, discipline was breaking down at an alarming rate. Groups of boys would simply disappear for hours, or occasionally, even overnight. Nicholas Ivanov, later one of the leading agronomists in the USSR and a specialist on lima beans, said he spent his days at the Museum of Natural History. Leonty Duebner took it upon himself to visit Red Cross headquarters personally and actually met many of the ladies involved in the colony work. In fact, his friendship with Mrs. William Draper proved instrumental later on in helping him to leave the USSR and finish his education in France in 1924. Attempts to control these trips only met with sullenness and muttering about "rights."

Pressure on Allen continued unabated. On the same day as the presentation of the Wilsons' letter, the Russian teachers sent him a petition declaring that all the teachers supported the children's protests and actions. They said that they would refuse to teach any more if force were used to send the children to France, and that they would not recognize the authority of the American Red Cross over the education of the Russian children. The document was signed by a majority of the teachers.

Dr. Keppel, who had come up from Washington on September 4th, had witnessed the Madison Square Garden chaos. He cabled Colonel Olds and Dr. Ferrand in Europe, outlining the American situation and saying it would be advisable to plan for an alternative English or Baltic port. Olds replied, still arguing for the French stay, but agreed to go to England to check out the possibility for a temporary landing. Allen also contacted Colonel Ryan, the ARC Baltic Commissioner, about the feasibility of going directly to Finland.

An executive committee meeting of the ARC held on September 7th heard Dr. Keppel present the situation and its problems in an organized manner. The committee gave Dr. Keppel carte blanche to go ahead and settle the matter as he deemed best. By now he had come to the conclusion that the destination of the ship had to be changed. He therefore cabled Colonel Olds of his decision. Time was getting very short because the *Yomei Maru* was supposed to sail on September 11th and her clearance papers had yet to be registered with the destination declared.

On September 9th, Keppel authorized an announcement to the newspapers and the colony that the encampment in France was abandoned. The ship, for administrative reasons, would not sail directly to Petrograd but would land at a neutral port on the Baltic. The Baltic port was unnamed simply because no one knew yet which it would be. The following day a final resolution was sent by the teacher-student committee of five, which Allen forwarded to Keppel. He had explained to the committee that most of the requests had already been complied with, and that Mr. Martins, allegedly representing the Soviet government, was in touch with Red Cross officials in New York and Washington. The resolution, as recorded in the log, reads:

Resolution adopted by the Petrograd Children's Colony on September 10, 1920.

We, the undersigned, Executive Committee, duly appointed by 780 children and 37 teachers who accompany said children, at a meeting of the said children and teachers held this day, September 10th, 1920, at Fort Wadsworth, Staten Island, United States of America, after being duly authorized and commissioned by the said assembly, do certify that the following resolution was unanimously passed by the said children and teachers and that we were directed to forward said resolution to the parties mentioned in said resolution.

During the year 1918, while a famine was threatening the city of Petrograd, we were sent by a committee of the Soviet Government and of our parents to the Ural district in order that we might receive proper nourishment and support. We were then settled in small colonies of children in that district. When the Czechoslovaks began their campaign against Russia in 1918, their operations cut off our colonies from communication with European Russia, and as Kolchak and his Czechoslovak allies began their retreat, we were moved along with the retreating armies across Siberia, without our consent and contrary to the repeated protests of our parents. We were shifted about in the vicinity of Vladivostok and finally were interned on Russian Island opposite Vladivostok whence 780 of us have now been brought to New York by the American Red Cross on the Japanese steamer *Yomei Maru.*

After many disappointments we were about to embark on a journey for a Baltic port which we were informed was to be Copenhagen. Realizing that no obstacles should ordinarily lie in the way of the Red Cross organization to get into communication with even a belligerent government, we cannot conceive of any reasons why a ship flying a Red Cross flag should not sail directly for the port of Petrograd, which is our home city. Having taken all these matters into consideration, the colony of the children and teachers, this day in assembly convened, has declared the following to be its unanimous resolution.

Resolved: that the colony of the children and teachers accepts the word of the American Red Cross officials and their promises, and interprets the same to signify that they will be returned to their homes in Petrograd without any further delay:

That the colony demands that a communication be sent to a committee of their parents in Petrograd, through the representative of the Soviet Government in New York. The colony is informed by the said representative that he will gladly cooperate with the American Red Cross to make that possible:

That having been taken by different belligerent forces without their consent, having been helped by Red Cross bodies for a period of about two years without their consent, having been kept away from their families for over two years, and shifted from port to port, the children's colony feels that in the decision of all matters of importance, such as the destination to which they are to be taken, they will not be obedient to any other body except their own parents' committee:

That the communication aforementioned to be sent through the representative of the Soviet Government in New York, shall be to the effect that the American Red Cross will meet the parents' committee at some convenient Baltic port and, through the committee of parents, arrange for the final transportation and disposition of the children's colony.

Further resolved: that a committee of five consisting of S. Dobrova, E. Mazun, L. Duebner, F. Zabedchekof, A. Kamenskaji is to be authorized to transmit a copy of the resolution to the

Atlantic Division of the American Red Cross, to the International Red Cross in Geneva, to the representative of the Russian Soviet Government in New York City, to the Secretary of State of the United States of America, and to the Committee of Russian Organizations.

Be it further resolved that the Children's and Teachers' Colony is deeply appreciative of the good care and hospitality of the American Red Cross and of the numerous favors and acts of kindness shown to them and that it is the hope of the children's colony's assembly that the children may take with them and cherish unimpaired this feeling of gratitude and appreciation to the American Red Cross.

S. Dobrova	A. Kamenskaji	F. Zabodchekov
L. Duebner	E. Mazun	

As the official announcement of the boat's schedule to go to a Baltic port seeped down among the children, tension noticeably decreased. Meanwhile, preparations to outfit and organize the children for the last lap of the journey continued. Many gifts of clothing had been presented to the children. Alexandra Gorbochova was given a white silk dress with a sash of embroidered roses on a blue background. When she returned to Russia, her family could not believe that such beautiful things still existed in the world, and she kept the sash all her life. Ivan Semenov remembered being given a beautiful suit which had a semi-military look to it, and which he wore proudly with a green army shirt that came with it. Of far more interest to Ivan, however, was the gift of a full set of instruments for a brass band presented to him and his friends. To him, the high point of this gift was the fact that it included a Neopolitan contrabass with frets, which at last replaced the one he left behind in Turgayak when they all had to get away hastily because Kolchak's forces had crumbled. Now he could finally join the orchestra of two mandolins, a guitar, and one contrabass and play some of the new songs he had heard in New York. Mr. Bramhall had taught the children the "one-step dance," and between New York and Finland the boat rocked to new melodies and dancing children. The tall lanky figure of Bramhall dancing with a little girl on the deck of the *Yomei Maru* made everyone laugh and was remembered by many of them later.

The organizing, buying, and checking of children's wardrobes fell to Mother Campbell. Since growing youngsters always outgrew their shoes, the Red Cross asked the Coward Shoe Company to come and measure each child for a "good sense" pair.

After getting 150 wriggling bodies into a long line, she turned around looking for the clerks and bellowed, "Come on you shoe boys! Snap into it! I can't hold these live wires indefinitely."

Everyone laughed but began working. Just before sailing, she went to the Coward store herself and was greeted like a long lost grandmother.

When she tried to pay, her money was refused by an older man who said, "Your money isn't any good here! You can't pay for these!"

Attempting to argue that donations to the Red Cross should not include her, the man answered, "Anyone who calls me 'Boy' as you did the other morning is welcome to a pair of shoes at my expense. Been years since that name's been used for me!"

It was Mr. Coward himself whom Mother Campbell had hustled to work with his workers at the camp.

The spirit of protest seemed to be contagious. During the second week at the fort, and at the height of the children's protest, two POWs walked into her office with the following paper: "We, the former POWs have signed a paper asking that we be given more full assurance that we will not be taken to France where we will, without doubt, be held as war prisoners again." Mother Campbell, much annoyed, told them they had the ARC's word that they would be protected, and had not the ARC kept its word so far?

This did not satisfy the prisoners and, in a moment of pique, she said sarcastically, "I presume that if we get a personal letter from our President Wilson you folks will be thoroughly satisfied?"

"Yes," they said. "That would please us very much." Clicking their heels and bowing, they left.

Mother Campbell turned that matter over to Allen when he returned from Washington, but he said, in effect, that he simply did not have the time to deal with the situation—and what did she think?

She was extremely irritated, and said, "They've done good work for us, but somehow I feel that it would be right to replace them. We took them from those horrible prison camps, we've clothed them and fed them well, besides paying them wages which they never could have had elsewhere. We've also given them letters assuring them of repatriation. In fact, I think we've carried them around on a silver platter, and there doesn't seem to be any appreciation!" Allen simply told her that she should make any decision she thought correct and he would back her up.

At this point, Mother Campbell called the New York Police Department and explained the situation. They promised to round up the POWs and dump them back on the ship—a solution which she realized would not exactly help with the rest of the work on the trip back. When appealed to, the Immigration Department offered to send them back to Vladivostok, but it would cost $1000 each. Finally, she appealed to Dr. Keppel to write a reassuring letter about repatriation.

But he said, tongue in cheek, "You'll have to take it and read it to them, Mother Campbell, because I know President Wilson is too busy!"

Within a day, despite his teasing, he gave her a letter. She then called all the POWs together, got up on a stump, and told them that she was hurt because they didn't trust the ARC after all the kind and generous treatment they had received, and that she didn't have a letter from President Wilson, but one from another very important man. She proceeded to read:

September 8, 1920

The National American Red Cross has no hesitation whatever in assuring the former prisoners of war who are employees of the Petrograd Children's Colony Expedition, that they are under the fullest protection of the ARC, which guarantees them safety and their repatriation to their homes without molestation or seizure by foreign governments. The *Yomei Maru* will not call at ports where these employees could be taken from the steamer as war prisoners. The ARC wishes to extend to these employees an expression of appreciation of their faithful services with the Petrograd Children's Colony together with the reassurance that so long as they continue in the employ of the Red Cross and during the time of their repatriation, they will be afforded the earliest opportunities for return to their homes through channels by which the ARC, in association with other American agencies, is already repatriating former prisoners of war.

Frederick P. Keppel, Acting Chairman

The letter was accepted with great relief. A few POWs did run away before the ship left, but the rest went back to work and got the ship cleaned up and ready to sail. The actual clean-up was led by Mother Campbell.

One day when she was covered by a big apron and scrubbing oilcloth covers on the dining tables, she suddenly heard Keppel's booming voice, "Well, well! Mother Campbell must have wanted to get to Europe in the worst way—and I'll say she got it!"

The ARC proceeded to outfit all the rest of the POWs, except the Hungarians who had already been taken care of by the Hungarian Relief Committee. Many of these men were doctors, lawyers, politicians, as well as a number of musicians. Just before the ship sailed, Allen told them that he estimated their length of service to be another 35 to 40 days from the date of sailing out of New York. After that they could expect repatriation.

One deeply tragic incident took place just before the ship was to sail. On September 9th at 7:15 A.M., Private Jack Berhim was coming off guard duty and on his way back to his own quarters. As he rounded the corner, one of the boys, 14-year-old Pavel Nicolaeff, jumped out at him with a broomstick simulating a gun and smartly presented arms. Falling into the game, Berhim unslung his own rifle from his shoulder, snapped to attention, and presented arms. Inadvertently, his finger touched the trigger, the gun went off, and Pavel dropped dead with a bullet in his head. The soldier shouted and ran to the guard house, grabbed a first aid kit, and then turned himself over to the guard, saying that he had killed a child.

Private Berhim, who was Russian born, had become a naturalized American citizen and then joined the U.S. Army. Speaking Russian, he had made friends with many of the children and often played with them around the camp when he was off duty. Thus it was not unnatural that Pavel had tried to surprise him.

Realizing the seriousness of the incident and how the publicity could adversely affect the whole trip, Allen asked for an immediate Court of Inquiry the same day. By 9 A.M. a board was in session, composed of three officers and three ARC personnel: Coulter, Ruaga, and Davidson. There had been several witnesses to the incident, and when Olga Nesdarova gave her testimony, she presented a written statement by two of the boys who witnessed the accident. She asked that the soldier be released. The ingenuousness of the document clearly showed its unquestionable veracity:

P. Nicolaeff with a stick in his hand was demonstrating to the soldier the military methods. The soldier began to demonstrate too, and when he was raising his rifle to his shoulder, it suddenly went off. The soldier did not expect this. Then they tell that he was looking for a bandage but could not find it. Some say he wished to stab himself but he could not pull his bayonet as he was very much excited. He ran to the office and exclaimed, "Kill me!" as the interpreter translated it to them. All the boys who knew the soldier say that he was very good to them and that he always used to play with them.

All the boys feel that the soldier did this without intention and this happened quite accidentally.

All boys of the eight barracks agree with this.

Signed for all boys—V. Souev

I herewith confirm that this is a correct translation of the statement of eyewitnesses of the above incident.

N. Pazlozkaya

The above statement was followed by one from the teachers:

Fort Wadsworth, September 9, 1920
To the Russian Colony
Today, September 9th, in the Children's Colony occurred a terrible accident, a member of the Colony, Pavel Nicolaeff, was killed by an accidental shot of the guard.

After having looked through the conditions under which the boy was killed and after having taken into consideration the constant friendliness of the soldier toward the children, the Council of Teachers and Educators of the Colony decided to apply to the Court Martial with the following petition.

After having discussed the accident in the Children's Colony which resulted in the death of a boy, the Council of Teachers and Educators of the Colony confirming in one voice the constant friendliness of the soldier toward the children apply to the Court of Justice to grant full clemency to the soldier.

In forming this the Council of Teachers and Educators of the Colony ask the Russian Colony to partake in their grief and not to believe any other rumors.

signed: Chairman, S. Dobrova
Secretary, A. Bouldireva

Detailed testimony was taken of all concerned—those who had witnessed the event, and there were several—those who heard it—those who treated the boy and later arrested Bernhim. They all told the same story, and when Private Bernhim was examined, his genuine grief moved everybody. A verdict was handed down that the shot was fired unintentionally, although the soldier should not have had his gun unlocked. The Board believed that the man had not been properly instructed.

General sadness, but accompanied by relief, was felt by everyone, particularly in view of the fact that the children's and teachers' documents could be used to answer any unseemly charges made by outside agitators. Funeral services were held at Fort Wadsworth late that afternoon, and the following morning at the Russian Cathedral in Manhattan, conducted by Orthodox priests. His body was buried with Elena Alexandrova at Mount Olivet Cemetery.

CHAPTER TWENTY-TWO

The *Yomei Maru* was scheduled to sail from New York at noon on September 11th. Steam had been kept up the preceding 48 hours, and at 10:53 A.M. the children began to board. Little Alexandra Medvedeva Gorbochova had other things to think about than just a white silk dress and sash during her stay in New York. During the passage of the Panama Canal, her older sister, Maria, who had been a teacher with the children from the beginning of the saga, had fallen seriously ill. The diagnosis was mastoiditis, an infection of the bone behind her right ear, and during the trip to New York, her condition had worsened. She had been taken from the ship in an ambulance to a hospital where an operation was performed. All during the stay in New York, Alexandra visited the hospital each day, but Maria's condition did not improve. Now there was a decision to be made—should the young woman sail with the *Yomei Maru* or stay in New York. But Maria herself had the final word, and the children were delighted to see her carried up the gangplank on a stretcher to the waiting ship.

As the last child was checked on board, Bramhall looked over the list and reported that eight children and nurses had remained legally in New York, claimed by relatives and friends. Two boys, Appolon Vorobioff and Dmitri Bouyanoff, deliberately missed the ship but were found later and taken care of by the Red Cross. Sixteen former POWs were absent without leave, but last minute negotiations with the Department of Immigration, and Commissioner Comminetti in particular, permitted the *Yomei Maru* to sail without them. The eagerness of the Immigration Department to get rid of the *Yomei Maru* at all costs, even though some of her personnel were in the States illegally, was evidenced by the letters and calls to the New York Bureau from Washington. At this point, the articles in the New York newspapers had reached a peak of hysteria, charging Red Cross administrators with kidnapping plots. Unscrupulous editors published hundreds of letters and editorials in both Russian and American newspapers accusing the Red Cross of dishonesty, political maneuvering, and downright criminality, which only resulted in the Soviet Government increasing their pressure to take the children. Word of Pavel Nikolaeff's death frightened government agencies enough to galvanize them into immediate action, so Allen's fears of red tape holding up the sailing came to naught.

The steamer was informed that she could leave at once, no matter how many were missing from the original list of children and personnel. Allen happily rejoined the ship for the last leg of the journey, accompanied by his wife and Dr. W. H. Gutelius, a dentist and former Director of Civilian relief in Eastern Siberia. To make up for the loss of eighteen people, older boys were selected to do dining room and kitchen work and put on the payroll at $5.00 a month each.

The first day out of New York was quiet. So many parting gifts had been given that the children spent their time opening, playing with, and repacking their new possessions. Inspection was not attempted until all the baggage could be rearranged. But at that time, and for no apparent reason, a general malaise and depression came over the ship. Allen attributed it to the excitement of New York and the barrage of propaganda to which the children had been subjected. Discipline was lax, and considerable sullenness was displayed by both the children and the Russian teachers. The POWs caused no further trouble, but some teachers asked for reassignments, claiming they were unable to control some of the groups of children. One of the girls, Larissa Vorobieva, had slipped away from Fort Wadsworth and had been gone for several days. She said she had been with friends but had refused to identify them. Allen had a stern talk with her and assigned her to work in the linen room without pay. He then wrote in the ship's log that over twenty boys had also been absent in New York without permission, "but it would be a hopeless task to penalize all of them." Double standards seemed unavoidable.

By September 13th the ship's routine was put into action, although the cleanup duty left much to be desired. New brass tags had to be issued because many had been lost. Also, new life boat personnel had to be appointed and trained to replace the 16 POWs who had deserted in New York. The sea turned rough the next morning, and the decks and hatches were lined with children bearing "expressions of mortal sickness worthy of a much more serious cause."

The older boys resorted to calisthenics up on deck to work off excess energy. Cables were sent from America and England to identify those parents who wanted to have their children dropped off in France and sent to friends or relatives. In spite of the children's and teachers' objections, a brief stop had to be made at Brest in France on the way to the Baltic Sea because it was necessary to unload and take on new cargo, as well as to refuel. This was a means of helping to defray the $5,000 per day cost of renting the ship.

On September 15th, the soul of Maria Gorbochova slipped from her body with no warning. Dr. Coulter was sitting in the dispensary that evening at 7:30 when a nurse's aide noticed that she seemed worse. Before Coulter could reach her bedside, she had passed away. Some of the Russian personnel were asked to take over and carry out funeral arrangements according to Russian customs. The nurses dressed the body, and it was placed on the poop deck. All night, relays of Russians read prayers. At 11 o'clock the following morning, and at 2 o'clock in the afternoon, small choruses of boys and girls sang hymns.

Allen asked Mother Campbell if she knew how to make a shroud.

Sorrowfully she replied, "No, I don't. But I'm sure we can fashion something."

Procuring sailcloth from the Captain, she made one with the help of some of the other women. The body was slipped into it and heavy iron bars were placed at the bottom of the sack. A group of the older boys asked permission to sing at the final service.

Just before 11 o'clock that night, the ship's motors were stopped. A Red Cross flag was draped over the small body which was then placed upon a sort of stretcher, and, as Allen recited appropriate prayers, it was propelled gently over the rail and into the water. It was a highly emotional moment for most of the colony who witnessed the funeral. One of the teachers even attempted to throw herself overboard but was restrained and taken to the hospital, while several children succumbed to hysterics. Most, however, remained calm and controlled. The location of the burial was carefully recorded in the ship's log as Longitude 50-20-0, Latitude North 42-12-0, SSE 310 miles from Cape Race. Many years later, Alexandra, her younger sister, spoke with bitterness of some boys telling her that they saw sharks jump up and grab the body. Poor Alexandra, at the age of 14, believed it.

Strangely enough, after that the mood of the ship completely changed. Although unrest was evidenced increasingly as they neared France, the general depression and sullenness disappeared. Sometimes wild rumors flew around the ship, but Allen soon found a way to cope with them. For instance, one story which was very prevalent was that the *Yomei Maru* was carrying munitions to France to help in the war against Russia. Allen simply repeated the story to the Russian teachers and personnel, treating it as a huge joke, and something so ridiculous that he knew no one would believe it. But in the ship's log he wrote that "in the present state of mind of the older and younger Russians, they were ready to believe almost any wild tale."

On September 18th, trouble again broke out between the Japanese crew and the older boys. Some of the latter, having had their regular drill under Mr. Woods, stayed on deck when it was finished and continued running up and down. The Captain's mess boy wanted to carry some food through the narrow passage by the ship's galley and tried to stop the running boys. When they refused to stop, he grabbed a small hatch grating, about three feet square, and brandished it. The boys bumped into it, and a pushing match ensued. Fifteen-year-old Peter Orloff ran around the grating and struck the Japanese boy in the eye with his fist. A three hour investigation took place in the Captain's cabin.

At first the mess boy said it was not Peter, but Peter confessed immediately. The Captain said the Russian boys had ill feelings against the Japanese seamen and that, during the hearing, they were nonchalant in their attitude. Allen disagreed with this on both counts. He believed that the incident happened in the heat of the moment. The Captain demanded that Peter be put in the jail. This, Allen said, was too drastic, because the whole incident arose from the boys bumping into the grate and both sides pushing and shoving. The Captain demanded that Peter apologize, and the athletics be restricted to one side of the ship. Orloff did apologize immediately and seemed genuinely sorry he had hurt the mess boy. But the mess boy, who was sitting at the table during the session with his eye bandaged and holding an ice pack to it, refused to accept the apology. Again an apology was offered both by Allen and Peter, who admitted it was his fault. The hospital said that the blow to the eye had done no serious damage, but the eye was swollen and discolored. The session ended, but the Captain was still noticeably upset.

The next morning Allen called all the big boys together and explained the gravity of the situation. They reported that the mess boy had thrown pans of water at them twice when they were sitting near the galley, and another time had thrown dirty water at them. Bramhall, who had seen the dirty water incident, testified that the Russian boys were not making fun of him as he claimed, but were minding their own business and talking quietly with each other. All passageways were to be kept clear from now on, but the boys were still allowed to sit on top of the hatches. That afternoon, when Allen had gone to his cabin for a nap—he had been patrolling most of the night—Dr. Gutelius burst in and told him that the mess boy had come out of the galley brandishing a gun at the boys. He was obviously looking for trouble. The Captain promptly sent for the boatswain who had a talk with the Japanese boy. But Allen also cleared Hatch #4 of boys from then on and said they could sit on Hatch #5 or the poop deck. Day and night watches were instituted, and all American men and women assigned turns. Mother Campbell was particularly angry with the boy for adding a watch to her other duties, giving her almost no rest at all. However, the Russian boys went out of their way to avoid trouble and to keep peace.

That evening Bramhall spotted the mess boy going to the quarters underneath the poop deck, where he pulled out a gun and fired three shots. Leonty Duebner still remembered the shots years later and the fear felt by the children. The Captain was alerted and, at the same time, Allen said he wanted to send some wirelesses to New York but did not specify their nature. This implied threat made its impression on the Captain who said he had taken the revolver away. He even showed Allen a small gun which was locked in his safe. Allen asked how it was possible for the boy to have just fired three shots if the only revolver was there in his safe. He told the Captain that the Russian boys were under control, and that Peter Orloff had been confined to his own hatch since the incident. After all, it was Japanese sailors who were causing provocations by flourishing knives or a revolver. The Captain still claimed that the Russian boys felt ill will against the Japanese crews, but Allen insisted that there was no evidence of that, and the boys were behaving admirably.

The ship's physician reported that the mess boy's eye was healed, and he did not need the eye patch any more—but he still continued to wear it. The doctor said that there was no evidence of any eye injury and just a slight discoloration remained. The mess boy went too far in his demands, even for the Japanese sailors, who finally turned on him and gave him a good old-fashioned spanking, much to Mother Campbell's delight. One last incident occurred during an evening movie on deck, when the mess boy appeared with a flash light and shoved it into the faces of various children, obviously looking for Peter Orloff. The Captain was informed within a few minutes and nothing more happened, but the strict guard was maintained for the rest of the trip.

By September 20th things seemed much improved. Allen recorded that a number of the Russian personnel were suddenly expressing fear of conditions in Petrograd and decided that they would like to stay in France or England. This, of course, was a complete reversal of their earlier objections to stopping in "imperialistic France with its warlike acts." Mrs. Mazun, who had led the fight against the Red Cross over the idea of landing in France and had demanded that the children and personnel be taken straight to Petrograd, now asked Allen to wire her husband to meet her in Brest and get visas to stay in France. But, although Allen wired ahead, the French government refused all permits except for the few which had been arranged in New York.

The *Yomei Maru* arrived at Brest on September 25th and quarantine officers came aboard with Major Eversole, who had gone to France before the ship had left New York. Several other Red Cross officials also came aboard. Allen had telegraphed earlier that it would be necessary to take the children off the boat for two days and bring the steamer to dock to unload the cargo and to take on more coal, but his message mysteriously had arrived only the night before, and therefore no preparations had been made. After much discussion, the Red Cross succeeded in getting a berth at a dock with a covered warehouse adjacent to a place where the children could be sheltered and eat their meals during the day and only sleep on board at night, leaving the ship free to be unloaded.

The following day tables were removed to the warehouse and dining areas set up. At the end of the dock, fences had to be erected hastily to keep back the curious and also to prevent any of the boat personnel from jumping ship. Major Eversole brought papers and documents proving that several of the children had parents in France and could be legally left there. Andri and Sergei Fede and Konstantin Frebelius, plus three Russian nurses, were all happily met by parents and relatives to begin a new life as emigres in France.

While the cargo was being unloaded, the Russian personnel complained bitterly about not being able to leave the wharf. The children were given the freedom of the warehouse and one third of the large wharf. They immediately organized games, their orchestra played, and some of them sang and danced to the music. The first day passed swiftly, but by the second, the grumbling and dissatisfaction of the Russian men and women began to affect the children who also started complaining.

In one corner of the warehouse, baled hay was piled high to the ceiling. Many of the children decided to climb up on it and then jump down. There were several bad falls, but no bones were broken.

The third morning Mother Campbell spotted a huge box of wool being unloaded with other Red Cross supplies being sent to the Paris headquarters. It gave her a brilliant idea. She quickly obtained permission to keep several cases out of the Paris shipment, as well as "liberating" a box of knitting needles. Soon all the girls happily lined up for wool and needles, and then, sitting on the bales of hay, got busy making garments to take to their families in Petrograd. Not to be outdone, a number of the boys joined in, and the occupation kept them busy until they got to Finland.

Behind this activity a real drama was being played out. On Monday, September 28th, Colonel Olds, the European Commissioner, arrived at the ship and spent the entire day on the *Yomei Maru*. First he inspected the ship, watched the children at play, and met many of the personnel. He then closeted himself with Allen for the rest of the day, eating lunch and dinner on board. Olds still claimed that he was loath to give up his plan of keeping the children in France until direct contact with each parent was made. He repeatedly stressed the dreadful living conditions in Petrograd. He again stated his belief that many of the parents were outside of Russia but admitted that he had no proof of this. He felt that if the ship landed at a Baltic port, the Red Cross would lose control, and the Soviet government would force its influence over the weak Baltic state and take over the children, with no guarantee of their safe return. The propaganda of the Soviet government would then know no bounds, and the Red Cross would be blamed for all sorts of imaginary crimes.

Allen had to go over all his original arguments again. He told Olds of the difficulties in New York with both children and personnel, and said that if Olds persisted, they would have to be kept within high walls with guards, for some of the children would be bound to escape. No contact with outsiders could be maintained, and the children would be subject to all sorts of pressures. In fact, all the constructive work that the Red Cross had done with them would be lost. The bitter resentment of the whole colony would vastly outweigh any feelings of gratitude or warmth that the children now felt. Even more, the ideally liberal but firm administration practiced over the colony for the past two years would be completely misinterpreted by the world at large, as well as the Soviet government.

Allen stated that he understood Olds' concern over the conditions in Petrograd but the Red Cross had given its word to repatriate the children and, the decision having been made, the question could not be reopened. Announcing that the *Yomei Maru* would now proceed to the Baltic, Allen steered the conversation into constructive ways to deliver the children.

Colonel Ryan, the Baltic Commissioner, was to be told to contact Baltic ports at once. Vyborg or Helsingfors were felt to be the two most likely ports, and the *Yomei Maru* was to start off immediately. Allen suggested that the Soviet representatives of the children in Petrograd and the so-called Parents' Committee be contacted to ask for their help. The more communication the Red Cross had with various groups, the harder it would be for the Soviet government to demand a wholesale delivery without any assurance that parents were waiting. Olds agreed with that and said that the Red Cross could not be tied to any strict deadline for the delivery, but contact with the parents had to be established first. Lists of children and parents were to be circulated as much as possible, especially to the Parents' Committee in Petrograd.

The conversation also touched on the needed contract extension of the *Yomei Maru*, the method of returning the POWs, and changes in agreements with the personnel to extend their working deadline and to assume responsibility for getting all of them home at Red Cross expense. To forestall further complications, Allen asked Olds for a written agreement of their plans and the line of authority. The meeting ended with their visit to the other Red Cross administrators on the ship to outline and explain their projected plan of action, which included the understanding that, once in the Baltic, Colonel Ryan would be in charge.

On Monday, loading and unloading continued. Six big boys, losing their fear of France and its supposed imperialism, ran off. They returned later in the evening, having seen the city and bought some postcards. Tighter security was introduced, and the only unpleasantness came from several Russian teachers who demanded to be allowed to see Brest, in spite of the fact that they were the ones who had originally led the protest in New York. Since they had no visas or passports, Allen refused their demand.

Early on Tuesday morning, the *Yomei Maru* left Brest. A French pilot came on board and stayed with them until they reached the Straits of Dover, after which an English pilot took over. Now the most dangerous part of the voyage began. Not only were the waters rough, the channel narrow, and the traffic on the water heavy, but there were still many mines being found which had broken away from their original positions. These would be floating around for years to come.

The second day out of Brest happened to be the name day for all Veras, Sophias, Nadejdas, and Luboffs. Legend said that Vera, meaning faith, Nadejda, meaning hope, and Luboff, meaning love, were the three daughters of Sophia, meaning wisdom. All suffered death for their faith in the early days of Christianity. The celebration that night included a dance and new movie shown on deck.

During the festivities, the twenty-four boys who were being paid to work went on strike. One of their group, Vsevolod Pravdin, had loaned his deck pass to a friend who misused it. The older boys had been forbidden the use of the main deck since the Japanese mess boy incident, unless they had special passes. Pravdin's pass was taken away, and the rest of the boys delivered an ultimatum — return Pravdin's pass or no work! Mother Campbell took them at their word and determined to manage without them. She worked one meal satisfactorily, and by the next meal they were back at their posts. The teacher, Peter de George, had an earnest talk with them, and they ended up apologizing and offering to work the rest of the trip without pay.

Meanwhile, Allen was anxiously awaiting news from Colonel Ryan as to their port of destination. The ship's papers said Reval in Estonia was where the ship was headed, but this, of course, was fictitious. Early on the morning of October 2nd, the boat entered the sluggish mouth of the Elbe River and anchored at the quarantine dock of Cuxhaven, Germany. The Red Cross officials expected to be delayed by tremendous red tape. But, although a doctor came out to the boat to check its hospital facilities, it was immediately passed.

By 8 A.M. the yellow quarantine flag was hauled down, and they headed for the Kiel Canal. They entered the canal by noon and reached the other end by midnight. The passage was so crowded with large vessels that the *Yomei Maru* had to pull to one side several times to let bigger boats, needing more draft room, pass. As they sailed along, they saw storks flying high overhead, and thin cattle, sheep, and pigs grazing on the adjacent, poorly cultivated fields. Evidence of great poverty was everywhere in Germany.

Wherever they stopped during the slow trip, they were accosted by Germans wanting to trade anything for flour, sugar, or meat. The German officials who dealt with them openly hinted for free food and bartered anything for cigarettes or cigars. Broker agents besieged the ship at both ends of the canal, waving their papers and shouting their qualifications. One German officer who boarded the ship, described the rigid rationing — one and a half pounds of bread a day, and two pounds of meat a week, if it could be procured. Flour and sugar were unobtainable, even with ration cards. When their canal pilot left, he begged for a little flour and sugar. From what Allen could see, prices were cheap in Germany, and the fact that the German mark was 57 to the dollar made things even cheaper. Whatever stop the ship made, there was no need to put guards at the gangplank, for none of the POWs wanted to slip away from the ship. At the end of the canal, the ship stopped for an hour and a half to take on supplies which had been ordered. Then the *Yomei Maru* put out into the Baltic Sea and rough weather.

On October 2nd, Allen again telegraphed to Paris for orders: "Yomei Maru passed Kiel Canal October 2nd stop all well stop have received no instructions yet stop if none received will proceed Helsingfors stop Allen."

Allen spent the next day trying to get in touch with Reval, Helsingfors, or any other Baltic port, to get through to Colonel Ryan for instructions. Finally, because he had received no orders since leaving Brest, he decided to go to Helsingfors which he and Olds had agreed on as the most logical destination.

By October 4th no word had come through, so Allen cabled Ryan: "Col. Ryan, American Red Cross, Helsingfors or Reval stop Monday Oct. 4th 9 P.M. Yomei Maru about 400 miles from Reval stop having received no instructions expect to proceed Helsingfors which expect reach Wed night or Thurs morning stop if you have different instructions please wire us immediately stop all well aboard ship will be prepared quick debarkation stop inform us if you have any information re charter Yomei stop Allen."

He also cabled that the Russian staff and colony wished to get in touch with the Parents' Committee in Petrograd as quickly as possible. The message was sent to B. Gukovsky, Centroesoya, Russian Cooperative, Reval, Estonia, with a request to send it on to the Parents' Committee.

October 5th proved to be a fine clear day. At 8 A.M. Allen finally received a wire from Colonel Ryan: "SS YM for Major Allen stop to what port are you headed now stop Helsingfors or Hango Finland will be ultimate destination of ship stop are you going to Copenhagen to unload coal before putting children ashore stop please communicate above info by wireless at once Ryan." With relief Allen now wired Ryan that he had received no message until October 5th and was therefore heading for Helsingfors which he expected to reach the next morning.

At 7:40 that night a rude wire came from Olds: "Wire received stating you proceeding to Helsingfors stop your orders were report directly to Riga for further instructions stop we have not heard from Ryan designating Helsingfors but you understand you are to take final orders from Ryan Olds."

Allen simply wrote the following in the log: "It is probable that Col. Ryan has sent instructions for me by wireless but they failed to reach the ship, although our operator has been constantly listening in the expectation of getting a message with information on which we could proceed."

That evening there was a dinner celebration on the ship with Captain Kayahara present, and special decorations made by the Russian staff helped to enliven the event. After dinner the Russians made speeches, expressing their thanks to the Red Cross for its kind treatment.

October 26th was a bright sunny day and the boat arrived at Helsingfors at 9:25 P.M., 14,622 miles from Vladivostok. When the Americans on board awakened the next morning, they found the following poem presented to each one from Allen, who had written it after dinner, before he went to bed:

> No longer I worry about the old Yomei
> As she bounds o'er the blusterous, billowing brine
> No longer I'm anxious for fear of the foamy
> Old ocean without wireless and SOS sign.
> No longer my thin and fast graying tresses
> Are standing on end in hideous fright.
> The reason therefore O you don't need three guesses
> We are nearing the end of our voyage tonight.
> The Petrograd trip is concluding,
> We're only one jump from our last port of call.
> So here's to an end of our feverish brooding
> From here to Finland is one night — that's all.
> For months when the youngsters would climb the tarpaulin
> My spine would grow chill, my features turn pale,
> In fancy I'd see them all slip and go sprawlin'
> A few seconds later to skid off a sail.
>
> For months when they shot up and down the steep hatches
> I expected to hear of a violent death,
> And see their small forms all done up in patches,
> Painfully, sobbingly, drawing each breath.

As calm as Miss Farmer as cool as Miss Snow,
To all cries for help I can only say "No."
We're only one night out—hip! hip!—let 'er go!

But in spite of it all, for a serious minute,
Are you not glad you came on the Yomei Maru?
Are you not glad from Vladi you've always been in it?
Mighty glad that you stuck and are seeing it through?
Not to speak of some more that you very well know,
It's been "interesno" to put it in Ruskie—
And although it's been tough, it has never been slow.

CHAPTER TWENTY-THREE

The entrance to the harbor of Helsingfors was through a narrow rockbound channel. On both sides were high pillars like medieval tower fortresses, with the glimpse of old stone buildings beyond, which reinforced the medieval aspect of the city. Dropping anchor a couple of miles off shore, Allen was disappointed when only port officials came out to the ship, but no quarantine officers. This meant that the question of whether the *Yomei Maru* could enter the port was still up in the air. Allen, Kayahara, and Bramhall went ashore and were surprised that there were no Red Cross officials to meet them. Allen telephoned the American Consul who knew nothing and had never heard of the *Yomei Maru*.

Next he went to the Red Cross office to locate Captain Elliott, the local Red Cross representative in charge of Finnish work. He had just arrived at Helsingfors, having heard the *Yomei Maru* was due to arrive. After lunch at the hotel, they all went to the Foreign office. Here they were told that the Council of Ministers was discussing the matter of the colony that very minute with the Foreign Office officials. At mid-afternoon, Allen had received word that the government had agreed provisionally to admit the children to Finland and that he would be formally notified by about 5 P.M. Returning to the ship, he informed them of the good news. He then made plans to go the next day with Mother Campbell and Bramhall to the place which had been suggested for housing the colony, Tevastehus, until repatriation could be arranged. Needless to say, the whole colony joyfully celebrated their arrival.

But Allen realized that enormous problems still lay ahead. Communication between Finland and Petrograd was meager, and there were no formal relations as yet between the Soviet and Finnish governments, except on such matters as the exchange of war prisoners.

The joint Peace Commission was sitting at Dorpat, Estonia, at the time, and they were expected to sign a peace treaty within a week. However, that would not make the peace official, for the treaty had to be debated and ratified by both the Finnish Parliament and the Russian Soviet. The border was completely closed, and there was no open commerce between the two countries. Thousands of Russian refugees had illegally crossed the border to escape the dreadful conditions in Petrograd, and the Finnish government had imposed rigid regulations on these people who were all being fed and clothed by the Red Cross. Captain Hopkins, who was in charge of Red Cross activities in Finland, outlined the considerable difficulties that lay ahead affecting repatriation, because of the extreme limitations.

The next morning Allen was ready at 7 A.M., waiting for a boat to arrive with Hopkins and Elliott who were to go with him to inspect Tevastehus. The two men arrived one hour later and told Allen that at 9 P.M. the night before, they had been informed that the Home Minister refused to give his consent to the landing of the children, and that they could not put the colony anywhere in Finland.

Allen and the two men went straight to the Foreign Office but found no one there. As a last resort, Hopkins called a very influential business man in Helsingfors named Jensen and told him the story. At the same moment, Allen was tipped off that the wife of the War Minister was very musical and a quick message to the ship produced an impromptu concert that afternoon, with the War Minister's wife as an honored guest. During the intermission of the concert, there were many little children introduced to her, and their touching story was related by attentive Red Cross personnel.

Back on shore Jensen understood at once. He commented that he would "light a fire" under the government and get back to them. Within an hour, Mr. Worenar of the Foreign Office, whom Allen had met the day before, arrived and said that the Council of Ministers had reopened the matter and were again considering letting the colony into Finland. If so, it would have to be located at a health resort near Unsidirko.

Then word came through that the final answer would be given that evening at 8 o'clock, and would Captain Hopkins and Allen come to the Foreign Office at that time. When they arrived, the meeting was still going on. But after half an hour, they were told that the decision of the ministers had been favorable, and it was now just a matter of finding the right place to house them. Apparently, Mr. Jensen's "fire" and the children's concert had worked. At 9:45 Allen, Hopkins, and the three Finnish representatives boarded a train for Vyborg.

Arriving at 7 A.M. the following morning, they were met by two cars and taken to a Red Cross staff house. After breakfast they were driven to Halila, the site of a former tuberculosis sanitorium. There they met the doctor in residence and an English speaking nurse who showed them around. There were many buildings and, although they had only been used for a short time after being built, and then closed for years, they were in remarkably good condition. The main building was selected as a house for the girls, and a second one was chosen for the boys. The immediate problem was to put the buildings into working order, including the immediate installation of a new pump to bring water from the lake a half mile away.

Now arrangements had to be made to transport the children to Vyborg as soon as possible, for each day they remained on the ship cost the Red Cross $5000.00. The Finnish government provided twenty-five passenger and fifty freight cars, which would be sent to the railroad station nearest the port of debarkation to transfer the colony to Halila. The *Yomei Maru* was instructed to make ready to sail at noon on October 9th for Koivisto, 170 miles east of Helsingfors, and as close to Halila as possible.

Mother Campbell was asked to go to Halila by train to get there ahead of the children so she could help get the place ready for them. She arrived very early Sunday morning, October 10th, with a young Czech, Mr. Hodek. Four flat tires on the way to the sanitorium did not give her a very secure feeling about the coming sojourn in Finland.

Architecturally the buildings were beautiful, having originally been built for the Czar and his numerous relatives, just in case illness should strike any of them. No amount of money was spared, since they were constructed when Finland was a Russian province. Dainty French furniture filled the rooms, but just the thought of letting 800 children loose in them made Mother Campbell panic, because the Red Cross would be responsible to the Finnish government for replacement and breakage.

As Allen showed her around, she turned to him and said, "It's a beautiful layout, but how is it possible for us to get all the work done before they get here?"

He replied, "Sorry, but I have to go back to Helsingfors, so the job's on your shoulders! You can hold the children on the ship a few days if it's really necessary, but that's all. We've hired a young husky Finn named Blackie, who came to us well recommended as a go-getter. He can get as many men and women as you may need for cleaning and moving furniture!"

With these words, he left to finalize the details of the colony business with the Finnish government.

Blackie soon proved indispensible. He hired five two-wheel carts and hauled all the furniture to a rented warehouse a mile away. About fifty men and women started cleaning the rooms as soon as they became empty and then went to work on the second building for the boys. That building had been temporarily occupied by Kerensky during the war and was badly neglected. Many more repairs were needed there. Because the water supply was inadequate, a new pump had to be installed and outdoor toilets hastily constructed for boys and girls, basically to conserve water. Stacy Snow, one of the Red Cross personnel, accused Mother Campbell of having these dug so far from the main building so that everyone would get the right amount of exercise. Five showers were also put into working condition.

Everyone worked hard to get the job done as quickly as possible. Mother Campbell and Mr. Hodek pushed and cajoled the workers to get the colony's new home ready. And Blackie turned out to be even more capable and efficient than his reputation. Mother Campbell had only one problem with him—he couldn't speak Russian, English, or Swedish, and she couldn't understand Finnish! Hours were wasted while she got Mr. Hodek to interpret Blackie's messages to her and her orders to him.

The last day before the children were due to arrive, they were having one of their three-cornered conversations when, without warning, Blackie broke into fluent Russian. Mother Campbell was furious and told him so in her best Russian and in no uncertain terms. He raised both hands toward the heavens and looked straight at her, tears streaming down his face!

"God! I ask your forgiveness. I swore to you that I would never again speak the dirty language and now I forget. Help me, Oh, God! Help me to keep this oath!"

Mamasha never heard him speak Russian again but would talk to him, and he would just answer by the motion of his head. She learned that his grudge was very deep because his whole family had been tortured and killed a few years earlier.

As soon as preparations were completed, light baggage and food supplies for a week were brought up from the ship to Halila. Then some of the children were moved in that night. For the first time in a long time, they had the treat of eating real Russian black bread baked by the Russian cooks who had been hired for the colony. The next morning they all exclaimed happily over sleeping on solid ground at last, without the tossing motion of the boat.

The rest of the children and the staff came to Halila that day, and they all settled down to await their repatriation. In spite of the water shortage caused by the inefficient water pump, their living quarters had many unaccustomed advantages. For one thing, they were delighted to dispense with daily bathing.

The kitchen and dining room were the pride of the sanitorium— gleaming white tables, copper kettles, double sinks and ovens made meal times quite efficient. The dining room had a balcony at one end and a speaker's platform where movies could be shown. The boys complained right away about the fact that they had to come all the way to the girls' building to eat. But Mother Campbell would hear none of that.

"You asked for it," she said, "by insisting that we change our port of debarkation from France to Finland, so just keep quiet and take whatever comes!"

That usually stopped the grumbling.

The lightened ship, carrying only POWs and some remaining cargo, went back to Copenhagen. From there the POWs were dispatched to Berlin, and thence to their respective countries, ending their service to the Red Cross. They were all clothed in new suits and carried a good deal of money. They wrote letters later to Mother Campbell and Riley Allen, most of them telling how shocked they were by the conditions of life in Czechoslovakia, Poland, Hungary, and other middle European countries.

Allen now turned his attention to the problem of repatriation. Ryan, responsible for the feeding of so many Russian refugees, was pushing as hard as he could to get it over with. But Allen refused to be steamrollered and insisted that no child be sent back to Petrograd unless there were families or friends waiting. Since there were still no direct negotiations possible between Finland and the USSR, all communications went through Estonia. Again, lists were sent to Red Cross headquarters in Tallinn, Estonia, to be forwarded to the Parents' Committee in Petrograd, with instructions that all communications from Russia must be sent through Estonia to Ryan's office in Riga, Latvia. The children would finally receive their correspondence via Hopkins' Red Cross offices in Vyborg, Finland. This highly complicated system was bound to lengthen the time it would take to accomplish the desired results, but now all they could do was wait.

At the sanitorium, the ship's routine of school plus varied forms of

entertainment again became their normal pattern of life on land—
much to the disgust of the teachers, whose only wish was to get home
right away. But the first dance after they were settled became the
highlight of the stay at Halila.

Just as the musicians finished playing the last number, Allen arrived
with a sack of mail from Petrograd. While one of the Russian teachers called out names, he began handing out letters that had just come
from Hopkins' office in Vyborg.

Before long everybody was weeping—those who received mail and
those who didn't. Many had had no word from Russia or their
families for almost three years, and there was both good news and
bad. Mother Campbell had her hands full consoling those who heard
nothing. She did her best to reassure them that the Parents' Committee was working hard to find each family and that they would be sure
to get a letter the next time.

Now plans were developed in earnest for repatriation, and the
children came to realize that they would soon be returning. The older
ones sensed how bad the situation might be. Vanya Semenov, who
had saved all his pocket money, began buying food and making
packages of sardines, cans of condensed milk, sugar, butter, and rice.
Some made things in the machine shop as gifts, and the girls seemed
to be knitting scarves, mittens, sweaters, and stockings non-stop!

The first delivery of children was to take place on November 10th,
after all arrangements had finally been completed, more or less to the
satisfaction of the governments involved.

There was a big farewell party on the night of November 9th.
Teachers, children, and administrators all came, and the young musicians gave the performance of their lives. At the end of the party a
knotty problem came up. Some of the musicians were returning to
Russia the next day. Who owned the instruments?

Leonty Duebner, as one of the acknowledged leaders of the group,
persuaded them that the instruments were common property and
should stay in Halila until he departed. Then when he got to Petrograd, he would form an association of the former colony members,
and the instruments could be played at their get-togethers. However,
although he did keep them for some time, they were eventually
divided among the various performers. His association only became a
reality many years later.

In 1920, the border between Finland and Russia, which had been
agreed to by treaty only a few weeks earlier, was the Chornaya
Rechka, or Black River. It is a tiny river, formerly crossed by a heavy

wooden bridge which had been destroyed during the war. With the coming of peace, a rickety footbridge over the river had been constructed.

There, on the morning of November 10th, the first group of children walked toward the Russian border. They were followed by carts loaded with luggage and boxes of food for each child to take home as a gift from the Red Cross. The Soviets were supposed to get there by ten o'clock, but it wasn't until noon that a platoon of Red Army soldiers arrived.

One Russian stepped onto the bridge and stopped midway. Riley Allen and an interpreter came from the Finnish side and met him right in the center of the bridge. At this point there was a minor dispute over the fact that no Latvian, Lithuanian, or Estonian children were being delivered, since the USSR claimed them as citizens of the Russian Socialist Federal Soviet Republic. Allen sidestepped the issue by saying that he had no authority to discuss the matter—that this group consisted of 138 children with 7 adults, all of whom desired to return to waiting parents or relatives in the USSR. The Russian, Commissioner I. Subotin, gave in on the point and wanted to take the group without further discussion. But Allen held out.

He demanded a signed receipt for every child and adult as they crossed the bridge. Each one was then called by number and gave his or her name as they went over in single file, usually pausing to murmur a "good-bye" or "thank you" to Allen. When the last child had crossed, Allen walked back to the Finnish side and watched as they happily marched off, loudly singing together.

Eight more similar trips were made after that, and, on January 26, 1921, the last 45 children crossed over the Black River. The question of the 30 Estonian, Latvian, and Lithuanian children never was brought up again, and they were finally returned to their parents in the newly free countries from the treaties recognized at last by the USSR.

Later reports revealed that all was not warmth and gladness as the children walked toward the city. Vanya Semenov told how the soldiers who carried their possessions had to be bribed with the white bread the Red Cross had given them. Leonty Duebner's possessions were all stolen before he reached Petrograd, which was only a few kilometers from the border. The guards were extremely harsh in their treatment of the children, sharply ordering them about and constantly complaining about the weight of their baggage.

The first sight of Petrograd was a terrible shock to the older children who remembered the city from 1918. No stores were open, and their windows were all boarded up. Public transportation did not exist. As they walked along the streets to their homes, Vanya kept remembering New York City.

As each group of children came into the city, a frail shabby woman kept running among them showing them a faded photograph.

"Do you know my son, Pavlusha? Have you seen him?"

Sadly the children would turn their heads away. She was the mother of Pavel Nikolaeff who had been killed in New York.

EPILOGUE

The dreadful famine and living conditions in Petrograd in the spring of 1918, which had sent the children out of the capital city in search of food and safety, seemed almost halcyon compared to conditions the same children found when they returned in January of 1921.

Trouble piled upon trouble. Russia was completely exhausted with four years of the European war followed by three years of civil war, and on top of that, a new and bloody conflict with Poland. Also, the revolution had destroyed all the accepted economic and political institutions, resulting in famine and a total breakdown of civilization. 1920 and 1921 brought two years of drought. Peasants refused to plant or plough because of forced requisition of crops by the Bolshevik government. All these things put the finishing touches to any more talk of world revolution.

Only massive food relief received from the American Relief Administration headed by Herbert Hoover stopped whole areas from being completely depopulated. Frightening statistics showed the drop in cultivated land to 62% of its pre-war level, with cattle dropping from 59 million to 37 million between 1916 and 1920. Cotton production fell to 5% of its prewar level and iron to 2% in the same time period. Strikes and uprisings took place everywhere, and the most telling incident was an uprising of the Kronstadt naval base against communist rule in March 1921. Oddly enough, 4 years before, revolutionary action by this very same base was credited with being the main body of the original force that had stormed and taken the Winter Palace on the night of November 7th. They had arrested the members of the Provisional Government which paved the way for the establishment of the Soviet government in 1917.

Lenin, the Chairman of the Council of the People's Commissars, had introduced the New Economic Policy which was a partial restoration of capitalism. Although the Bolshevik government retained control of heavy industry, small factories hiring no more than twenty workers were permitted to operate under private control. Peasants were again allowed to farm their own land, but the hated requisitioning of crops was replaced by a heavy tax in kind. Peasants, however, were now permitted to sell the remainder of their crops on the open market.

Lenin's death in January 1924 unleashed a four year power struggle among the commissars centering around the charismatic figure of Trotsky, still wedded to the idea of immediate world revolution, and the more plodding peasant Party Secretary, Joseph Stalin. In spite of this struggle, economic life began to improve throughout all Russia, and shops, factories, and schools reopened. The colonists, now at home, continued their education and ultimately entered into their respective professions. Many of the boys became engineers, a somewhat loose term used to describe anyone engaged in technical activities from running a train to becoming an electrician. Some of the girls went into clerical or library work while several became teachers. It was a remarkable fact that their schooling during the two and a half years under the Red Cross had put them ahead of many of their friends who had remained behind in Petrograd.

Then political events again impinged on the lives of even the most ordinary children. Stalin won out in the power struggle, and Trotsky fled into exile in Mexico only to meet a hideous death there in 1941, orchestrated by the long bloody arm of his rival. Stalin promptly scrapped the New Economic Program, and all those who had dared to profit from it were stripped of all their possessions. Over five million peasants, angered by the government's harsh collectivization of all land and animals, burnt their crops and killed their livestock by way of protest.

That brought on the establishment of the notorious concentration camps where untold millions were enslaved for the rest of their short lives. No one was spared—factory workers, farmers, government clerks, army and navy personnel, even the intelligentsia. Stalin's government introduced a five year economic plan intended to pull Russia out of her "medieval past" into the 20th Century in one big leap. Again a dreadful famine hit the land. Rumors of cannibalism were reported. Since the goals of the plan were not achieved, the government continued into a second five year plan. Several of the colonists were caught in this holocaust and only one of those lived to tell the tale.

The purges continued throughout the thirties and only slackened slightly when Russia became embroiled in World War II, first on the side of Germany. But eventually, when Germany changed its mind and attacked, the Russians fought back heroically against their former ally.

During the long siege of Leningrad by the Nazis, many of the colonists stayed in the city the entire time, almost starving to death and seeing many of their families die either at the front or from the devastating conditions caused by the war.

When peace came in 1945, the government stubbornly attempted to push Russia into new and greater heights based on economic and military power but with little regard for the personal needs or wishes of the Russian people. In spite of the troubled times, a few of the colonists continued to send messages to Burle Bramhall, Riley Allen, and, in particular, Alfred and Katia Swan. Even during the blackest time of Stalin's maniacal despotism, Vanya Semenov, Kotya Ivanov, and Vladimir Smolianinov, after he was released from a concentration camp, sent guarded letters describing their work, their lives, and their families.

In America also, those who had been a part of the adventure took different paths. Riley Allen returned to Honolulu and became a lawyer but, unable to forget his old love, ended up as the editor of the Honolulu Star Bulletin. He and his wife, Susanne, were involved in a great deal of civic work until his death.

Mamasha Campbell, on leaving Finland, returned to the United States after a visit to her native Norway. Dad was already working in China, but her return to the United States was necessitated by formalities involving a homeless child she had adopted in Vladivostok. Evdokia Gorelkina, fondly named "Ida", had been found wandering in Tomsk by an American Vice-Consul and his Russian wife. They brought her as far as Vladivostok, then leaving instructions to return her to her family in Tomsk, left her at the Red Cross headquarters in Vladivostok. With the destruction of the Trans-Siberian railroad line out of Vladivostok, Mother Campbell took her with the children all the way to France. Leaving her with friends in Brest, she picked up Ida on her way back to the States. After considerable delays because of complex legal difficulties, Ida joined Mother Campbell and travelled to China to join Dad and their own two children, Junior and Helen. Dad had obtained a position with the Otis Elevator Company in Shanghai, and Mother Campbell became a house manager at the American Shanghai school. After Dad's retirement in 1940, the family returned to Woodland, California, where Mamasha opened a restaurant and became a member of the City Council. Her contributions to this community were soon warmly appreciated, and a town park was named in her honor. Mother Campbell died on June 27, 1975, at the age of 94. Dad had predeceased her by just 16 days.

Alia and Katia Swan traveled from Vladivostok, via the United States, to England. They had hoped to settle down there with Alia's family, most of whom had left Russia. Alia soon realized that he could not earn a living in depression-ridden England. Returning to the United States, he obtained a teaching post at the University of Virginia and eventually accepted a dual appointment as professor of music at both Swarthmore and Haverford Colleges in Pennsylvania. Here he rapidly became known for his scholarship in Russian folk music and the Znamenny, or ancient chant, of the Russian Orthodox church. His compositions in secular and church music were performed with increasing frequency in America and Europe. His wife, Katia, became a specialist in Linguistics, with particular emphasis on the old Slavonic language of the church and state in Russia during the medieval ages. Katia died in 1943.

In 1947 Alia married Jane Ballard, one of his music students who was fascinated by Russian history and became a professor of history at West Chester University in 1955. Her Master's Thesis was a description of the first part of the odyssey of the Lost Children. With the death of Stalin, communication with the "children" was increased, with many more daring to correspond with the Swans and, as a result of the letters and easing of travel conditions, the Swans returned to Russia in 1963 and 1966. After the death of Alfred Swan in 1970, Jane Swan was requested by the "children" in Russia and by some American friends to return to Russia. In 1975 she did, and made oral tapes of the stories of about a dozen of the children. Thus, this book was begun. The heartrending stories told on tape and in the diaries of some could fill another dozen books.

Vanya Semenov was 17 when he returned. Mostly self taught, he joined the orchestra of the Maly Theatre and rose to the position of first cellist. It was this position which helped him to survive the awful famine during the siege of Leningrad during 1942–43 because all artists and musicians were given special ration cards so that they could continue to perform for the soldiers and sailors during the war.

After the war, the increased paranoia of Stalin had everyone spying on everyone else and the resulting dissension and suspicion took a toll. Vanya felt unable to continue playing in the orchestra and took early retirement at 55. His wife, Sophia, and he lived in two small adjoining rooms. Actually, he never could officially marry her, for they would have lost one room. Gradually, he began collecting autographs, pictures, original manuscripts, furniture of Russian musicians, etc., paying for them with money earned from one night performances at local dances or concerts as a fill-in cellist. They lived a mouse-like existence on his and Sophia's pensions. Ironically, his collection of original manuscripts by Moussorgsky, Cui, Balakirev, Tchaikovsky, Rachmaninov, Stravinsky, Swan, and others, had become so valuable that it has been recognized by the government and listed as a private museum. It was his intention to leave it to the Russian people.

Nicholas (Kotya) Ivanov also rose to a fairly high position as the leading agronomist of the U.S.S.R. He introduced original methods for cultivation of the lima bean which became an important crop in Russia, breaking the monotony of the endless beet and cabbage vegetable diet. He also became a leading local historian of old St. Petersburg and wrote several articles on the subject. He died in 1974. The author still remembers leaving Russia in 1966 with an armful of three-foot tall black gladiolas, a hybrid developed in Kotya's government greenhouse. Their enormous size took up three seats on the airplane.

Katia Kozlova became a librarian in the Pushkin Museum and spent a quiet but productive life until her retirement. She, more than anyone else, remembered her years with the children's colony, and it is from her oral tape taken in a hotel room in Leningrad at twelve o'clock at night, plus a dog-earred diary, that much of the information about life in the nunnery at Troitsk and life on Russian Island was reconstructed.

Vera Schmidt, the little girl at Kuraii who witnessed the taking of the town by the Czech soldiers and the public execution of the captives, the child who from hunger tried to milk a cow and was caught and beaten by an enraged peasant, also survived and told me her story in great detail.

Yuri Zavatchukov, who became an electrical engineer, wrote out his memoirs and, in a long conversation, told of later meetings with the colonists and attempts to organize them into yearly get-togethers. He had been one of the lads who spoke in New York at the riotous meeting in Times Square and rather ably defended the Red Cross in spite of all the haranguing of Martins.

Burle Bramhall, of all the Red Cross personnel, perhaps had the most interesting life. With the return of the children to the USSR, Bramhall, although originally from Canada, settled in Seattle, Washington. He married Jessie Drury in 1923 and settled down to a long and successful career in the investment field, eventually forming his own company of Bramhall and Stein. He remained active in the National Council of American-Soviet Friendship and for a time continued to correspond with some of the children. In World War II he reentered active military service, serving with the military civil-affairs government in London and Paris with the rank of Major. But the high point of his later days was a return to the Soviet Union to see some of the children. He had tried to see some of them on a trip in 1967 but had no success, for he had lost contact with them since the War. Attracting the interest of a *Pravda* editor, Vladimir Bolshakov, who ran a series of articles in the newspaper, several old colonists wrote letters to the editor and a committee was set up to locate other colonists. In 1973 Bramhall and his wife returned to Leningrad, and there was a week-long celebration by the government, climaxing in a great reunion in Leningrad's Hall of Friendship. Gifts were exchanged, music played and poems read, but most of the children were kept away from Bramhall except for perfunctory handshakes, and Bramhall was shown the usual list of required sightseeing musts. Later during the week of the visit, many of the colonists were able to get to see him by joining the obligatory tours. During one of these tours a note was slipped into Bramhall's pocket with the name of Jane Swan, her address, and a request for her to come back and take down the rest of the stories of the colonists. Somehow a copy of the shortened version of her published Master's thesis had gotten into Russia, and the colonists wanted to have the whole story told. It wasn't until a year later that Bramhall found the note and passed it on. This triggered Swan's trip in 1975 after many letters to and fro. Life has a strange way of ending stories, and perhaps in Bramhall's case the end defies understanding. Retired and living happily with his wife, Burle Bramhall and his wife, Jessie, were brutally slain by the mentally ill son of a neighbor. The boy was well known to the Bramhalls and had been in their home many times. Left unfinished on his desk was a letter to one of the colonists.

After Bramhall's visit to the USSR, some of the colonists got together once a year, and many of them began to put their memories down. One of these was Misha Denisov who still had his old diary and added onto it his impressions of Bramhall's visit. As late as 1980, there were about eighty colonists still accounted for and a few still in

Burle Bramhall, member of the Siberian Commission of the American Red Cross.

touch with the outside world.

In writing this book, the author has visited the Soviet Union three times, become close friends with a number of colonists, and discussed this work with them. I even brought them the most precious of all American gifts—dungarees! It might be difficult for Western readers to understand, although it would be crystal clear to Soviet citizens of that time, why most of the colonists expressly asked that their names not be used, even though they told their tales freely. I have honored this request to the best of my ability. It was, however, a fact that most of these discussions were held only late at night over many cups of tea and quite a few tears.

Leonty Duebner, one of the older boys involved in the colonists' revolt in New York, left Russia in the middle 1920s. He was educated through the kind auspices of Mrs. William Draper, who had met him at the Red Cross offices during the children's New York experience. He spent the rest of his life in France. Ending this saga, I think that no words of mine could be as fitting as those quoted in his memoirs:

"For I was hungered and ye gave me meat. I was thirsty and ye gave me drink. I was a stranger and ye took me in. Naked and ye clothed me; I was sick and ye visited me. *** And the King shall answer and say unto them: Verily, I say unto you, inasmuch as ye have done it to one of the least of these my brethren, ye have done it unto me."
(Matthew, Chapter 25: 35, 36, 40)

MAPS

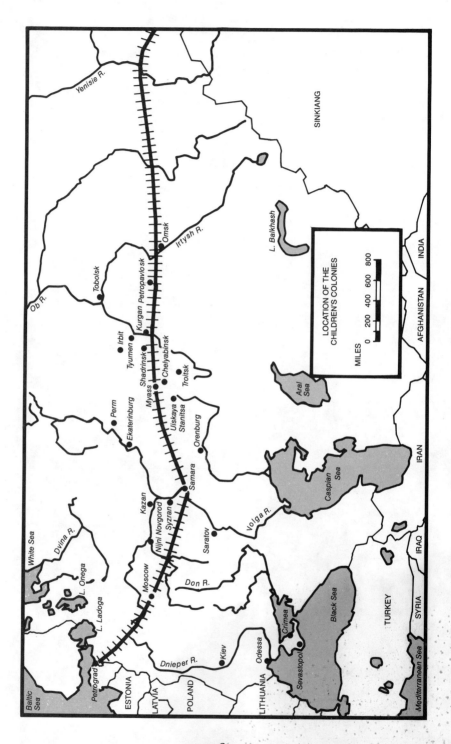

LOCATION OF THE
CHILDREN'S COLONIES

MILES

0 200 400 600 800

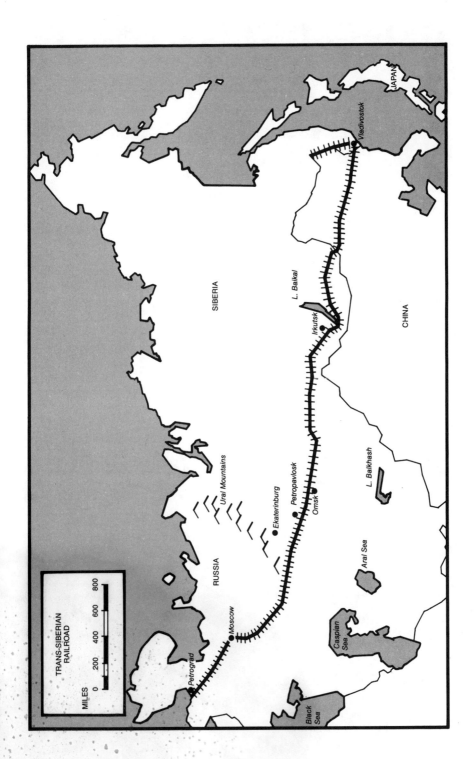

INDEX